OTHER WORKS BY BOB PARIS

Beyond Built
Flawless
Straight from the Heart
Natural Fitness

Gorilla Suit

Gorilla Suit

MY ADVENTURES IN BODYBUILDING

Bob Paris

ST. MARTIN'S PRESS
NEW YORK

Left endpaper photographs (*clockwise from top left*) by Albert Chacon, Art Zeller, Mike Neveaux, (school picture), Art Zeller. Right endpaper photographs (*clockwise from top left*) by Art Zeller, Tom Bianchi, Art Zeller, (family photo), (family photo).

Design by Ellen R. Sasahara

Library of Congress Cataloging-in-Publication Data

Paris, Bob.
    Gorilla suit : my adventures in bodybuilding / Bob Paris. — 1st ed.
        p.   cm.
    ISBN 0-312-16855-1
    1. Paris, Bob.   2. Bodybuilders—United States—Biography.
    I. Title.
    GV545.52.J33A3   1997
    646.7'5'092—dc21
    [B]   97-18564
                                                                          CIP

First Edition: September 1997

10   9   8   7   6   5   4   3   2   1

To my family—blood and extended—
for all the years of love, kindness,
and understanding

C O N T E N T S

Author's Note   ix

Acknowledgments   xi

1   Edge of a Cliff   1

2   Middle of Somewhere   16

3   Rediscovering the Accidentally Discovered   41

4   Even Muscles Have Memories   55

5   Getting Out of the House a Bit   67

6   Next to Death   80

7   I Get Educated   94

8   Southern Excursion   117

9   Mr. Olympia Calls Me by Name   132

10   A Week from Next Tuesday   148

11   I Decide to Stay   162

12   Grasshopper Turns Some Corners   177

13   World by the Tail   202

14   Second Thoughts   224

15   First Comeback   246

16   Mountains and Green Pastures   257

AUTHOR'S NOTE

This is a true story. However, because so many of the people portrayed in this book are not necessarily public figures, many names have been altered. So have a few locations. I have performed this task—hopefully—in a way that keeps the story factual, without incidentally hurting the feelings of any innocent bystanders. Most actual public figures retain their real names.

ACKNOWLEDGMENTS

I must first, without hesitation, thank my editor, Michael Denneny. Beyond our friendship, he was a patient guide during the time that I wrote this book. Michael, from the bottom of my heart, thanks.

Also I give deep thanks to my agent, Basil Kane. He's also a man I feel fortunate to call my friend. He believed in me from the start and has been a role model of enthusiastic encouragement throughout the time I've known him.

And finally, I want to thank John Clark for his patience with me and his hard work on behalf of this project.

Gorilla Suit

1

EDGE OF A CLIFF

Friday Evening,
Midsummer, 1994
Seattle

Are you ever going to compete again?" he asked, completely changing directions, after we had spent forty minutes venting our frustrations about America's being taken over by religious nutcases and the power-hungry maniacs who pander to them; what archconservatives would call liberal whining.

Tommy's question seemed out of place. I wanted to ignore it, but he asked again, "Well, are you?"

"I don't know," I replied, hoping he wouldn't push. I'd been giving everyone this vague answer, while bitterly realizing that people thought bodybuilding was all I could do with my life.

"What does *that* mean? Who do you think you're talking to?"

I should have known; it wasn't his style to let it drop. I'd known Tommy since the early eighties, when we'd both trained at World Gym in Santa Monica. We had started talking politics one day and struck up a lasting friendship.

"That lame shit won't work on me. Be specific—you know, s-p-e-c-i-f-i-c," he said, as if he didn't understand I was intentionally being vague.

"Same old freak-show bullshit. I can't justify it anymore."

"Listen to that sorry excuse of an answer you just shoved off on me—like I'm a fan or something. You are being so goddamn weird. What is up with you and this sport? You don't want to compete, then don't. Doesn't matter to me. But it is what you did for all those years. You can't change that. Why do you want to act so repelled by it now?"

"First, don't put down my fans—they're about the only reason I hung in as long as I did—"

"Don't get off the subject."

"Second, I don't know. If I did, I'd tell you . . . maybe. It changed. I did too. Look, I don't want to talk about this right now, okay?" I said, signaling that it was time for me to go.

"I wasn't putting down your fans, Bob. But I deserve a little deeper answer than one you'd give to a stranger at a seminar."

"Yeah, I know," I said, quieter.

"Fine. Go, avoid it, don't talk about it, whatever. But seems to me, you need to figure this out and then deal with it—period. One last question, then I'll let you go."

"What?"

"You didn't always feel like this—like you're feeling right now, but won't let me in on—did you?"

"No. No, I didn't."

He hung up. Forty minutes of nonstop pontificating on the state of our country and I'd managed to bring the conversation to a sudden stop because I couldn't speak honestly about an old passion gone bad. Tommy was right: I would have to deal with it. I hadn't always felt like this.

I once loved the sport of bodybuilding. In a strange way I still did. It frustrated me and at times I hated it, but for sixteen years I tried to balance love, frustration, and hatred while watching both the sport and myself change. Convincing myself that I'd outgrown this obsession was impossible. One simple truth held us together: bodybuilding had saved my life. It was a guardian angel who found me at seventeen hazarding seas of inner struggle without a compass.

At thirty-four I had the luxury of distance, remembering those struggles that had led me to want to be big and strong, but I couldn't run from the truth of what had happened along the way. My frustrations may have grown into hatred, but the love came first. It began simply. I found authentic purpose the moment my hands wrapped around a cold iron bar. All else fell away and my spirit knew it could do anything. I built my American dream one repetition at a time. That much could never be taken away.

After hanging up, I stood in the kitchen and watched the sun go down behind the Olympic Mountains. I poured myself the last of a bottle of '92 zinfandel I'd opened before answering the phone.

It was an early August evening, around nine o'clock. Across Puget Sound, the sky was on fire, the flint edge of the mountains rising jaggedly against the evening sky. I'd been in the Northwest five years now. On the surface, my life appeared successful. All the trappings seemed to be there: beautiful home high on a waterfront bluff; a highly publicized marriage; a growing career. Not even my closest friends knew that in reality I felt like a slave to a huge mortgage and my marriage was quickly sliding toward a divorce. I didn't live in a home filled with love anymore, but in a house stuffed with things. I had a lot of things. I even had my own fully equipped gym now—in the house—it filled a huge room on the lower floor. It had been a major consideration when looking for a house in Seattle: there had to be room and ceiling height for all the equipment. It ended up being a room with a fireplace and big windows that let the light swarm in, revealing a slice of Puget Sound and mountain views.

In the last month I'd used it four times. I kept swearing to myself I'd start back again, full bore, but lately, when I went down there, I mostly puttered. At seventeen or eighteen I would have done anything to have access to equipment like this. Now I'd do a few sets and stop.

Buying that equipment had been a subtle step in my move away from the sport, even though I'd wanted it so I could train in privacy, without having to deal with the traffic of a commercial gym, especially after I'd left World Gym behind in L.A. I couldn't blame the equipment though; my move out of professional bodybuilding had been set in motion years before. Now I missed many things about the sport, but couldn't figure out where it fit into my life.

I took that last glass of wine up the winding stairs, to the sunroom, perched like a lookout tower over an expansive, 180-degree stretch of beauty. The sunset was at its peak. Snowy shadows on Mount Rainier were pink and purple, every glacial crevice darkening. I looked for the mass of crevices known as the deer head, which resembles the right profile of the neck, head, and antlers of a buck with its snout turned downward, as if licking the snow. Northwest legend said that if you could find the deer head in the side of the Mountain (up here, Rainier went mostly by "the Mountain," as in, "Oh, look, the Mountain is out today"), it would bring good luck.

Elliott Bay glowed navy blue, mirroring the sky. A freighter ship, with *Hanjin* in white letters on its bloodred side, moved toward the city, followed by two trails of blue-silver wake. Dozens of boats skimmed the calm summer waters. Two ferries crossed paths midway in the Sound. One came from Bainbridge, the other went from Seattle toward that island. The Olympics, in the background, were stony black. It was the perfect spot and time to think about life.

It would have been easy to blame my growing nostalgia on Tommy's irritating questions, but I'd already been wondering the exact same things. What the hell was up with me and this sport?

Sitting back with my feet up, I laughed a little at the irony of the night. My legs—which hadn't been shaved in two years—hung out of a pair of worn-out cutoffs. Another drink of wine. A night like this.

September 1979
Southern California

At four in the morning, an Anaheim cop shined his flashlight in the window of my car. I was asleep.

I'd made the grave error of trying to follow my dreams, and one turn of bad luck kept creeping up behind the last, leaving me three shades beyond blue. My car was camped behind the Body Shop gym, where I trained. I pulled up off the front seat, both hands in his clear sight. Already sized up as vagrant scum.

The eyes of a deacon in a church of snake handlers dissected my license and registration. Did I know it was illegal to park overnight in back of this place of business? Did I have a local home address, and why, if I did, was I in possession of a Florida driver's license? His voice slicing, like the blue and red lights that smacked the buildings, Dumpsters, and telephone poles surrounding us. His two-way radio pierced the night air with staticky blasts of official code.

"Well—what's your story?" he demanded.

It's a very long story, I thought, standing there in nothing but a pair of raggedy cutoffs.

"Well, sir, I just came over, er, down from . . . Big Bear. That's where I live. . . . I moved there a couple weeks ago from that address on my license," I said, trying to think fast. I needed to whip up a quick mix of truth and tall tale to establish my perfect bumpkin innocence. A pure dose of the facts might land me in jail.

"Why the Indiana plates on the vehicle?" he asked, unwilling to be convinced.

"That's where I grew up, sir," I quickly responded, enhancing my previous lie with the truth. "After I left college, I moved down to Florida, settled in and all . . . then was called out here . . . Big Bear, actually, to, uh . . . care for this great-uncle of mine—on my mother's side—Bill . . . emphysema. Great old guy. Family wanted nothin' to do with him. Well, I went right on up to Big Bear. Been there couple a weeks now . . . like I said, and he's doin' much better—my uncle, um, great-uncle, that is . . . sir."

I had returned to lying right after the bit about Florida, but the cop softened some—or got bored with my rambling and decided that I was

4

pathetic, but harmless. Either way, it looked as if I'd worn him down and would avoid any real trouble. I was on a roll though and wanted to finish the story, just to be sure:

"Yes, sir, I came out here just for that, but I got this college buddy—works here at the gym." I pointed at the brown building in front of my car, while trying to get rid of a piece of broken glass on the bottom of my right foot by wiping it across the instep of the left. "I drove down this evenin' so we could work out together and decided to save money by sleepin' in my car, instead of gettin' a motel room. His girlfriend is pretty shi—um, cranky about him lettin' people stay over at their apartment. I'm going to church with them tomorrow—before I head back up to Big Bear."

No such buddy, or his girlfriend, existed, any more than an ailing great-uncle in Big Bear did. I had no intention of seeing the inside of a church anytime soon, but threw that in at the last second, in case my instincts about his being a born-again were accurate.

He looked at his watch, shined the flashlight into the front and back seats of my car, which were piled high with all my clothes and everything that wouldn't fit in the trunk, moved the light right into my eyes to reinforce the point, and said, "Leave this spot now. Do not park here again."

He got in his car and left. So did I, crossing the Anaheim city line into Fullerton. In a more secluded alley, I curled up on the front seat and slept fitfully until the sunlight startled me awake.

From the first second I opened my eyes, every instinct screamed, "Jump off a twenty-story building." That faded later in the day as I drove up to Will Rogers State Beach on still-unfamiliar freeways. I guessed my way back toward Santa Monica, only becoming seriously lost three, four times. By the time I passed Lincoln Boulevard, the physical feeling of defeat had retreated. The Fourth Street exit from the Santa Monica freeway flew toward me. I got off and drove through town to Ocean Avenue. I had to see the waves crash at Will Rogers, like that first day here. I went three blocks farther, instead of turning left when I got to the California Incline, the steep hillside street that curved down the cliff to the Coast Highway. First stop, Palisades Park—another accidental discovery on my first day in California. To gather perspective.

Coming up from Orange County had definitely been out of the way, but an intense two-hour chest and shoulder workout, and a forty-five-minute, blistering-hot shower at the gym didn't crush the pain. Sitting for six hours in my car, steaming, thinking about what to do, I decided to head back to the source. Parked all day in the miserly shade of a textured block wall cascading with crimson bougainvillea, I tried to figure out what I would tell everyone back home—especially the ones with a "told ya so" ready. I sank into the muck of disappointment and decided to quit.

When I'd set out for Santa Monica from the parking lot of the Body Shop in Anaheim, I figured that I'd had my last workout in California; maybe my last workout ever. I needed to go sit by the ocean for a while, since I was in a hurry to go nowhere. I didn't have to drive the fifty miles up to L.A. There were beautiful beaches in Orange County, but I needed a dose without compromise. I had already compromised enough. One final memory of how it was supposed to be; that's all I wanted.

Past the T intersection where Idaho Street ends at Ocean Avenue, I swung the car into a diagonal space, found two quarters under the passenger-side mat, jammed them into the meter, and cranked the handle around while looking down at my bare feet and the stubble of hair coming back on my calves, which I'd shaved two weeks earlier. I crossed the sidewalk and wet grass of the park to the fence right on the edge of the cliff. The sun was beginning to set. I stood there for thirty minutes before it finally occurred to me exactly what this changing sky reminded me of. Not only the sky, but the whole picture. The mountains surrounding the bay had the hard edge of flint. In that instant I knew—no matter what—I'd stay.

I was remembering an arrowhead Pap-pa Clark had found for me in a tobacco field when I was seven. As I walked along beside him, he gave it to me to keep. I held it up sideways at arm's length, eyes squinted, imagining it was a set of jagged mountains on the horizon. Pap-pa asked what I was doing, and I told him. He didn't think I heard, but as he lit another Winston, he mumbled, through a crooked smile, that I was such a dreamer. He was right.

Now, here those mountains were, up against that sky, curving their way out around the bay to Malibu. This was obviously a place of great magic. I'd figured it would be. I had certainly dreamed about it long before actually standing along that cliff, with my arms resting across its white concrete fence, far above the Pacific. Looking down from the cliff, I had to wonder about the descriptive sanity of the adventurer who had so misnamed the most violently seductive thing I had ever seen in my nineteen years of life. According to my memory of European explorers, the Pacific's namer was Ferdinand Magellan, who thought it looked peaceful and tranquil. That started me thinking about other possible differences between Mr. Magellan and myself. Other than the way we saw the Pacific Ocean, our biggest differences came in how we got to see it in the first place. Ferdinand came from Spain in the early 1500s, on a wooden sailing ship, navigated the globe, and fought crushing storms rounding Cape Horn at the southern tip of South America, to find this magnificent body of water, which probably did look serene after what he'd been through.

I had simply driven west, for the most part along interstate highways, in a beat-up, maroon '73 Monte Carlo, from a little town in southern Indiana. Those minor differences aside, I couldn't help but wonder if he had also stood somewhere similar to where I was now, on an eroding cliff at a far edge of the continent, contemplating his destiny. Impossible to know really, but I figured, yes.

High above the beach in Palisades Park, crystal September twilight all around, hard-ass cop long forgotten, and completely wrapped up in dreaming of arrowheads, magic, ancient-world explorers, and my own destiny, I remained pragmatically clueless, especially concerning petty details such as where my next meal would come from. Trivialities regarding how to survive nearly penniless and twenty-five hundred miles from home were suddenly beside the point. I was nineteen and I was sticking around to live out my dreams—no matter what. On this one brilliant night every possibility on earth lay right in front of me.

I had mistakenly thought it started years earlier, when I first discovered that rusty weight machine in a dank corner room of the high school gymnasium, but now I knew. It was just beginning. Just now. This whole adventure was developing into something far beyond simply building up my muscles. I had discovered the promised land. I was, however, unprepared for the price this piece of heaven would require.

*Saturday Morning,
Midsummer, 1994
Seattle*

I fell asleep on the sunroom couch and only woke up when my right arm ached from being numb too long. Three thirty-six A.M. The bay had gone as black as the glitter of city lights would allow. There was a sliver of the new moon. The stars were out.

Shit, I thought, massaging the part of my neck that had gone stiff from falling asleep with my head cocked to one side. I'd been slightly tipsy, but not drunk, when I nodded into a sleep filled with strange dreams, while lying there enjoying the twilight and thinking, several hours earlier.

In the bathroom mirror I saw that a deep red groove had grown down my right cheek from the edge of the couch pillow, and I had drool drying in a line from the corner of my mouth to the jawbone. I hadn't shaved for several days. I had strongly resisted shaving since I first sprouted a beard as a teenager. I looked like a squinty-eyed bear waking from hibernation.

"Hmm," I grunted, heading toward the bed, before I swallowed down on the sour taste in my mouth. I went back and brushed my teeth. Then as I headed across the room, being careful not to step on one of the dogs, I pushed the button activating the house alarm, set the alarm clock, and fell into bed.

I woke up thirty seconds before the alarm clock went off.

How does that happen? I wondered, debating whether or not to roll over and get some more sleep. Samantha, as usual when she was hungry in the morning, came around to my side of the bed and began licking my face. So I got up, turned off the house alarm, and went downstairs to let the dogs out. Got their food ready and made coffee without having to think. The daily routine of a life so settled that it was unsettling.

After I'd had my first cup of coffee, I took the empty wine bottle from the night before, a short pile of newspapers, and three empty diet Pepsi cans out to the recycling bin in the attached garage. On the way back in the door I noticed the stack of filled moving boxes along the left garage wall.

One of these days those boxes need to be unpacked, I thought, for the hundredth time in two years. I opened the nearest box on top of a stack of three. It was filled with old magazines. On top was an *Ironman* from May 1983. Frank Zane was on the cover. I flipped through and found an article about me, "The Last Time I Saw Paris." Writers always tried to make catchy tag lines out of my last name. It was about how this writer had met me for the first time (the last time he saw me was also the first time he saw and met me, thus a double pun—plus some) at the '82 Mr. America in New York, where I had placed third in the heavyweights. He figured that I could just as easily have won the contest, that I was a major force to be reckoned with and had a bright future in the sport. There were three black-and-white photos of me that the writer had taken in a studio the day after the contest. I met him in a rented studio space, at noon on a cloudless September Sunday, after I'd taken a long walk around Central Park, gone to the zoo, and then inhaled a big, off-diet, late breakfast of cheddar cheese omelette, bacon, and fried potatoes with ketchup. In his photos I looked very young.

I tossed the magazine back in the box, and my eye caught on a reflection. The box was filled with some of the physique mags I'd been in over the years. There were four or five more of these boxes, jammed with magazines I'd been in, or on the cover of, during my career. What caught my eye though was a strip of metal glinting from the glare of the overhead garage light. It was the metal strip off my National Championships trophy from 1983. I had won the heavyweight class and the overall title the year that the name of the competition was changed from the Mr. America to the National Championships. The actual trophy had been a six-foot-tall, plastic-and-imitation-wood cheapo that had fallen into ruin many years before, so I'd pulled the little plate with the title, year, and my name engraved on it off the base and threw the rest in the trash. Over the years I did the same with all but a few of the trophies I had won; kept the nameplate and pitched the rest.

I still had the whole trophy from my Mr. Universe win. It was more substantial than usual: a brass, art deco, funnel-cloud-shaped, covered vase, mounted on a teakwood base. Only the little physique man mounted on top was plastic, so I kept it around. Not displayed. Collecting dust in a hall closet.

The one from winning the Mr. Southern California was a silver-plated champagne bucket with the title and year engraved on it. It sat on a corner of my desk. Since it easily held fifty or sixty pens and pencils, it had some utility.

The silver-plated punch bowl from winning the California Muscle Classic was outside in a flower garden, filled with carefully selected, smooth agate stones and being allowed to go old and mossy, because I thought it looked English or French or something. That one was getting the best second life an aging trophy could ever want.

All the other nameplates from all the other contest wins were in one of these boxes in the garage—except for the one from the '82 Mr. California (but that wasn't a win, just a rip-off, quarter-point-from-winning second place). That trophy had been violently smashed on the pavement of a back parking lot, right outside the backstage door, behind the auditorium in San Jose. The splintered pieces, nameplate and all, were then thrown, like an old hamburger wrapper, into a nearby Dumpster. I was young and ambitious.

There were no trophies from all the years on the pro circuit, after winning the Mr. Universe. Then the trophies were checks, some small, some large, but long since cashed and spent, or invested.

I put the thin and tarnished piece of metal that I had fought for so hard back in the box, closed it, and went in the house.

What a waste, I thought.

But it was a lie that I told myself to keep from feeling the full weight of the memories.

G O R I L L A   S U I T

Right inside the garage door, I stood staring in the bathroom mirror, my hands braced on the sides of the sink, bleary morning eyes and wild hair looking back.

"It was not a waste," I said quietly, arguing with myself. "I could go back to it right now—if I started training full bore again. I came back from a long layoff before. I could do it again."

"Yeah, right," I said after a few seconds.

Looking in the boxes of old magazines always had this effect on me. A mixture of something someone who didn't understand would call sour grapes, blended with my own blurry nostalgia, and the stone-hard slap of reality.

Why would I even want to go back? That sport is so choked with petty politics and drugs, I thought as I came back to the kitchen and poured another cup of coffee.

I went upstairs and changed into a pair of baggy, yellow gym shorts and a battered, gray World Gym T-shirt. Barefoot, I headed downstairs to the gym.

It was going to be another amazing summer day. The light came shining off the water, blasting in from early morning until sunset, across the back of the house.

I was determined to get back into my workouts again. The last one I did was a half-assed arm session on Monday, and my biceps and triceps had been sore and stiff for four days after. I'd also tried to go out for a short run on Wednesday, along the boulevard park that lined the edge of the bluff, high above the bay. I thought I'd soak up a little fresh air and sunshine, enjoy the scenery, and get some exercise, so I started slowly down the hill to the park, a long block away. Then I jogged along for about five minutes. It felt good to begin with, but I quickly ran out of steam and slowed down to a fast walk for another couple of miles, while my heart pounded out of my chest, before I eventually headed back home. The next morning my back was completely out of whack, pain shooting up from the left hip to the right side of my neck, and my knees ached, as if they had been beaten with hammers.

I felt as if I were in the worst physical shape of my adult life. I wasn't really fat at all—a bit love-handlish perhaps, but certainly not overweight. I looked good in clothes, better than I did when I was muscularly forty pounds bigger, but I was beginning to feel like an aging jock, going to seed.

In the gym, I stuck the Eagles' *Hotel California* into the CD player and cranked up the volume. I only liked to listen to old favorites while I trained. While the title song played, I warmed up my chest on the incline bench, pushing the empty Olympic bar up and down for twenty-five or so reps, getting up after and stretching the muscles a little, then putting a forty-five-pound plate on each side of the bar and starting another set.

It didn't take much to remind me why I had done this for so many years. The squeeze of my muscles as I pushed against the weights had meant freedom. I would lose myself in the whirling flow of blood that rushed through every vein, never knowing at what point my body would collapse from pushing too hard, and the end result was a hardened sculpture, a suit of warrior's armor, that could only be taken away by quitting or death. My bones, skin, and meat were rockets, lifting me past the fading planet where a father will call a son an unwanted loser within that boy's earshot.

I turned the volume of the music higher. *Hotel California* moved into the deepest stretch of its heart.

As soon as I had pushed against pieces of iron, the world made sense. I only had to squeeze to find it. Every time the pain came, I washed it away with cold iron and surging blood. Doing that day after day made me stronger, harder, more immune.

I did a set of incline bench presses with a weight that three years earlier I would have warmed up with, but it still felt great; stretching and squeezing, working against an object that would crush me if I didn't find the strength to push it off my chest.

God, how I used to lose myself inside those bonfire-intense sets during a workout.

Summer, 1985
World Gym, Santa Monica, California

Two more, Bob. Two more, come on, you got it," Eddie growled East Coast, like a Brooklyn thug, right behind me.

I was either going to pass out or puke. My lungs were exploding. I paused between the reps to try to suck a thimble more sweaty air and could see in the mirror right in front of me, on the other side of the squat rack, that my face looked as if I were swinging from a hangman's rope, veins popping out of the crimson skin.

Slam it. Slam it, was racing through my head. Eddie's voice seemed to come from across town. *Fuck it—yeah*, I went in my mind, the beast voice raging, like a warrior leaping from a trench to charge the enemy, the long iron bar bending across the base of my neck. My knees bent and I dropped slowly, the bar bending more, its ends sloping toward the floor. I went to the bottom of the squat and without hesitating—even though I should have given out three reps earlier—shot back up and started back down for the bottom again the moment I reached the top.

"Paaaaa—uuhhh," I pulled the air. I aimed the bar at the squat rack, stepping shakily forward on Frankenstein legs. Eddie helped guide me. I rolled out from under the bar as soon as it was safely back on the supports, fell to the ground, and moaned. A cheer went up from two people standing by the leg-extension machine that stood behind where I was lying, unwinding my knee wraps. Twelve reps with five hundred pounds, in strict form.

"Jesus, Bob, great set," Eddie said as he headed toward me with his hand held out, to give me help up. "Very impressive."

I looked up at Eddie, grabbed his outstretched hand, got up, and began retightening my knee wraps.

"You ain't seen nothin' yet," I said, heading to one side of the deep gray bar, bent under five hundred pounds of plates. I was still struggling for breath. "Help me yank a couple these plates off, Eddie."

"You got it." We stripped the bar down to four hundred and five pounds and laid the two forty-fives we'd pulled off against the side of the rack. I slid back under, planted myself evenly, looked in my eyes in the mirror, let out a power grunt, and backed the bar out of the rack.

I had only paused maybe fifteen seconds between the sets, but was raring to go again. I pounded out ten more reps with the four hundred, struggling hard to get the last three and then collapsing after I put the bar back. I undid the wraps that wound tightly around each knee, to keep those joints from flying through the room like loose hamburger under such a load—and got up after two minutes so Eddie and I could finish our workout.

I measured everything in the gym against sets like the ones I did that day. Even more than my muscles, I used my mind to lift the weight. I'd see myself separate from the thing actually moving the load up and down, but intertwined as well. On squats, my whole body was a giant, heavy-duty spring, compressing as my knees bent and my hips moved toward the ground, a tremendous energy and pressure building with each inch I descended, until right at the bottom, when my butt was nearly touching the floor, the pressure of the energy would explode and thrust me back up to the top. The weight lifted itself; I simply controlled its momentum. This kind of workout was common in the days when I was ravenous for success.

Not an unusual day. Typical June, Santa Monica beach weather: foggy morning, low gray clouds hugging every light pole and house. It burned away later, letting the blue air unveil itself in a slow striptease that ended by noon or one. Then it got hot, especially if there wasn't any wind to keep the smoggy desert air pushed back on the other side of the 405. I lived far on the other side of the 405, inland near the hills, where the June heat and thick air would wrap around every living thing, so I enjoyed coming down to the beach to train in the early morning, if only for the change in weather.

I was part of the "early crew," as Joe Gold called the gang of guys who made up the informal shift between seven and nine every morning at his gym. My sights were focused on getting ready for the Mr. Olympia in October, and I'd been training with Eddie Giuliani for a couple of months. He had worked as the manager at World Gym, in Santa Monica, since Joe Gold first opened it a few years before. Eddie had been a great amateur competitor in the sixties and seventies, even winning his class in the Mr. America. He had come to the West Coast, from New York, in the early sixties to see Dave Draper and the other top guys of the day train and never moved back East again.

Sometimes Eddie's best friend, Ira (who just went by Ira and had been a training partner of Lou Ferrigno's, back in Brooklyn, before Louie had been in *Pumping Iron* or had been cast as Bill Bixby's monsterish, green alter ego on the *Incredible Hulk* TV show), joined us in the workouts, but Ira yelled too much while I was doing my sets and I complained to him about it, since I was a more quiet trainer, so he had been training on his own lately. I felt bad. I'd hurt his feelings. He meant no harm; he was just used to encouraging Louie through his workouts. Lou was legally deaf and didn't wear his hearing aid during training, so Ira yelled his encouragements at him in a loud voice and, after so many years, was unable to adjust the habit to suit my ears.

Joe Gold, who owned World Gym (and also started but sold Gold's Gym, several years before opening World), had been one of my biggest supporters, ever since I had shown up at his gym three years earlier as a shy kid who had just won the Mr. Los Angeles. Over the months leading up to the '85 Olympia, he gave me a hard time about training with old-timers, but Eddie and Ira were great training partners (if I could just convince Ira not to yell at me during my sets). I told Joe that I didn't mind training with old-timers at all and asked him to join us for a workout sometime if he thought I wasn't working hard enough. He declined since he was plagued by severe back problems and hadn't trained seriously for many years, but he watched me none the less, to make sure that I was working hard enough to capture my potential.

Saturday Morning,
Midsummer, 1 9 9 4
Seattle

I turned off the shower, shook some water out of my hair, flipped it straight back, and climbed out, grabbing a towel. I liked using the shower downstairs by the gym because it made me feel as if I had gone someplace other than my own house to train. The cocoon was feeling a bit claustrophobic on this bright morning. As I dried off, I turned toward the mirror above the sink and toilet. Standing up straight, as I would onstage in competition—pulling the stomach in, the shoulders back, and lifting up the rib cage—I checked out my shrunken body as the steam melted from the mirror, then laid the towel across the sink, stepped back so I could see the whole upper body and legs down to right above the knees, and did a double biceps.

"What a geek," I said, giggling a little.

The basic structure was still there, but the muscles had gone on a long vacation.

"You're thinkin' about the past too much." I finished drying off.

The workout felt good; not long or heavy; pathetic by my older standards, but not bad. I still had the stuff if I ever wanted to use it again.

I discovered that I had the stuff by accident. All my life I wanted to create. I used photography, painting, theater, and writing, and eventually my own body. A moving piece of marble. The marble, however, lived and breathed and had second thoughts, because the sculpture was not a pure work, but instead a confusing manipulation, using an alchemic blend of science, art, and sweat to push past the limits of nature and into the world of monsters.

Bodybuilding was not even a blip on the radar of life where I grew up. Musclemen were oily, nameless enigmas on the covers of seedy magazines; seemingly the men on those covers popped up from nowhere—probably less than nowhere—since their existence did not merit any thought about roots or background; greasy, worm-packed circus freaks who must have been born hairless and overbuilt, contorting their plastic-looking arms and legs—and for what purpose? The sight of them made people want to grit their teeth and look the other way, probably throwing out a derogatory comment about grotesqueness, or hair-combing abilities.

This was not a real thing, any more than sword-swallowing was a real thing, so there was nothing to even think about in any accidental newsstand encounter. Someone might giggle nervously, look around to make sure no one saw what he was looking at, flip through a few pages, then stuff the weirdness back where it came from and move on to *Guns and Ammo* or *Esquire*—magazines that were about something.

It's a different world now. Today, if a kid—even living where I grew up—wanted to build up his size and strength, he'd go join the local Gold's Gym or one of the other places like that. Then, there wasn't a gym where I lived, so going to one wasn't even an option.

I don't know if I'm a gifted athlete. Many experts in the physique world have told me that I had a tremendous gift—among the best that anyone had ever been given. I'm only partially sure, even now, exactly what that meant. Probably that I had a physical structure ideally suited for this particular sport. But, aside from physical structure, I don't think that I had the perfect gift for bodybuilding because I lacked one key quality. I was only able to do it without question for a few years, and then I began to be conflicted. I began to wonder if I shouldn't be doing something more important with my life. I don't consider myself a snob. I never—well, rarely—thought that I was too good for the sport. My conflict rose, in part, from wondering about the value of all sports, not only this one. Yet, I was pulled toward the life of singular devotion that my sport required, using my physical skills to try to block out an overactive mind that seemed to grow louder the more successful I became.

The ideal mentality for this sport is one of never thinking—certainly never thinking about life's deeper meanings or, for that matter, anything more than the right combination of factors necessary to get in peak condition. You have to shut off your brain, close your eyes, focus solely on the task at hand, and do whatever it takes to win. That's not the personality that emerged as I grew into manhood, deeply absorbed by this sport.

It wasn't a fear of being different. I was always different. The devil of this thing was in its details, many of which I only began to question after I was so deeply involved that to cut loose would be to sever an artery. And I really did love it.

It's usually assumed, by someone who doesn't understand bodybuilding, that anyone who is successful at it must have been born that way, or at least most of the way there. I wasn't. The right bone structure was there, but not the muscles. I adapted well to hard exercise and, as I came out of puberty, had a moderately fast metabolism, which kept me from getting too fat or staying too skinny. But if someone had looked at all the boys in my town, in my age range, and had predicted which one would eventually become a Mr. Universe, I would have been ranked in the lower half.

2

MIDDLE OF SOMEWHERE

I used to think that I had the world all figured out. I knew that, during my life, I wanted to be the best on the planet at something. I chased a dream. Behind every dream—every stretch to reach beyond mediocrity—there is a story. This is the story behind my dream. It's not neat or tidy. I can't even say for certain whether it is a tale of success or failure. Perhaps it's both.

I was born a boy who never fit in, raised where conformity was expected. That fact has colored every move I've made, both intelligent and foolhardy, throughout my life.

I was brought into this world at a hospital in Columbus, Indiana, and lived, until I left home at eighteen, mostly in Bartholomew and Brown Counties, a region in the southern part of Indiana, dominated by hilly woods and farms.

Columbus is the Bartholomew County seat. Begun on the swampy, mosquito-infested floodplain of the White River, it grew into a small agricultural and manufacturing town that gained a national reputation for progressive architecture in the 1950s, when diesel-engine industrialist J. I. Miller decided to grant funds for renowned architects to design innovative public buildings. Over the years, other civic leaders followed Miller's path, and along with a meticulous restoration of the original classic downtown, a model for small-city urban planning was achieved.

Columbus is also my father's hometown. Generations of our relatives came from farms in the area. His parents left their family farms to build a life in town. Cities such as Indianapolis or Louisville represented too great of a change for them after having been raised on the land, so a nearby town the size of Columbus presented a workable compromise. You could find work other than farming and still remain rooted, both physically and spiritually, near childhood homes.

The Brown County seat is the small village of Nashville. The two-lane State Route 46 winds fifteen miles through rolling hills covered with sycamore, poplar, oaks, and pines to connect Columbus and Nashville. Small corn, soybean, and tobacco fields quilt the valleys between the hills.

Along with other, even smaller towns in that county—with such names as Gnaw Bone and Bean Blossom—Nashville was held in great regional regard because of its rustic beauty and ability to attract artists and other creative types to its hilly woodlands. Tourists saw the area as a charming place for escape, but many natives and longtimers hated being invaded by outsiders. The county thrived on the tension. Crustier locals would complain bitterly when the roads were clogged each fall with gawkers chasing after colorful autumn leaves, but the galleries, antique shops, inns, and restaurants would prosper, and that made a lot more folks happy for the money than angry about the crowds.

This area was my mother's birthplace and her family's before her. I was raised to understand that creating a home in Brown County was, for the people who belonged there, the greatest way of life possible. We always looked with pride whenever driving past the white farmhouse, weathered barn, and log cabin clustered together at the edge of a clearing, where my mother's family lived when she was a girl. It lay just across 46 from Salt Creek (we said it "Saw Crick") where, as a boy, I would skinny-dip and flip over big flat rocks looking for snakes and crawdads.

I grew up roughly midway between Indianapolis and Louisville. It's forty or so miles down through Madison, Indiana, to the Kentucky state line. The place was one of those subtle culturally gray areas that occur on the border between two regions. Crossing the Indiana-Kentucky state line meant, only by a cartographer's definition, that you were among Northerners on one side and Southerners on the other, especially on the southern-Indiana side of that line. The people of northern Kentucky knew that they were Southerners. On the Indiana side of that state line, you grew up with the same culture, but were classified Midwestern.

Everyone I grew up with, if they came from the area, had a Southern accent, including my family. Not like a Georgian, but far more a Kentucky drawl than the flat Chicago twang northern Hoosiers wrapped around their words.

My family was mostly working-class Democrats, Baptists and fundamentalist Christians. In an area that was, if not the buckle of the Bible Belt, at least an edge of that buckle, I was raised to understand that hellfire and damnation crouched behind every shrub. I grew up hearing that not even Mahatma Gandhi would get into heaven, since he was a heathen who hadn't been "washed by the blood of the lamb."

I loved the place where I was born and raised, but plotted escape from an early age, anxious to flee the mildew of familiar claustrophobia. It didn't matter that it was beautiful or that visitors would come from all over the area to admire it. I was drowning there as surely as if I'd fallen into a deep pool of a river with a giant rock tied around my ankle. No matter how far I eventually ran, though, I was attached to a time and place, and its shadows would always stay with me.

I was named Robert Clark Paris. Eight pounds ten ounces; ten fingers, ten toes. I was a happy-eyed infant, with wheat-brown, almost blond, thick hair, and a light olive cast to my skin. My eyes went from infant blue to brown with natural ease. My hair would gradually darken too.

Everyone called me Bobby, until I made a getting-past-boyhood transition—against strong resistance—to Bob, in my midtwenties. I was my parents' second child, born in December 1959. My sister Lisa was born in August of the year before.

My middle name, Clark, was Mom's maiden name. Constance Diane; she went by Diane. The middle child of three, Mom had jet-black hair, blue eyes, and fair skin. A Brown County high school cheerleader, an all-American country beauty, she made up for what she may have lacked in urban sophistication with the charming ways of a working-class debutante. Liz Taylor might have been cast to play her in a 1950s movie about simple rural life.

My first name came from Dad. Only his middle name, Gene, kept me from the nickname Junior. Thank God.

Dad had been an athletic young man, with a dark olive complexion and black hair, who ran track and cross-country for Columbus High School. He was a Lucky Strike–smoking, Budweiser-drinking man of his times, with a flawed genius for math. The first person in his family to graduate from college, he become a CPA the hard way. He went from high school to college, but left after a year; was drafted into the Marine Corps during the Cold War times between Korea and Vietnam; and was then discharged one year later because of severe migraine headaches. He married Mom, started having kids, and began night school at Butler University to get his degree, while working full-time as a bookkeeper at an asphalt plant in Indianapolis.

Mom and Dad had been introduced by a cousin of my mom's who had married a friend of my dad's; she thought that Bob and Diane were made for each other. They went on their dates in Dad's '56 T-bird. After a short courtship they were married, on Christopher Columbus Day, at the Nashville Christian Church—Mom's family church—in 1957, and had Lisa ten months later. I was conceived during a time when they lived in Baton Rouge, Louisiana. They divorced for the first time when I was three.

We called our grandparents Mam-ma and Pap-pa. Those names simply appeared in our family vocabulary. Both Mom and Dad's parents were hardworking, devoutly religious couples who saw the world from rigid cultural perspectives and raised their children in the best ways they knew how. Hard, physical punishments. A spared rod (or razor strap) spoiled a child. It's how they were raised. Children were always to be controlled, even if they feared you. Grandkids were regarded differently: pure love. It was up to parents to control their own.

Between my parents' first divorce and their eventual remarriage, Mom, Lisa, and I lived with Mam-ma and Pap-pa Clark in their house on Tuck-Away Ridge, outside of Nashville. It was our safe harbor, since all Mom had been prepared for in life was being a wife and mother. She graduated high school, found her mate, created offspring and a home, without exterior ripple. She played by the rules: no drinking, no smoking; all service and loyalty.

Dad got an apartment in Indianapolis so he could be close to work and school. We hardly ever saw him. He was trapped between having a family to provide for and being overwhelmed by the burden of working full-time while getting his college education. I don't think he ever really wanted the responsibilities of a wife and children, but in those days it was simply what any respectable person did with his life and was rarely questioned.

This time marked his life in destructive ways and, as a consequence, mine and my family's as well. He was shut out of the soul of his family and did not possess the skills to work his way back in. Distance and ice, warmed only by a raging temper, were his solutions for us; alcohol was the answer for him. My father was not a bad man; he was just squashed by what he was told a real man had to be and damaged his life, and the lives of those around him, by trying to live up to unreasonable standards. He numbed his mind and heart with booze when they objected to those standards.

From the youngest age I can remember, I had an extremely shy, quiet exterior, hiding an exploding, imaginative interior. I found refuge in my

imagination, a fantasy world where Jules Verne adventures or the bat-
tlefield of an obscure war came to life. My internal life contrasted so
sharply against my external one that many people who knew me as a
little boy were amazed that I would become, at times, such an extro-
verted personality as I grew up.

To most adults, I was a one- or two-word child, answering most of
their questions with a "Nothin'" or "I dunno." In occasional bursts, I
would open up my world a bit, rattling on about my take on the shape
of a deer's antlers or anything else that captured my imagination, but if
I got the least bit embarrassed, I'd retreat.

Pap-pa Clark built the house on Tuck-Away Ridge with his own hands,
and I fell in love with a patch of woods that began at the lower edge
of the backyard. The trees and undergrowth went down a hillside to a
dirt road and continued down to a ravine, where a small stream trickled
and bubbled beneath mossy, exposed-tree-root overhangs.

I kept my first horse in that ravine and visited her every day, riding
her magnificent chestnut flanks—that only I could see—up and down
the hills, chasing rabbits and deer, hitching her behind a cluster of trees
while I shot at enemy soldiers who had crossed behind our lines. She
was my only best friend during that little-boy time when things just
weren't right, so each morning I'd pull a battered, ready-for-the-
Goodwill, felt hat of Mam-ma's down on my head—imagining that it
was a ten-gallon Stetson—strap on a six-gun and holster, and head out
to find a place where everything was clean and muddy. At the end of
each day's adventures, when I'd come out of the woods for supper, everyone would ask me how my horse was doing.

I learned to read early, beginning at around four with the basics and
being able to get through a third-grade-level book by kindergarten. The
words came easy and I loved everything about language. By the time I
was four, it was also established that I was artistic. My early drawings
were done exclusively in black crayon. Since black was the color of
funerals and depression, some family adults wondered if my color choice
might be tied to how I was responding to Mom and Dad's divorce, or
some other deep-seated mental mystery. I discovered the other colors
of crayons and paints eventually, although I felt that I had been using
them all along. I saw the colors even if no one else did.

My parents got remarried. A child could see that their attitudes toward each other hadn't changed, but Lisa and I were happy to have
them back under one roof anyway. Mom produced (with some help from
Dad) a set of fraternal twins, right before Halloween: a happy, healthy

girl, Leslie, and a boy, Todd, who died less than a day after birth. Ten months later, at Thanksgiving, another boy, James, came along, and he was the last.

I was vigorously promised by Mom and Dad that I'd get to name my younger brother, but Dad refused to go along when I decided on John, because Mom's last serious boyfriend before their first marriage was also named John. Dad didn't have much hesitation in going back on his word, especially to his family. We were his property and his was the final word, regardless of any promises. So my younger brother was called Jim, after Dad's brother.

Spring, 1965
Southern Indiana

Bobby, what are you doing?" Mom asked, coming around the side of the house. Her voice was gentle—changed.

"Nothin'," I said.

It seemed as if she weren't mad at me anymore.

"Do you want to tell me about what happened last night at supper?" I shrugged my shoulders. "Do you have *any* explanation?" The sweetness in her voice inched closer to cracking.

I was only five, but still understood that she was trying hard to be careful and patient. If frightened, I was known not to say a peep for days at a time.

"No, ma'am."

I looked down from her face at my muddy clodhoppers, the plastic submachine gun I'd been playing with hanging from my small right hand.

"Mean to tell me, young man, that you've been out here this whole time and still haven't come up with an answer for me why you wouldn't swallow that bite?" The edge came stronger.

"No, ma'am." I kept looking down, but every few seconds tilted a quick, sideways look up. A lock of her dark hair hung, separated from the rest, over her eye like a comma.

"Do I have to keep telling you about those other little children going to bed without supper every night?"

"I dunno."

She was losing me and knew it.

*   *   *

The night before, sitting at the dinner table eating a dry roast, left too long in the oven because Dad had stopped *somewhere* on the way home from work and was late for supper, I had quietly refused to do more than push my food around on the plate.

"Eat," he growled.

"Yes, sir," I said, forcing another bite in, never looking up.

Mom and Dad had battled in whispers that sounded like angry vacuum cleaners hissing in the kitchen, the minute Dad came in the door. The occasional "goddamnit" or "drunk" or "shut up, bitch" flared like the high arc of a heartbeat chart up over the sound of the TV, which we small ones sat in front of on the oval rug, hungry and waiting for the tornado to pass, Lisa crying, holding baby Leslie between her legs.

I had forced down nearly every bite, but on the last one lost my ability to swallow, sitting there with the hunk of unchewed beef pouched in the side of my mouth.

"Eat," he said again. I froze. Everything shut down, the stubborn response coming involuntarily over me. Everyone else finished eating and left the table.

"You will not get up from this table until you swallow that bite," he snapped, shrinking me with his eyes.

Two hours passed; then three. Mom begged him not to tan my hide—but good—as he was itching to. They swirled around. Suddenly I decided that I would outlast them. At ten-thirty, the bite of beef still in my cheek, they broke down and sent me off to bed. Mom came in and gave me a short lecture on starving children in foreign lands and ordered me to ask Jesus for guidance. Her voice was strangled with quiet anger.

In the morning, I came into the kitchen with the bite still there. Mom told me to spit it out in the trash can, which I did, and gave me the choice to go to my room or outside to think about my prideful behavior and then ask for forgiveness.

She came out to find me in the side yard two hours later and never pried an answer from me about the incident, which found its way—after the freshness of their anger about my severe stubborn streak wore off—into family lore: the night Bobby decided to play a squirrel with a piece of pot roast.

It was no wonder my imagination flourished. I lived in a home where I was frightened most of the time so I needed a refuge somewhere. I chose the inside of my head.

But imagination was for little boys. Creativity and artistic talent were supposed to wilt on the vine when more practical interests developed. I was raised with a complete disregard for the arts. No symphony, ballet, museums, theater, or poetry. Living in the cultural sticks, we were to find practical, "sweat of thy brow" ways through life. In spite of this, I drew my pictures and read all the great adventure stories I could get my hands on, studied the works of the great writers and artists in library books, and my imagination continued to flourish.

Mom put, by far, the greatest efforts into helping each of her children try to develop new interests, but she wasn't raised with any understanding or appreciation of the creative arts either and so didn't know how to help me grow in this area. I was too stifled to tell her what I needed, so a circle closed around that only further separated me from my family.

Now, when the early American settlers fanned west over the Appalachians, they felt it was their divine right to take whatever they saw," my eighth-grade history teacher, Mr. Marvin, said, as he moved his hand from Pennsylvania westward across the roll-down map. "They modeled the ethic of this westward expansion after their European ancestors. The land and the setting sun belonged to them. The means were always justified. It was theirs to take. They called it manifest destiny. And so now we have America."

His hand came to rest two inches below San Francisco.

I was soaked to the bone by those words: *manifest destiny.*

I believed that it was my destiny to be the best in the world at something. As soon as I figured out what it was, I'd grab on to it and take what was mine. Nothing—not location or poverty or lack of knowledge—would stand in my way.

Autumn, 1973
Southern Indiana

The woods dropped yellow and red leaves on hills rolling out past the valley covered by a hundred tents and campfires. Four times each year all the Boy Scout troops in the district gathered and made camp. I was a Scout because I loved the trips, but there were always events at these camporees. I hated them, especially the competitive ones. The theme of the events for this fall's camporee was fitness.

At thirteen, living in a body with forearms the size of chicken bones, I possessed a mixed bag of physical traits that made the Scouts' idea of fitness both abhorrent and appealing. I was a good runner. Decent speed, great endurance.

On the way into the campground I ran beside our scoutmaster's nine-year-old, black '63 Chevy station wagon, used to pull a small trailer of troop camping gear. I ran, panting and proud, right outside his rolled-down window as he gave second-by-second updates on my speed, for two miles along a dirt road. He marveled at how I could keep going. That was Friday evening.

On Saturday morning I stood underneath a chin-up bar, staring up with tears in my eyes. I was going to jump up for the fourth time and try to pull myself up. The first three tries had yielded shaking arms, no upward movement, then a fall into the dirt. Just before I went, Mark—a superb gymnast from our troop—had easily done twenty-five chins, then pulled himself up over the top of the bar, locked his arms out, and rolled over the other side as if crossing a bed from one side to the other.

I couldn't even pull myself up once.

I joined the Boy Scouts in the sixth grade, a year after my family moved back to Columbus from Nashville.

Mom and Dad had been planning to build their dream house on several acres of forest land in an area called Deer Trails. Plans for building the house were canceled when the marriage again began to crumble.

I dreamed that I would grow up to be six foot ten and play in the NBA. This was a natural dream, since I grew up in basketball country. Beginning in the fourth grade, I went to basketball camp during summer break, at Hanover College, a campus of ivy-covered red-brick buildings and towering oaks, forty miles from home, overlooking the Ohio River. I went for two years. I was the kid in camp who, when they had the awards dinner for all the campers' families, got a Most Improved Player ribbon, which everyone knew meant that you were, while not the biggest loser on a team, at least a second-, or third-rate talent. After two years at basketball camp, and a season spent mostly warming the bench for both the fifth-grade team and a Boys' Club team, averaging only two or three buckets a game, and being scowled at by both teams' coaches whenever I had the nerve to attempt a shot and not pass the ball to a go-to boy, I realized that no NBA scouts would ever seek me out.

Little League baseball was the same. I joined a team that immediately saw my value as a right fielder. The coaches held their breath whenever a ball came my way. One swampy summer evening, mosquitoes and june bugs swirling in the overhead lights, I reached my glove up, closed my eyes, and came back to earth with the ball in my mitt on a bases-loaded, last-inning third out. No one could believe it, cheering as I trotted back to our bench. It was the absolute peak of my baseball career, based on a shut-eyed fluke.

Little league football was better, but by the time I discovered it, I was into the nasty habit of breaking my bones. I broke so many bones that the doctors in the emergency room knew me on sight. I fell out of trees, got flung off horses, snapped my leg on the first day of eighth-grade football practice.

Everything fell apart. The pieces would melt back together occasionally, but as I became a teenager, I was mostly spinning out of control. I remember thinking when I was eighteen and freshly away from home that my whole life had been lived in a fog. An impenetrable winter drizzle had wrapped its arms around everything I came in contact with; colors were diffused; true meanings hidden.

I became my own Siamese twin: a budding hood, attached at the chest to a shy alien. I didn't kill any teachers or rob any liquor stores, but I did drink, smoke, do drugs, and get caught shoplifting. Eventually I had to leave Mom's house and go live with Dad because I was getting into so much trouble. At the same time I was still in Boy Scouts, playing football, in school musicals, on the speech team, and had won National Scholastic awards for my drawings. But all the good things couldn't prevent me from tumbling into dark holes of despair and those holes seemed to appear every few steps. I knew something was wrong with me. No matter what I did, I couldn't make myself fit in. In one destructive situation after another, my life quickly began to slide downhill. First there came smoking.

Summer, 1973
Southern Indiana and Kentucky

I stole them from Dad because I didn't know where else to get them. Every morning I'd look at his pack of Luckys lying on the end table beside his recliner and estimate how many it was safe to make off with—how many I could get without his noticing—and pull out one or two. I rarely ventured three. My paper route was directly tied to my learning to smoke. I delivered the *Louisville Courier Journal* to subscribers in my neighborhood every morning for three years. I was not an early-morning child, and pulling my sleepy body out of a warm bed at four in the morning, seven mornings a week, four seasons a year, was like dipping a chocolate ice cream cone in vinegar, but I was instilled with a work ethic from early on. I was never, or rarely, without employment from the age of ten or eleven on.

I delivered the paper to about seventy houses—close to ninety on Sundays. The first year I had the route the local distributor, a Mr. Rummple, told all his carriers about a subscription-gathering contest that could yield a free trip to the Kentucky State Fair and Mammoth Cave. I was extremely motivated to win this trip since I had only been to the Indiana State Fair and wanted to make an informed comparison between the two. I'd also never been to a place as grand as Mammoth Cave, so naturally this contest stoked the furnaces of my imagination.

I rang the bell on every door in all the neighborhoods I could reach by bike and sold subscriptions. By the end of the contest, I'd won my trip.

One early morning in late July—a day that already held the potential to bust the top off a thermometer—Dad took me to the Greyhound station on his way to the office and I got on the bus with the other carriers from the area, headed for Louisville and the State Fair. I had saved forty dollars from my collection money—a fortune, a key to every conceivable lock—and had it stuffed in my underpants, since I didn't know what sorts would be on the bus or in the city when I got there, and I didn't want to be robbed or, worse, pickpocketed.

On the bus, I sat next to a kid from the east side of Columbus, Sherman. He was a sort of Jerry Lewis, nutty-professor-looking kid, and we made sporadic small talk all the way down the interstate, until the bus pulled into the Louisville station. We stuck together as we were met by Mr. Rummple. All of us got on another bus with a new bunch of strangers, who turned out to be paperboys from other parts, and we headed for the fairgrounds. Once we got there, we were given a meeting time and place, an emergency contact, and then set free. Surprise. I had thought we would be supervised, but we were on our own. Sherman and I looked at each other disbelieving our good fortune.

"Come on, Sherman, I'll race you to the gate," I said.

"I don't know, Bobby, I probably shouldn't run. I have flat feet, and besides, I don't want to get any blisters. Mother said I shouldn't exert myself."

I couldn't believe what I was hearing. *Why'd I trap myself with this guy before I even knew him?* I thought.

I took off running for the front gate, forgot that I had left my small duffel bag sitting on the ground next to the bus, stopped, turned around, went back to get it, and found Sherman sitting on the dusty pavement crying.

"Ah, jeez, Sherman, what's a matter? Why ya ballin'?" I was just going to grab my bag and leave, but suddenly my Sunday school upbringing—against my deeper, better judgment—kicked in. "Come on. I'll stay with ya."

I put my arm around his shoulder and led him, as he sniffled a bit, into the Kentucky State Fair.

What a mistake.

He couldn't go on any fast or swirly rides because he claimed to have an ulcer. He didn't want to do the spinning gravity ride—where the floor drops out from under you—on account of his dizzy spells. He couldn't eat hot dogs or caramel corn—ulcer. He was afraid of the haunted house, claiming it might give him nightmares. I said that it was supposed to give you nightmares—that was the point. He wasn't swayed.

So we played games of skill and chance for most of the day: ring tosses, duck shooting, ball pitching. I had no concept of budgeting my money, and before I knew it, I was down to less than five dollars. It was then that I noticed that Sherman hadn't really played any games, so much as watched me play. He had plenty of money left. I got mad and called him a cheapskate—without any real reason other than the fact that I was angry about not spending my money on rides and being so low on cash so quickly. I broke away from him and stormed my way through the crowd and went out to the bus. I plopped down with my back against a front tire and waited—sitting on the shady side—till six o'clock, when all the other guys began filtering back from the midway. I pouted over the fact that I'd spent my day obligated to a cheap hypochondriac, especially as I overheard other guys' stories of adventures on the rickety roller coasters and in the sideshows. Two of the Columbus boys—one whom I knew from church—pulled out Winston cigarettes and went around the side of a beat-up Pontiac.

"What're you lookin' at, Paris?" Burt, the one from church, asked. "I'll betcha never even smoked before, Paarr-iiss—have ya?" He said my name like an insult.

"Course I have," I lied, and looked away.

"Been hangin' out with that weirdo all day, Paris," the other guy, Kenny, said. I felt my face go all hot.

"Lemme have one," I said. "I've been waitin' all day to have a smoke."

I went over around the car and Burt held out a cigarette, pulled it back when I reached for it, then gave it to me.

"Gimme a light," I said.

"Light it from mine," Kenny said, tapping the ashes, then handing me his smoke. I took it and held it up to mine as I'd seen my dad do and got that fresh-lighted tobacco smell, which only lasted for a couple of seconds. I coughed a little, they laughed; I only pulled the smoke into my mouth; I didn't dare breathe it.

I sat with Burt and Kenny on the bus ride down to Mammoth Cave. They were my first smoking buddies. Sherman sat near the front of the bus and kept looking back at me the whole trip, as if I had betrayed him or something.

When the bus arrived at the national park, we all filed out and were directed to giant group cabins, where we would live for the weekend. Burt and Kenny and I went out exploring the woods behind our cabin and puffed a couple of smokes, trying to blow rings like seasoned pros. All weekend, even deep inside the cave, which stretched dozens of miles through the middle of the earth, we would steal away to smoke. Finally those guys got sick of my bumming smokes from them and demanded that I buy a pack. Well, I'd never thought about that, but it seemed, in some uncomfortable way, fair enough, except that I had no money left.

They began to refuse to give me any cigarettes, those creeps. I tried to figure out how to get myself a desperately needed smoke, even resorting to asking some of the older guys I didn't even know (they just laughed at me and told me to get lost). By the time the weekend was over, I was hooked.

Dad picked me up at the Columbus bus station and asked me how my time away was. I told him it was fun and suspected that he could tell that I had been up to no good, but he didn't say anything else until we got home when he asked me if I had brushed my teeth all weekend. I froze waiting for the shit to fly, but he got out, went into the garage, and never said another word about it.

I was thirteen when I began scoping out Dad's pack of Lucky Strikes each morning as I'd head out to deliver the paper. Riding my orange Sting-Ray bike through the streets of my neighborhood, a canvas paperboy's bag slung over my shoulder, I could sometimes be seen on the darkest mornings only as a small, glowing dot coming around a corner.

Early Spring, 1975
Southern Indiana

We came out early on a Saturday morning and finally began working after an hour of exploring the old barn, which to our young imaginations was like a dilapidated medieval castle. All around were the guys in my Scout troop. We were cleaning out the scoutmaster's father-in-law's barn as one of our community service projects, although it was a bit unclear exactly how cleaning up after someone's in-law's animals was serving the community. But we were all, for the most part, in good spirits.

We settled into our good deed with the enthusiasm of an engine that's slow to warm up. Sputtering and wheezing to begin, not sure if the task will catch, but moving into smooth, easy hard work after exploring all the options for just fucking off the whole day. One of the other guys my age got us working, since those of us who were contemplating riding away on a few of the horses out at the pasture fence line didn't want to take the fall for the disharmony that could result if the stalls weren't squeaky-clean by sundown. I was the strongest objector to the work, athough even I eventually settled into it with a sweaty rhythm. Playing would've been more fun, but the shoveling and hauling weren't all that bad either. We were Boy Scouts after all, so what did I really expect to come of the day, bank robbery?

When the day finally ended, all the stalls were clean and we waited in the corral for our scoutmaster, Mr. Turner, to bring his pickup around from the house. He had spent the day working in another barn, but showed up every couple of hours to check on our progress. His oldest daughter, Lizzy, who was eighteen or nineteen, stood around with all of us, leaning against the corral fence, shooting the breeze and waiting for her dad. She was home from college for the weekend and had been bringing us Cokes and various other things to drink throughout the day.

One of my buddies, Jimmy, said that he and I should go look at the horses, and I went around to the other side of the barn with him, telling the others that we'd be right back. Jimmy and I were the sort of pals who had conspired to steal little bottles of booze out of his dad's liquor cabinet to take with us to summer camp the year before. We'd each drunk three of them and got puking sick one July night, back in a deep pine and cedar woods. We'd also become smoking buddies.

We rounded the side of the barn. The horses were right there, a dozen of them, an odd assortment of wild lookers shuffled in with muscular beauties—their tangled chests and tails and moving legs right on the other side of a three-wire fence, only a small hill between it and a hundred-acre pasture. Jimmy and I went down-fence about twenty feet and crossed it by a post and then walked right up into the middle of the bunch as if we belonged there. Two of the wilder ones split off and went around the corner of the barn, not violently, but like rough cloth dragged through weeds. I picked my favorite of the ones that stayed: a tan and dirt-brown mare who had a look in her eye of a mother who'd had a wild younger life.

"I'll ride her," I said to Jimmy while I stroked her nose.

She threw her head back. I took her gently by the mane and, before I could even register a thought, slung myself up on her back, preparing to head out into that pasture—fuck the world. I looked up and saw that everyone else had come around the barn to see what Jimmy and I were up to. They looked like a flock of penguins crossing dirty ice, the summer shimmer and the movement of my ride tossing my vision into a stir of dust and pounding veins. I saw Jimmy running around in a tight circle, then the mare kicked up her back legs and took off toward the hill at a gallop. Two seconds later she stopped short; I lost my grip on her mane. She raised up on her back legs and, in one smooth motion, bucked me forward. I was in the air a year before reaching forward with my right arm, trying to push the packed earth out of the way. The bones from the elbow down to the wrist gave way. Crumpled. By the time everyone had surrounded me and my sense of time had come back in shards, I saw that my hand was torqued backward so that the knuckles of my dusty fingers were resting only inches from the top of my forearm and bones were coming through the skin, where seconds before a boy's hand had been.

The mare galloped away over the crest of the hill. I saw this, with my head flopped over to the left, away from the smashed arm, right before I vomited up a liverwurst-with-mustard sandwich on Wonder bread and some Ruffles potato chips, then passed out.

"Oh, fuck. Oh, fuck. Jesus, Bobby, hold still, man—you're hurt really bad, man—oh, shit." I heard that as I came rippling awake again. I don't know who said it; it sounded like all their voices combined, but it couldn't have been—there were guys there who would never use that kind of language. I went black again.

Get the truck around here."

"Oh, Dad, he just took off. I didn't see him go."

I was coming back; my feet felt elevated and my hand had flipped back into an only slightly perverted position; the bones were still out and my mouth tasted like bullets. Mr. Turner was telling Lizzy to go get the truck and pull it up to the gate a hundred feet away. I tried to get up but couldn't move my legs. They were wrapped in a plaid horse blanket.

How appropriate, I thought.

Then I realized that I'd been treated for shock and my arm had been partially wrapped in a splint made out of bandannas and a broken tree branch. It looked like birch. I *was* surrounded by Boy Scouts, so the treatment—for shock and other first aid—wasn't surprising. I had a pang of slight envy, since someone would earn major brownie points toward a first-aid merit badge by way of my stupidity. I started to black out again, but accidentally bit down on the inside of my mouth and snapped back.

"Paris, can you get up?" Mr. Turner asked, pulling the blanket away.

"I . . . um . . . think so," I answered as he supported my upper body and I tried to put my feet underneath my legs. I made it up, lunging forward, riding the momentum as we headed toward the gate. I began to go down again, straining against his grip.

"Damnit, don't you pass out on me," he yelled straight in my ear, and I stopped myself from falling, moving faster toward that truck seat, where I collapsed. And right then the anvil of pain descended.

Lizzy headed straight to the emergency room in the old pickup; her dad stayed behind to make sure everyone else got home all right. We were at least fifteen miles out in the country. As we drove into town, I tried to make some jokes about bareback riding and luckily being left-handed, since I had a social studies report I hadn't started yet due on Monday. She tried to go easy across railroad tracks and chuckholes, driving as fast as possible toward the hospital where I had been haplessly building a reputation for several years. An empty styrofoam coffee cup was rolling around down by my boots.

I told her about my first serious injury, which had happened when I was four. I was a climber from early on, I told her, trying to calm her, and had been scaling the ladder on the tallest slide in Brown County State Park, where Mom always took Lisa and me to play. While I laughed at nothing else but the joy of being in the wind, my right foot missed the top rung of the ladder. I fell headfirst to the pavement, sustained a severe concussion, resting dead to the world for several hours after being rushed to the clinic, which acted as the hospital in Brown County. In those days, Mom worked as the clinic receptionist, and the head nurse told her that if it weren't for the hardness of my head (a quality, the nurse said, that seemed generously distributed on all sides of my family), I might have smashed open like a late-November pumpkin.

"I'm really sorry, Lizzy," I slurred with my head bobbing around. "I didn't mean to get hurt. Tell your dad I said I was sorry too, will ya?"

*   *   *

Mom and Dr. Schnieder (our family physician, who was completely familiar with my emergency-room visits) got to the examining room, where I had already been stripped, gowned, shipped off to X ray on a gurney, and brought back again. Fifteen minutes later, Dad came in wearing golf clothes, right before another doctor slipped a needle filled with some painkiller into my arm and told me to count backward from one hundred. I got to ninety-five and faded out. Right after the needle went in, a sudden insight hit me. Mr. Turner and I seemed to be oddly connected through my broken bones.

Two years earlier, after I'd broken my left arm by first falling from a high branch of a tree in our backyard and then playing middle linebacker in a little league football game the next day, I first encountered Michael Turner at an Indiana University football game.

A couple of weeks into my first serious cast, our troop had usher duty at an IU home football game. When we weren't escorting fans to their seats or otherwise trying to look vaguely official, some of us would toss a ball or stand around in doorways shooting the breeze. Some of us would also sneak off to smoke cigarettes and explore the possibilities of other general mischief while fifty thousand people watched the game. Before the games began, however, all the troops would gather by the old basketball field house to get their assignments and sections of responsibility (as if ushering a football game were D day or something).

The old field house was a grand gymnasium that rose five or six stories and was supported by a line of enormous concrete arches that ran, spaced perhaps twenty feet apart, the entire length of the building, vaulting over the roof and lined up like a loose tunnel.

We always had parent drivers who took us to these things. Michael Turner was a parent driver this trip. He was the Cub Scout leader at the same church where our Scout troop was based.

All the adults had wandered off to fix their collective caffeine jones, which left a hundred milling adolescent boys to get up to no good. I was the biggest duck in the puddle. Challenges were begun regarding who could climb to the top of one of the arches, which were less than a foot wide and rose high above the pavement. I immediately began to scale the one closest to us, in spite of having a cast on one arm. A guy from the troop standing next to ours hopped on the next arch and began to race me to the top. I grappled on with my good and bad arms, looked straight ahead only at the piece of arch right in front of me, and went up. Suddenly a third of the way up the guy on the next arch let out a little gasp and picked his way slowly back to the ground.

"Ha!" I yelled. "And I've got a busted arm—chicken!"

I lost my grip for one small piece of a second, swallowed my intestines back down, focused in again, and made it to the top of the arch. I stayed there a minute trying to decide if I wanted to cross the roof and follow the arch down on the other side of the building. After a couple more minutes, I'd picked my way back down the same side I'd just climbed. Immediately another challenge came and I started up again, racing another sucker, who like the last one didn't even make it halfway before heading down. This went on three more times; on each successful descent I pointed out my cast, which was covered in dirt, doodles, and autographs. I decided when no more challengers came forward to do one last victory climb. Right when I got to the top, Michael Turner came back to see what all the commotion was about.

"Get down from there," he screamed up at me. "And be careful. Are you some kind of an idiot?"

I made a swift return to the base of the arch, where he met me, bright red in the face, ready to boil. My explanation that I'd been up and down nearly half a dozen times (trying to show that I knew what I was doing) only seemed to enrage him more. He threatened to have me kicked out of the Scouts, prosecuted for recklessness and so forth. Luckily, as I tried to decide whether to laugh in his face or shrink away from humiliation, some of the older guys found our scoutmaster (during the time before Mr. Turner took over), Louie Evans, coming back— sipping on a paper cup of coffee and smoking a small cigar—and reported to him on my feat. He came over all proud, put his arm around my shoulder, and said, "Jesus H. Christ, that's great! And you with that busted-up arm and all. That's a hell of a goddamn thing, that is."

He said that last part looking straight at Mr. Turner, then led me away from the smoldering Cub Scout leader, who had no sense of the victory this had been over all the other troops.

I woke up several hours later on Mom's bed with a complicated fresh cast on my entire right arm. *It's a hell of a price for a ten-second horse ride,* I thought.

Dad came in. He told me how lucky I was that I hadn't been hurt worse and bent forward, as if he were going to kiss my cheek (he smelled of sweat, tobacco, Scotch, and worn-down Aqua Velva), and then while he was right by my ear, said, "You ever pull a stunt like that again and I'll break your other arm."

When he stood back up, his eyes had gone hard and black. I could see the hairs in his nose moving as he breathed. He turned around and left.

My life was changing. I didn't climb on the bare back of an unbroken, unfamiliar horse for nothing. I didn't steal Dad's Lucky Strikes just for kicks. The overwhelming specter of total collapse hung over me, and I couldn't really even have said why; whatever made me feel this way seemed foggy, indistinct, and distant, but also familiar.

I wished that when that needle full of Demerol had gone in, and I'd counted backward from one hundred, that the next thing I'd seen was God. I wanted to ask God why He made life so hard. If He could do anything—as my Sunday school teachers had always insisted He could—then couldn't He make life a lot easier? I just wanted to ask Him that, and if He said that He couldn't—or worse, wouldn't—then I never wanted to wake up again.

Late Summer, 1975
Southern Indiana

Do you know why you're here?" Dad asked with his back toward me, pouring himself a highball glass halfway full of J & B Scotch. "And I know what you're thinking too," he added, glancing back over his shoulder. "I'm making myself a drink while you're here because of booze. Well, my answer to that is that I'm an adult, and I can do this if I want."

He turned around and held his glass up in the air—a barroom gesture—toasting me. "You're just a kid and you can't. So, do you know why you're here?"

He took a sip of his drink and looked at me, squinting his eyes.

Mom had nabbed me, claiming that I'd once again stuck a knife in her heart. How could I keep doing this to her, she had asked me.

I'd reverted back to a childlike "I dunno."

I had been such a sweet little boy when I was young, she had thrown in; so innocent, so trustworthy; how did it all go wrong?

"Yes, sir," I told Dad, looking down at my bare feet—tanned and grass-stained—wanting to be anywhere but here, now, my scrawny fifteen-year-old arms poking out of a dirty gray T-shirt.

"Didn't you bring any goddamn shoes?" he asked, following my eyes to the floor.

"Yes, sir, they're in my bag over there."

I hated shoes, especially from May on. They were a crime against the nature of summer, or any other season, as far as I was concerned.

I sat there not fully listening but instead trying to imagine Dad as a small boy. I'd seen an old black-and-white photo of him: little, black-haired four-year-old, standing in front of the corner of a hazy barn and chicken pen, wide, unblemished eyes, faded overalls with big cuffs turned up, the whole future rolled out before him like an open prairie. *What was on his mind when that photo was taken?* I wondered.

"Where the hell are you?" he asked. "Off in outer space again. You better wise up or I'm gonna tie a goddamn knot in your tail."

I snapped back and realized that he'd been talking to me.

"I ought to stick you in the goddamn Boys' School. You know that, don't you? But, I'm not going to. You're movin' in here with me. We'll get all your shit this weekend."

The plan had been so simple. Joey Lynch and I were going to camp out down by one of the rivers and tried to plot a way to get a couple of bottles of Annie Green Springs. The only person either of us could think of to get the wine was a young woman named Wendy who lived in the neighborhood. She was maybe twenty-two or twenty-three, husky voiced, bottle blonde, and mostly wore short cutoffs and small halter tops in the hot weather. She also flirted with me when no one else was around and basically let me know that when I was ready to lose my virginity to come look her up. One afternoon she'd offhandedly said she could get me booze if I ever wanted it. I eventually took her up on the offer. Joey and I pooled our money and I went on a Wednesday afternoon and asked Wendy to get us two bottles. She said that she would have them for me that Friday afternoon.

Every Friday, all summer, I cut three lawns, Mom's included. I had five or six others spread out through the week. I was just finishing our back-yard when Mom came driving up from work an hour early, a mad, soaked-hen look all over her face.

"Get in the house," she yelled over the mower noise. "Now!"

"What?" I yelled back, reaching over to shut down the engine, which sputtered and coughed to a ragged stop. "What?" I asked again when the engine finally quit, pretending that I hadn't heard Mom the first time—being fifteen.

"Get your ass in the damned house."

This was serious. I began to shake as I left the mower behind and headed toward the back door. I heard the wooden screen door slam shut behind her. *Maybe she's mad 'cause I'm mowin' barefoot*, I thought. Dad had a total complex against this, a regular pet peeve. *Couldn't be that*, I thought, *she pulled up mad*.

"Get in here!" she yelled.

It hadn't been a trouble-free summer for me. I had already been caught stealing a *National Lampoon* from a grocery store a month before. I took the magazine—which my parents had declared off-limits because of its smutty contents—into the rest room and stuck it down the front of my shorts. An assistant manager saw me take the magazine into the rest room and come out seemingly without it, so he followed me through the store and nabbed me just as I made it out the front door. I hadn't noticed him.

Both Mom and Dad were called at their respective places of work. They arrived, both mad as hell, and came up to the store office, where I had been left to wait out my fate, a two-way window giving full view of the store. I watched them meet in the front by the checkout stands, exchange several animated words, then work their way back on the cleanser and pet-food aisle. The manager came in with them. "Do ya believe on the Lord, son?" the manager asked me.

"Yes, sir," I answered quietly, pretty much willing to say anything to get out of there.

"Then I suggest you get down on your knees and pray for His forgiveness," he said.

Dad dug his hand into my shoulder and led me down the stairs, through the store, and out toward his car. When we got to the side of his red Cadillac, he glared at me and said, "When you get back, put a bag together."

He got in his car and sped away across the lot. I stood there a few seconds, turned around, and Mom was several yards away crying.

"I didn't raise you to be a thief, Bobby." The tears rolled down her face.

When we got back to the house, I went down to my room in the basement and put a change of clothes into a small duffel bag I'd had since before I won the trip to the Kentucky State Fair. I'd bought it with my paper-route money.

"Guess what came today," Mom said when I came upstairs.

"I dunno. What?"

"You got that job with the Parks Department."

I had applied for a job as an apprentice groundskeeper with the city. It would pay three-fifty an hour, when most of the jobs someone my age could get paid less than a dollar an hour. I had been waiting for the letter to come in that day's mail. My lucky day. I had grown exhausted looking for jobs. I had to have one, but every time—for the past three years—I'd go to apply, it always seemed as if the minimum age was one year older than I happened to be: at thirteen, I needed to be fourteen; at fourteen, fifteen was required. I just wanted a job. So I hustled up lawn-mowing gigs during the week and caddying work on weekends.

"I'm gonna call them and tell them you can't take that job," she said. "That's gonna be your punishment from me."

She had gone icy cold.

I stayed with Dad for three days. When I first got to his place he yelled and made threatening movements, as if he were going to beat me up, but didn't. I caddied two rounds of golf for him on Saturday for free; he didn't bring up money and neither did I. By the time two days had passed, the shoplifting seemed to have faded away and I returned home to Mom's the next day. When I was caught stealing that magazine, I had thirteen dollars and forty-seven cents in my pocket.

You'd better get your butt in here or else," she yelled again, right when I was drying off my legs and feet.

"I'm comin', Mom," I said, heading in the back door, which led right into the kitchen. "What's up?"

I was shaking more, trying to hide it.

"Wendy called me at work today. Says you came and asked her to buy you wine. Is that right?"

The room closed in around me. This was the last thing I would ever have guessed this was about.

"Narc bitch," I mumbled slightly under my breath.

"What did you just say?"

"Nothin', " I shot back, trying to be defiant.

"Well, it doesn't matter. Your Dad's makin' you move in with him. He's on his way over right now. Be warned—you're about to get your ass whipped. Probably a couple a years too late."

I didn't get my ass whipped. Surprisingly, just the opposite happened. After he initially got in my face over my stupid behavior—a stern lecture that teetered on the edge of physical harm, lasting about half an hour and four double Scotches—things got calm and stayed that way all week.

We rented a small U-Haul truck the next Saturday and moved my bedroom furniture, my drawing board, books, and clothes out of the basement bedroom that Mam-ma and Pap-pa Clark had helped build for me, down in the raw, unfinished lower level of Mom's house. I never lived with Mom again; she cried as I left, the day we moved my things; Dad's calmness didn't last.

Autumn, 1975
Boy Scout Fall Camporee
Southern Indiana

Jimmy and I were sitting around a fire, over by our tent, pitched away from most of the others. We had just gotten back from walking through the woods, sneaking a couple of smokes, and were poking at the fire with sticks. Jimmy asked if I had ever heard of a particular guy at school—Donny Bilig. I told him I had—and, oh, wasn't he supposed to be a dopehead?

"So you know who I'm talkin' about, right?" Jimmy asked.

"Right."

"Well, anyway, did you ever think about smokin' grass?"

"No! You're not doin' that, are ya?" I asked, getting a little concerned and confused. "Donny Billig, now he's a pothead. I heard that his older brother shoots up too. Why you askin' me this?"

"'Cause, I just thought you might wanna try it sometime. It's not gonna put ya on heroin or nothin'."

"Don't do it, Jimmy."

"Sorry I brought it up."

"Hey, man, I just don't wanna see you get hurt."

"That's cool."

We didn't talk any more about it.

Two months later, behind the high school basketball gym, right before the crowd came out at halftime, the guys I went to the game with lit up a joint as we stood around in a circle. I didn't freak; and when it came around to me, I took the burning joint—as if I knew what I was doing—and pulled a big cloud of smoke down into my lungs, tried to hold it down, and let it come flying back out with a violent cough and flying snot. Everybody laughed. On the next round I took a smaller toke. The weed belonged to a guy that I'd never hung out with before, friend of a friend. I had no idea that any of my friends had done this, but now I was one of them. I'd suddenly lost my cherry—in the dope-smoking department—but tried (as usual) to act as if I knew exactly what I was doing.

Toward the end of my sophomore year, right after spring break, every-thing changed. That might be a slight exaggeration, because life still slid, even after the change. It was like when you're drowning in a swift river, and you suddenly find a floating log to grab on to, but you still have to contend with the rapids—and that arching waterfall up ahead; you are still swept by momentum, though somehow you begin to feel as if you might just make it out of this thing alive after all.

In spite of being lost and feeling as if I had been abandoned at birth in a Dumpster on the dark side of the moon, I knew what I loved in the world. I loved the woods; their confusing but solid chaos enveloping me at every turn. I loved my creativity. I loved the smell of baby powder, sweat, mildew, and mentholated balm, in the football locker room.

But I hated myself; that simple. My limbs were in all the wrong places, my teeth were weird, the hair on my head from outer space, the hair sprouting on my chest embarrassing. And I was a fag.

I'm gay. Perhaps you knew. I have known since the age of ten or eleven, the same time most adolescents slowly discover their sexuality, which, in my youth, was well before ever understanding the concept of sex.

Like you couldn't guess, right? Artistic, sensitive, creative, self-destructive—ipso facto, Q-U-E-E-R, fag.

I didn't go into bodybuilding because I'm queer. And I'm not gay because I took up bodybuilding. Those are simply myths invented in the fifties to degrade anyone who took care of his body, especially to the extent bodybuilders did. It was part of the old psychological mumbo jumbo that equated narcissism with homosexuality, and of course, in that time, anyone who worked out—any man who violated the ethic of hiding his body behind a suit, tie, and hat—was automatically consid-ered suspicious and narcissistic, and abracadabra, homo. Since calling someone queer was a big insult, it made a convenient criticism for those wanting to make fun of this fledgling sport.

This sport has a lot of silly myths attached to it that grew out of people's insecurities with anything dealing with the mostly naked human body. It is amazing to realize now that there *was* a time before Arnold was one of the biggest movie stars in the world and before there was a gym in practically every town, but there was.

Contrary to popular belief, few gay athletes are at the top of this sport. I can only think of one, besides me, who in the history of body-building ever made it past the amateur level. However, the myth that all bodybuilders were gay caused great psychic unrest among the straight men who ran the sport, great strivings to prove what a wholesome heterosexual pastime it was. Comic, from a distance, really.

The sport does have a big gay following. After all, it revolves around men's bodies taken to the arguably hypermasculine limits of physical development, and that appeals to some people.

Personally, I don't find elite competitive bodybuilder's bodies sexy. Quite the opposite. I think they are overbuilt caricatures and a bit grotesque, but I guess that's not really relevant to my point, aside from getting it out on the table.

3

REDISCOVERING THE
ACCIDENTALLY DISCOVERED

Sunday Morning,
Midsummer, 1994
Seattle

What if I told you that I was thinking about competing again?"

"Good morning to you too, asshole," Tommy said, obviously not awake yet.

Seven-thirty, Sunday morning. I was all cranked up; feeling impulsive.

"Well, what would you think?" Silence; I was impatient. I didn't have a reason to push, but it was how we talked to each other. "Say something."

"I'm thinking, all right?"

"Sorry. I trust your opinion. . . . So?"

"Where are you coming from on this?"

"What?"

"Why would you be doing this after everybody who knows you has had to hear how you've moved on and all that happy horseshit?"

"You're testy this morning. Maybe I should call ba—"

"Answer my question, then I'll answer yours."

"Honestly? I don't know. That's part of the problem. I'm getting this urge and trying to figure out if it's nostalgia or insanity or . . . I dunno."

"And?"

"I want your opinion. You told me Friday night to think about why I was so weird about competing. You raised the issue."

"I remember."

"Well?"

"Do what makes you happy."

"Gee, thanks for the platitudes."

"Seriously, Bob. If you think competing will make you happy, then do it. I just wanted to hear why you wanted to go back after—what's it been? A couple a years, right?"

"Two years and two months since my last show. You are correct, sir," I said with an excited English accent.

"Jeez, you're wired. Too much coffee?"

"Yeah, that's it," I sighed. "Oh, I don't know. Pretty lame, huh?"

"What, your English accent?"

"Yeah, right—anyway, you know, getting onstage again."

"Not if it makes you happy."

"Listen to you," I said, then changed the subject.

Right before we hung up, Tommy said, "You're gonna hate me for saying this, but if it feels right, do it."

"You sound like a tennis-shoe commercial. Thanks anyway. Bye."

As I went on with my day, I thought, *Ah, fuck it. Forget it.*

Late Spring, 1977
Southern Indiana

Hot weather came weeks early and turned our un-air-conditioned school into a big pot of boiling saltwater. It was bound to get worse before school let out for summer vacation.

My sophomore biology teacher, Mr. Cleghorn, asked me to come up to his desk at the start of the next-to-the-last period and stage-whispered, conspiratorially, how he knew that an extra electric fan was stored in a back room of the basketball gym, over behind where they kept the wrestling mats. He asked me to go get it and joked that I shouldn't conveniently get lost along the way, then wrote a hall pass for me so that I wouldn't get busted by one of those teachers who substituted catching students in the hall without a valid hall pass for a satisfying sex life.

Naturally, I went the slow way to the gymnasium, stopping by my locker first, standing and looking inside at nothing in particular, then getting a roll of wintergreen Life Savers from the cafeteria candy machine. I crossed the covered breezeway that separated the school from the basketball gym. Surprisingly, no PE classes were going on when I came into the cool darkness.

It was a big gym for a high school. The floor threw spots of white reflection where stray pieces of light hit, contrasting against the darkness. I lay down on the floor, right inside the out-of-bounds line under the basket, and felt the cold of the polished wood seep through my clothes. I closed my eyes and imagined that I was lying on an iceberg in the far North Atlantic. I stayed there a couple of minutes, sinking toward a serious nap. Suddenly, I remembered the fan Mr. Cleghorn was expecting me to fetch and shot up from the floor.

"Now where was it?" I thought, maybe said out loud. "Ah, closet behind the wrestling mats, right. Where the hell do they keep the wrestling mats?"

I made my way through the gym and headed down a hall toward the room where the wrestlers practiced. The double doors were locked. I tried the door next to them and it was open, leading into a storage closet, where, after a two-minute search, I found the fan—a dusty steel oscillator that looked as if it hadn't been used in this century. As I left that closet, I turned around and saw another door that I hadn't noticed, where the hallway jutted out at a short right angle. It was only obvious when you were headed out of the corridor and back toward the basketball floor. I was feeling nosy. I could always claim that the fan was much harder to find. I tried the door. It was unlocked. When I opened the door into the room, a musty, rivery smell, with a tinge of sour cottage cheese, came back; the stagnant air was hot. I got tangled up in a spiderweb, or something like that, across the doorway, and panicking, I spun around swatting away phantom tarantulas. Dancing in place, picking the web off my face and hair, I did a fast body check to ensure nothing was crawling on me, then felt foolish for the overreaction. It was dark in there, but I could tell that the room was bigger than a storage closet. I found the light switch, flipped it on, but thought that the bulbs were burnt out when nothing happened. After a few seconds, I decided to go farther into the room and fluorescent lights sputtered to life.

"Well, I'll be goddamned. What have we here?" I said, being a tad dramatic, my voice hitting the concrete walls with a thud.

Around the corner inside the room, which was smelling more like a sulfurous tidal marsh every moment, was a machine unlike anything I had ever seen in this school. I had already played a year of football there, changing into pads and uniforms in a locker room a hundred feet from this spot, and never knew—never had a coach or another teammate point out—that we had a weight room. The entire dusty room was filled with a machine that had weight stacks and pulleys and gizmos galore. A roll-up, metal garage door was behind the machine, and the walls were a mustardy color that looked as if it might have passed for white at one time.

I felt my heart begin to race and set down the fan outside the doorway, looked down the hall and listened toward the still-empty basketball gym, then went back inside the room. I ran my hand across the rusty metal finish of the machine, walked all the way around it, looking at it, as if I were photographing every detail, and then when I got back to the same side where I'd started, I lay down on a bench under one of the bars that was attached to a solid stack of metal plates and tried to figure out how the damn thing worked. I pushed. I'll remember that push for the rest of my life. The bar didn't budge a single inch, but I felt my chest strain; my arms and whole body shook.

"Three hundred fucking pounds," I mumbled when I twisted around, while still lying on the bench, to read the markings on the weight stack. "No wonder I couldn't move the sucker."

I twisted farther around so I could reach down and figure out how to change the pin that set the amount of weight. I changed it from three hundred to one hundred and lay back down to try again. This time the bar went up, and I fell instantly in love. I had no idea what I was doing but knew that I was definitely on to something major. I pushed at the whatchamacallit a few more times—*What would I call this thing I was doing?* I thought—let the stack slam back down and jumped up off the bench, looked at my watch, decided that I'd pushed my luck far enough, flipped the light switch off, picked up the fan with one hand and shut the door with the other, and ran back through the halls—avoiding any roaming teachers—to Mr. Cleghorn's classroom. He was explaining the mechanics of osmosis in a cellular structure.

"Get lost?" he asked as I silently brought the fan up to his desk, the sweat running down my arms and from under the shaggy hair hanging over my forehead. "Mr. Paris," he said as I walked back toward my desk, "would you mind explaining what that is all over your back? Despite what my wife may say about my memory—or lack thereof—whatever that is wasn't there when you exited this class some twenty-five minutes ago. Must have picked it up during your adventure. Explain please. Did you spelunk for this fine wind machine?"

"Sir?" Completely lost.

"The back of your T-shirt . . ."

I reached over my shoulder and pulled my shirt up to see what in the hell he was talking about. The back was black with dirt. I had never thought to wipe the thick layer of dust off the bench I'd lain down on to try out the machine.

"I musta rubbed against a dirty wall or somethin' lookin' for that fan. But I was real happy to get it for you, Mr. Cleghorn—should keep it real cooled off in here, right?"

"Yes, I suppose. Sit down please. Would anyone care to bring Bobby up to speed on the details of osmosis? Yes, Kerry."

One of the teacher's-pet types droned on awhile about the transfer of liquid through the walls of a cell—or some shit like that—and class finally ended.

I went through the last period of the day in a trance, thinking the whole time about getting back to that room to try out the equipment for real. Would it still be unlocked? The clock's minute hand seemed to drag through thick mud, until at last the bell for the end of the day rang.

I raced through the crowded halls to my locker, where a couple of my buds were already hanging out. They asked if I wanted to go with them and wrangle up some weed for the weekend.

"Nah, gotta run. I'll fill you guys in later. Oh, yeah, here," I told them, pulling a wadded ten from my jeans pocket. I tossed it up in the air toward them; both reached forward to catch it. "Take care of me for the . . . you know . . . if you guys go huntin' timber."

"Where the fuck you headed, man? Off to do some brownnosin' or one of them speech-team deals or somethin'?"

"Yeah, that's it. I'll catch up with you all later. Take care of me, remember—don't conveniently mistake that ten spot of mine for gas money." And I headed off down the hall past the offices and the cafeteria and into the gym.

The building was much busier now; the people on the track teams were slowly filtering into the locker rooms on the far side of the gym, and the gymnastics coach was fiddling around with some of his team's equipment. A custodian stood on a high ladder replacing bulbs in one of the scoreboards. He whistled the theme music from *The Bob Newhart Show*. I flew past, headed straight for the back corridor, offering all the money I had to God if He would just make sure that door wasn't locked and that nobody else was in there.

"Yes!" I said a bit too loud when I found the door unlocked. Still dark. Still stunk. Still empty. I did what anyone in my position would do: I locked the door behind me.

"Goddamn, it's hot in here. Feels like the hinges of hell," I said quietly. I was talking to myself an awful lot lately—a sure sign of insanity. The lights blinked to life, since I'd only turned them on once I was inside with the door locked. I didn't want to attract any attention, maybe be told by some authority bean-head that this place was off-limits, or some other equally annoying nonsense. I pressed my ear against the door for a minute or two, wishing that I had a drinking glass handy, since in the movies they always showed you how to listen through walls and doors by holding an empty glass against the object you wanted to listen through and it always seemed to work—but from what I could hear, I'd made it in unnoticed.

And then, when I turned around, there it was. I circled the machine again, taking in all of its distinct features, making mental pictures of which did what where. After a couple of minutes of that I threw myself at it with an energy that took me by surprise. I began on the same bench I'd tried earlier and moved that stack up and down over and over. After doing this a few dozen times, stopping from time to time to catch my breath and wipe sweat out of my eyes with my T-shirt tail, I decided to see how much I could push up in one all-out try. I made it up to 160 pounds and couldn't budge an ounce more. *Enough of that,* I thought. *Let's try out these other contraptions.*

For the next hour and a half I pushed and pulled and shoved and stretched, using every bit of that machine in every way I could imagine, tossing myself headlong into a fit of spontaneous improvisation. I pressed with my legs and pushed up over my head and pulled down other things, for hundreds of repetitions. Since there weren't any windows in the room and I had the door closed, there was hardly any air, and what was there might as well have been bottled in a fetid jungle. I looked as if I'd just walked out of a lake with my clothes on. Right under the skin, the fibers of my body felt as if I'd shot them full of hot coffee; pinprickly xylophones ran up and down.

When I looked at my watch, I figured that I'd better get the hell out of there, since Dad would be picking me up from Mom's house in less than a half an hour. He had me go over there when I didn't have an after-school activity (legal or otherwise, but he was seemingly none the wiser to the distinction) since Mom's house was two blocks from the school. He'd come and get me on his way home from the office, or sometimes I rode my bike, or other times Mom might take me home—usually with a look in her eye like, wasn't I ready to move back to her home, that I'd respond to by acting clueless.

I walked to Mom's house through the gravel alley—where, behind a falling-down garage, I'd first attempted to inhale cigarette smoke—and my legs began to shake on every step, and I was overcome with a bone-weariness that seemed to manifest itself a couple of inches above my belly button, and I was starving. When I got to the house, my sisters and brother were already there, and their energy tumbled with that fresh-from-school feeling, moving around the living room—where the TV blasted a *Gomer Pyle* rerun—and in and out of their bedrooms. Nobody seemed to notice me come in. I went immediately for the bread, peanut butter, and jelly, made three sandwiches, grabbed a big handful of chips, and headed downstairs into my old bedroom, which was now mostly empty. I spread a blanket out on the concrete floor and sat down to pull the food in. The deep tiredness spread until, after a few minutes, my fingers wouldn't move to wrap around the third sandwich. It took a lot to prevent me from eating, but I set it down with only a bite out of it and lay back, thinking about what I'd done over in the gym, and fell into a silent hole of sleep.

Dad was standing over me. Lisa and Mom were standing behind him in the doorway, looking over his shoulder at me. It seemed as if it might be dark out.

"What's goin' on?" I asked, lying still. I had wrapped myself up in the blanket. My bones and muscles felt as if I'd been beaten with ball bats.

"Well, nobody knew where you were," Dad said. "You might try telling people before you come down here to hibernate, you know."

"They saw me come in. I fixed food in the kitchen."

"I didn't see you, Bobby, and Leslie and Jim didn't either," Lisa said.

"We figured you'd ridden your bike back to your dad's," Mom added. "You okay?"

I was trying to sit up. No part of me would cooperate. "I think I'm gettin' a cold," I said, finally coming up painfully into a sitting position, then standing up by putting one hand against the wall and rising as if all my limbs had been sewn on in a junior high school science lab.

"Let's get home," Dad said.

Mom looked at him hurt, wanting to say that I was home, but instead she felt my cheeks and forehead. "You're burning up, Bobby. You'd better go straight to bed when you get back to your dad's. Maybe I should take him into the doctor's tomorrow," she said to Dad.

"He'll be fine. It's just a damned cold, Diane."

"Really, Mom, I'll be fine."

"What the hell happened to your clothes?" Dad asked.

"I dunno—I fell or somethin'."

My legs didn't want to carry me up the stairs, but I finally made it up and out to Dad's car, and when we got back to the apartment, after riding silently across town (was it my imagination or did he try to smell my breath on the way into the apartment?), I collapsed into bed and fell immediately back to sleep.

I woke up at ten-thirty the next morning. Now the feeling of a severe beating was fully there. I could neither bend nor straighten my arms and legs, and it took me ten minutes to swing my feet onto the floor and push myself off the bed to go take a pee. When I did make it up, I was hunched all over, as if I were 125 years old. How was I this sore? I wondered. This was beyond sore, and I was shivering, which only made everything hurt more. Dad had left a note on my nightstand saying that he had headed to the office; he'd tried but couldn't wake me and had called me in sick at school, so I should rest—and I wasn't to leave the apartment.

Leave? I thought. *I can't even make it to the kitchen. Hell, I can't even lift my arms to blow my nose.*

I burned with fever for two days, and especially the second day, I couldn't get out of my bed at all. By the fourth day I went back to school, but still couldn't reach my arms above waist level without tremendous concentration. It took my body eleven days before it felt normal again.

I needed to climb back on that horse as soon as I could. My enthusiasm during that first workout, and the consequences that came after, could have forever extinguished the fire I felt on that first day. But I was on to something. I'd simply overdone it and chalked it up as lesson number one: don't go out and run a hundred miles if you've never even walked around the block before.

I went back to the weight room, after class, on a Thursday afternoon, locked myself in the room, and did the same things I'd done the first time, but about a fifth as much. I tried again to push as much weight up in one all-out effort on the exercise where I lay on a bench under handles connected to a big iron stack and managed to work my way up, with a touch of struggle, to 170 pounds; but even more important was that I began to figure out—by focusing in on the areas I could feel straining under the load—what parts of my body were being affected by doing it. As I moved on to do other exercises, I tried to establish, through the same kind of concentration, where those efforts were directed. Clearly, each apparatus had a different part that it worked. When the coils of my body were telling me to push on, I forced myself to stop, lest I suffer the same consequences as before, and enthusiasm aside, I couldn't be paid to go through eleven days like that again.

That night I was sore and tired, although not nearly as badly as before; the next day I was even more sore but not so tired, and after two days had passed, I decided to go back in again. I kept this up, working my way through all the exercises I could think of doing, given the blinders I was trotting along with, and I began, after a couple of weeks of this, to understand these things I was doing. It came quickly for a couple of reasons: first, I was an athlete and my body seemed to adapt well to the stress, if I simply kept my naive enthusiasm reined in; and second, because of art classes I had rudimentary knowledge of how the human body was put together.

I returned nearly every day after school. After a month I finally told my friends—who kept asking me where I was running off to each day— that I'd found the room with the weight machine in it. Of course, they all made out as if they knew it was there all along. We were riding around out in the country getting high on a Saturday afternoon when I told them. The approaching smell of summer vacation was cranking up the engines of our hearts. We were all getting stoned a whole bunch more as the spring progressed. These guys had various opinions about the weight lifting that I was getting hooked on. One said that I'd get muscle-bound—all bunchy and stiff—and wouldn't be able to play football right, another said that he thought it was cool, and another asked if he could start going in with me after school. I knew he never would, so I shrugged it off, passed him the half-burned joint, and changed the subject.

Time passed and I began to do more and more serious drugs.

At a party, a friend said that someone else there could get us some coke, if I wanted to try it. I didn't have any money with me, but thought, what the hell, why not. I asked him if I could borrow his car for a few minutes, and I went to a nearby grocery store that I knew kept their empty pop bottles stacked in a relatively hidden place behind the store with nothing except a cornfield to keep me from them. I drove up the dirt road, on the opposite side of the field from the store, and smashed a path through the low corn—the field a low, golden-green carpet broken only by an ancient maple tree smack in the middle—going against the grain of the carefully planted rows, up to the back of the store, and began to carry load after load of the bottles back to the car, being careful and quiet so as to not attract attention. After I'd loaded up, I tried to turn the car around and got stuck in some mud. It took an hour to get free. I took my bounty of empty bottles to another nearby store and turned them in for the deposits, scoring a pretty good wad of cash. The clerk wanted to know where I'd gotten so many bottles, and I said that my family drank a bunch of the stuff and had been saving them up for a couple of years, and that now we needed the money to buy food. I put on my most hangdog look as I told my sad tale; he was sympathetic. By the time I got back to the party, it had broken up and my friend was pissed at me for making him wait for his car, so I told him where I'd been and split the cash with him, and that soothed him.

*   *   *

Cummin's Book Store was in downtown Columbus. They had the best newsstand in town. I went in one afternoon looking for the latest issue of my favorite backpacking magazine and ran across a copy of *Muscle Builder* on the shelf. On the cover was a picture of some guy named Schwarzenegger, doing an exercise with his gigantic arm up over his head and a straining grimace on his face. His sweaty, dark hair hung down in his face, and he had on a light-colored tank top, and the arm and hand that wasn't over his head was grabbing on to a bench of some kind, the fingers squeezing into the brown leather, fingernails white from the pressure. I began to pore through the pages, devouring the pictures of these guys training and showing their tremendously muscled bodies, bursting out of T-shirts or without shirts on or flexing on a beach with mountains in the background. A guy named Joe Weider kept being mentioned, and a bunch of different musclemen, who were said to be the great champions. According to what I could tell, standing there and flipping through this magazine, these men occupied a terrific kingdom all their own, out in California. It looked as if all they did was work out in a magnificently complicated gym, go to the beach, and get great advice from this Joe Weider fellow, who many of them claimed was a sage trainer. There were a lot of ads for cans of powders and brown-glass bottles of things, and bendable contraptions, which I supposed helped these men, who were dependent on Joe Weider's wisdom, to sculpt their tremendous bodies. Wow!

After flipping through the pages for fifteen or twenty minutes, I put the copy I'd been reading back on the rack and took a fresh, unbrowsed copy from halfway back of the dozen or so that were neatly stacked. I paid for the magazine, after carefully searching the rack to see if there were any other muscle magazines. There weren't. The clerk who took my money knew that I always came in looking for backpacking magazines, so she asked me if I had forgotten to pick up the latest issue of my favorite one. I told her that I was more interested in reading this one, since I had been lifting weights lately. She asked to see my muscle, expecting me to flex my arm I suppose, but when she saw me blush, she quickly backed off and told me that the newest crop of these muscle magazines was due to arrive in two days. I said that was great, went out, hopped on my bike, and started out of town toward Dad's new house. It was a ten-mile ride out there, and I had the magazine in my knapsack and couldn't wait to get to the house to read all about my latest discovery.

I pored over every page and photo in that magazine, until it was dog-eared and worn. Now it made sense. I decided right there on the spot that I was going to become a bodybuilder and live in the kingdom of muscle. In one brief visit to the newsstand, I had found my future.

Spring, 1995
Seattle

After talking with Tommy that Sunday morning last August, I let several months pass trying to turn my back on it. Tommy never brought it up. Other friends asked less frequently if I planned to compete again. Everything indicated that I'd moved on.

Through the winter I wrote another fitness book, but still mostly piddled around when I went down in the gym.

The shadow was there though. It was a vague feeling that somehow it wasn't finished yet, that there was still more to be done. Whenever the feelings would come, I'd ask myself what I expected to accomplish by getting back onstage again, when it seemed as if I'd finally managed to escape from being completely defined as a person according to a sport that most people thought was weird.

There were no real stars now, I'd tell myself. The sport lacked a spark, in spite of how the magazines tried to turn the current crop of guys into demigods. One or two athletes had a hint of the charisma necessary to break out of the pack, but from what I saw, most of the current breed of top competitors were like sacks of potatoes with arms and legs. You'd never want to sit down and have dinner with them. What would you talk about, sets and reps? These guys couldn't carry Arnold's gym bag, regardless of whether or not their physiques were better or more developed.

I'm not being fair. I realize that. I don't like it when I begin to sound like a sour old man, and that's what it feels like I'm becoming. So I have to stop and ask myself where I'm coming from when I get this way. I crave simplicity. I want to return to a semblance of my younger days and have that kind of simple, uncluttered focus again.

Clearly, I'm having a midlife crisis. There, I've said it. Do people have these things at my age? I mean, I'm thirty-five and wanting to shed my complicated life and return to something that I did well for many years, in order to try to do it even better—while there's still time. If I had been a baseball pitcher, maybe this twinge would be coming too late, or maybe not. Look at Nolan Ryan. Not everyone can do that, though.

The other question I ask myself, besides why I would want to do this in the first place, is, can I gather the focus and drive I'll need to take on men ten years younger than me who eat, sleep, and shit this sport? Could I go up against someone like I had been, someone beyond driven and confident? Right now I don't know, and that may be the answer to my question.

When I discovered this sport and decided to chase it at a blind gallop, my life was hard, but I prevented it from collapsing through sheer laser-beam focus. Nothing was able to keep me from getting what I wanted, and I wanted to be a great pro bodybuilder, as Arnold had been.

Late Spring, 1977
Southern Indiana

I went back to Cummin's Book Store two days later, looking for more muscle magazines. The same clerk who had asked to see my muscle the last time was working again and smiled at me as I came through the door. Monday, late afternoon. I'd come downtown with Dad, after he picked me up at Mom's, where I'd walked after school and a quick work-out. He needed to go by his office to wrap up some work, so I walked over to the bookstore from his building, several blocks away.

"We got in all the new weight-lifting magazines," the clerk said as I headed for the magazine rack.

"Yeah?" I replied in that nonchalant way shy young men use with adults, that's meant to say absolutely nothing is any big deal. Inside I was bursting with a raw energy that had built up from watching the clock tick off the seconds, until this moment, for two excruciating days.

There they were. The new *Muscle Builder*, a small, cheap-looking one called *Ironman*, and another called *Muscular Development*, which looked even cheaper, like something put together in someone's garage. I snatched fresh, midstack copies of all three.

Then a bizarre sensation compelled me to pick up a *Rolling Stone*, lying on the flat bottom shelf. I set my three magazines carefully aside and picked up the one I was being drawn to. I looked at the cover. Nothing remarkable there. I flipped through the first few pages, began to lose interest, and as I set it back down, out of the middle of the magazine flashed a fragment of a picture that caught my eye. I turned right to the article and smiled.

The magazine had done a feature story about Arnold Schwarzenegger, the massive muscleman I had been reading about in that lone copy of *Muscle Builder* I had bought two days earlier. The *Muscle Builder* had left me wanting to know more, since the articles were about his training, and although I appreciated finally figuring out that that exercise I'd initially done in the high school gym was called a bench press, the articles gave me the impression that everyone else reading the magazine already knew everything about this man, except me. And here it was. There were photos of him, done by Annie Leibovitz, whose work I knew from Mr. Wellman's photography class, and a long article that on first glance seemed to be about some contest over in Africa.

I picked up the other magazines, kept the *Rolling Stone,* and paid for them. The clerk smiled at me some more and asked if I had also joined a rock-and-roll band, to which I replied no, I had not, and she smiled some more, gave me my change from a twenty, and wished me a very good evening. I ran back to Dad's office, all the way thinking that I knew how those early California gold miners must have felt after they first found one shiny nugget in a bubbling creek, then a couple of days later hit the mother lode.

When I got back to Dad's office, he said that he had a little more work to do than he originally thought, and I'd just have to relax and wait for him to finish. No problem, I told him, and went into the smaller, empty side office, behind the secretary's desk, to read my new magazines. I started with the *Rolling Stone* article. It was about Arnold mostly, and some of the other guys. They were in South Africa for a contest called the Mr. Olympia, which was explained to be the pinnacle event for the world's best musclemen. Joe Weider had started this contest in the 1960s as a place for former Mr. Universes to continue to compete. A grand overall championship. A thousand dollars' prize money. This Schwarzenegger guy had been winning it for several years running. He also had a lifting pal named Franco Columbu, who was much shorter and as thick as a bull. He came from an island off Italy and was a boxing champion.

I wouldn't mess with him, I thought.

In one picture, taken as Arnold was facing away from the camera, standing there casually talking to someone, wearing a black, Speedo-looking bathing suit, his back looked like a cross between a relief map of the ocean floor and the spread-out hood of a Duesenberg. The caption on the photo said something to the effect that his back muscles appeared carved out by an ice cream scoop.

An hour later Dad and I went home. By that time I had looked at all my new purchases a couple of times. And when I got back to my room, I read them a couple times more, until I eventually fell asleep.

Until that week, the things that I had been doing in the school gym were a distraction, but now, out of nowhere they had meaning. I would build and sculpt my body. I had to find a way to keep training during summer vacation, especially now that I was determined to become a muscleman myself.

I went to the football coach, Mr. McCaa, and enthusiastically asked him if there was any way to get into the weight room during the summer. He said he'd been thinking about opening it for a couple of hours in the evening, three days a week, during the whole summer and had almost decided against it because he didn't know how much interest there would be. I told him that I, for one, would be very interested.

Three days later, at a meeting of all the guys on the football team called by the coach to discuss taking care of ourselves during the summer—especially staying out of trouble, since much of the team were among the hardest partyers in the school—Mr. McCaa announced that the weight room would be open from five to seven every Monday, Wednesday, and Friday evening, throughout the summer, and strongly suggested that others follow my example—pointing straight at me—and use it. I didn't know anyone, except a few of my friends, even knew that I had been lifting. My body had already begun to change, and people were talking about it.

4

EVEN MUSCLES HAVE MEMORIES

July 1995
Seattle

We push the edges of what is possible. We look at what nature gave to us and say, "This may be nice, but it's not enough. I can improve this." And we set ourselves to that task.

Each athlete seeks his edges, a flying pass closer to the sun than ever before. That is where the silliness of an endeavor fades and the naked, holy quest for human possibility emerges.

"Why did you become a bodybuilder?"

I have been asked this question more times than I can count, by people who ask in tones ranging from incredulous to gleaming, depending on what their intentions are.

"Why did you become a human?" I always wanted to ask them back if they were being too snotty or smug. I never did, though.

I have had gleaming eyes ask me the question of why as well. I know where they're coming from. When I answer them, I try to show them the horizon. I did this thing because I loved the edge, I might tell them, and this is what lies out on the horizon.

I started working out again. People who know this sport understand what takes place when someone who was once in prime shape comes back from a long layoff. Muscle memory. The cellular structure of the muscles remembers how they were before. It works in both directions, building up and coming back down. When I stopped training seriously, my muscles shrank down; my body took on its more natural structure and size, as if I had never been 245 pounds. It took time of course, and I couldn't pig out, otherwise I would just have gotten fat.

If a guy stops training and keeps eating as if the world's going to end tomorrow, chances are he'll blow out—he'll get fat. Now, that isn't lending truth to the false old tale that says, if you work out and then stop, your muscles will turn into fat. That's not physiologically possible—muscle and fat have different cellular compositions; one cannot become the other. This isn't biblical, after all. The only miracle is simple science. The old myth grew out of a misinterpretation of circumstances. Some guys who stop training get fat. It's not the muscle turning to fat, though; it's the body adapting to being more sedentary. But then most people who never worked out at all get fatter as they get older too— they eat too much and don't get off their butts to burn it off.

When I stopped, I went back to eating normally—not obsessed as I had to be while competing, but not eating cheeseburgers and fries five times a day either. Slowly, over a couple of years, my body went back to normal.

I saw Mam-ma Clark a month ago. I hadn't seen her for about three years. The last time she saw me I was at my off-season weight—about 245 pounds. This time I weighed maybe a few pounds over 200.

"Now, Bob, where'd all your muscles go?" she asked, her eyes laughing with good nature.

"Well, Mam-ma, I haven't been working out much lately. Life's been too busy. I haven't been down in that gym for, oh, I don't know how long."

"I always wondered what would happen to all your big muscles once you stopped."

"They shrank. Do I look bad?"

"No—you look normal. Tell you the truth, I think you look better."

Muscle memory goes even stronger in the other direction, though. When someone comes off a long layoff and begins to train again with intensity—assuming there are no major injuries to deal with—this cellular memory kicks in and the muscles come back at a lightning pace. It's intoxicating, watching your body blossom once again. You think, "If only it had been this fast and easy when I first started." You revel in it. And then you reach a threshold where the hard work and routine of the thing descend, because the fast return of lost strength and size slows back to its normal plodding pace.

I began back in the gym with some amount of rusty vigor. I started slow and worked the dust off. Everything seemed to be functioning still. It's early, still too early to catch the thrill ride of my muscles flying toward their old home again—doing somersaults through the atmosphere. There's a feeling I have, back in a corner of the attic of my brain, that tells me this time I might keep it up. But I'm experienced enough to realize that I'll need to wait to see if this leads somewhere.

The Late 1970s
Southern Indiana

After I discovered that there actually was a sport of bodybuilding and that musclemen had a reason for being that way, I started buying all the magazines every month and eventually began to dream of the day when I would finally get to meet Joe Weider in person.

At nineteen, while halfheartedly attending Indiana University, I started working out at the first real commercial gym I'd ever trained in. The owner of the gym told me he'd heard—never citing the source of the information—that "Weider SOB," as he called him, "just used the guys like so much cheap beef and then tossed 'em aside once he'd made a fortune off their hard work," but I knew that Joe would play some major role in my life.

Joe knew exactly how to kindle the dreams of boys such as me. His magazines were packed with these magnificent Artie Zeller photos, works that for me held both the intoxicating artistry of tone and contrast that was possible in black-and-white photography and also captured the gym life that made the world of Muscle Beach and Gold's Gym glitter with strain and reality. I had to live in that world. In my mind I was already there. I'd imagine Joe Weider, greater than reality, cheering me on through sets of heavy squats in the silence of an empty gym. I was positive that when I finally made my escape, he'd be waiting to welcome me at the California state line.

Spring, 1980
Southern California

The first time I saw Joe Weider in person I was twenty. I'd been in California less than a year and had become friends with a rising amateur star named Rory Leidelmeyer, whom I'd met while training at the Body Shop gym in Anaheim. Rory would come in from time to time to work out, even though it wasn't his regular gym. I knew from reading the magazines that he'd placed a controversial second in the Mr. Los Angeles that year. We struck up a friendship because beyond being an upcoming competitor Rory also helped inexperienced young athletes get ready for shows, helping them with diet and training advice, and he commented one day on how much raw potential he thought I had and offered to help me, if I ever needed it.

I saw Joe Weider the night Rory was onstage competing as the favorite to win the Mr. California. It was also the first time I had been to a show at the aging Embassy Theater in downtown Los Angeles, which had a history of housing physique contests as far back as the early fifties. Nearly every star of each generation since then had competed there. The ghosts of these men's lat spreads and double biceps poses seemed to seep out of the rococo paneling of the place. Legendary muscle wars had been fought there.

Less than a year later it would be me standing barefoot and oiled up, onstage, with hot lights glaring down, blinding away the fifteen hundred screaming, seen-it-all L.A. fans, as my name was being announced as the 1981 Mr. Los Angeles.

But on this night I sat three rows from the back, main floor left, as Rory beat local hero John Brown by one point to become Mr. California. At the time it was assumed that whoever won the Cal in May would be the odds-on favorite to win the Mr. America in September.

Joe Weider sat front row, left center—next to the judges. He stood up a few minutes before the finals began to acknowledge the audience when the emcee announced his name as one of the VIPs in attendance. One-third of the crowd, including me, cheered. Simultaneously the other two-thirds booed—loudly. A guy four seats over yelled, "Asshole!" through cupped hands. I was dumbfounded. I assumed that everyone in bodybuilding, especially here in L.A., where they were much more savvy than the hicks in Indiana, would see him as a hero. I never forgot that booing.

After the contest was over and Rory had won, collected his trophy, and headed backstage, his wife, Cythnia, asked if I wanted to go backstage. Once back there, I watched from a distance as Joe squawked orders to a photographer doing shots of Rory, for *Muscle Builder*, in a voice similar to an out-of-tune accordion under the back wheels of a dump truck.

I was shocked by the sound of it. I'd heard it before, but not in person. A year earlier, I'd sat captivated by *Pumping Iron*, the documentary that revolved around Arnold Schwarzenegger's getting ready for the 1975 Mr. Olympia. In one scene Joe directs a photo shoot for one of his products, a bendable Krusher Bar, with Arnold and some female models. I assumed there had been some difficulty with the sound quality and dismissed the strange nasal twang of his voice in favor of the sound I'd invented for him in my head.

Backstage at the Embassy, I stood as still as the wall, watching. Suddenly the energy of the backstage shifted and pulled toward me in a rush. Joe and a small pack of athletes, writers, fans, and leeches were headed right at me. My eyes went straight to an oily, dye-stained towel at my feet, and I tried in vain to mentally project an escape. I was standing right in front of the door, a squirrel frozen in the headlights of an oncoming bus. I couldn't move.

"That's quite an arm you got there, gonna be a cham-p-ion, eh?" His right hand squeezed just above my left elbow, sort of trying to push me out of the way; and that voice.

"Yes," I squeaked.

"Maybe I'll put you on the cover." The procession moved past me as I staggered a step to my right.

"Thanks," I said, but no one heard me.

Later that night I wrote a letter to an old training buddy back in Indiana: "The most unbelievable thing happened tonight. Joe Weider told me I was a future champion and offered to put me on the cover of his magazine. . . . I'm really starting to get somewhere now. This place is amazing."

Spring, 1995
Seattle

On May 7, 1995, I wrote the following passage on the first page of a new journal:

> Perhaps if I return to competitive bodybuilding, I can correct some of my mistakes from the past. When I look back now, I see so much that could have been done differently, probably better. The same moral issues continue to surround my attempt to make this decision, however, and contribute to my inability either to fully commit to making a comeback, or to finally forget about it and move on with my life. I don't know how to cross the fence of some of the more complicated of these issues, and I am feeling

bogged down by this indecision. Maybe if I simply launch into full-bore training, the momentum will build and create its own sustaining energy and enthusiasm. Either way—doing it or not doing it—I must decide soon and stop this mushy vacillation. The bottom line is: make up your mind, Bob.

I have been keeping a journal off and on (mostly on) ever since I began training seriously. I have a large box filled with notebooks of information recorded about my training, eating, and personal observations, going back sixteen years. Each one is labeled according to the significant event that particular journal was leading up to: "Mr. Los Angeles 1981, final four weeks," for example, or "Mr. Olympia 1985, off-season." I've really used these notebooks too. When I first began, I wondered if they'd ever come in handy, but eventually they did. I developed several seminars and wrote three fitness books based on what I could go back and learn from my journals.

Over the years I've also gone back to those same journals looking for other things, many times having to read between the lines to discover who I was then, and what motivated my actions.

In my earliest journals I recall constantly referring to "destiny." There is something extremely teenaged—wide-eyed and enthusiastic—about those early journal entries. What exactly did I mean when I wrote that I felt it was my destiny to become the best in the world at this sport? If I were a coldhearted cynic reading those journals, I might think that the kid who wrote them was suspiciously egomaniacal. After all, talking as if fate and divine plans played into something as mundane as muscle building might be interpreted as a sign of lunacy. But it was all pretty innocent stuff, this prediction that my destiny would lead me to greatness in my chosen sport. Also, when I first gave myself over to body-building, I was a kid who was almost completely lost. Latching on to the notion that if I worked hard enough, hung in there long enough, stuck it out when the way got tough, and believed that I was capable of accomplishing whatever I set my mind to had kept me from tumbling.

When I look hard enough at those old journals, I discover what it was that gave energy to my life in those days: I threw myself into doing one thing well and did it with all my heart. I believe that this absolute focus and force of will—all bundled together—was what I meant by destiny. And wide-eyed teenage daydreaming or not, that energy had helped save my life.

The Late 1970s
Southern Indiana

That summer cemented my commitment to training. It also showed me how limited the equipment in the school weight room was. In the magazines they showed guys training on all sorts of intricate machines, and with massive barbells and dumbbells that looked as if they could crush boulders. I was hungry for more: more equipment, more knowledge, more size, more strength—more of everything. I wanted it all, and fast.

I carried that *Rolling Stone* with the article about Arnold everywhere. I told my friends that I planned to look like that in six months—pointing to the pictures of Arnold, and being, in a cockeyed way, sincere. People humored me, but my body did begin to change drastically.

One of my friends and I decided to go backpacking in Nebo Ridge, a wilderness area outside Nashville, and spent the night at Mam-ma and Pap-pa Clark's, so that Pap-pa could take us out to the fire tower on the ridge to drop us off and then pick us up there three days later. I took the *Rolling Stone* and showed it to Mam-ma and told her the story about how I was going to look like that in six months. A week before I'd also spent a night at Mam-ma and Pap-pa Paris's house and did the same thing. About a week after my backpacking trip, Mom pulled me aside and said that both sets of grandparents had told her that I was talking weirdness, and acting mighty big for my britches. All I could do was shake my head as she told me this. If I had been talking about how I was going to become a great surgeon, they would have acted proud of my spunk, but I'd latched on to a hobby that was to them too bizarre to describe, something suspicious, to nip in the bud through discouragement. It made me want it more.

I would show up at the school every Monday, Wednesday, and Friday at five o'clock, usually arriving before Coach McCaa did. He'd drive up and tell me that if I was this dedicated on the football field next fall, he'd be real happy. Then he'd unlock the metal, rolling garage door that let you into the weight room from outside the building, push it up, and I'd have at it. A few of the other guys would show up too. They all laughed and had a great time, occasionally doing an exercise. I, on the other hand, burned as I focused in on each set and each repetition, the sweat pouring from my body, rarely stopping except to move to a new station on the machine. And I did that for the whole two hours, making endless circuits around the thing, pushing myself to the point of dropping over.

But the limitations bothered me, so I got Dad to take me to JC Penney's one night, and I bought a 150-pound barbell set. When the clerk showed up with a dolly to help us out to the car with the box of weights, I quietly asked Dad if the guy was crazy and hoisted the thing up on my shoulder—it was a lot heavier than I thought 150 pounds would be—and staggered from the sporting goods department out to Dad's car, where the box made the shocks bounce when I dropped it, a bit harder than I wanted to, into the trunk.

Every spare moment when I wasn't at my job tossing pizzas or hanging out and getting high with my friends, I was either at the school weight room or in my bedroom using my new set of plastic-coated weights.

I found a place inside myself that would go *click* whenever I was in the middle of an exercise. This door would open and out would come a dervish who could push and push and keep going, beyond the place where the fatigue and the fiery ache would try to take control. My new enemy became gravity; and I was a boy who felt the pull of gravity in everything, so when I wrapped my hands around a barbell or the handle of a weight machine, I fought the pull of gravity with all my heart and disappeared inside the fight.

By July I had put on nearly twenty pounds. I began to bulge. The time came for me to go to the yearly week of Boy Scout camp at Camp Louis Ernest, about twenty miles south of where I lived. I would not, could not, miss a single workout, so I'd take my barbell set along to camp. Our troop's campsite was up a wooded trail, a couple of miles back on the far side of the lake that dominated the center of the camp.

First I made the trip back to the campsite and left my backpack, which was filled with all my usual gear for the week. Then I went back up to the parking lot and fetched my loaded barbell—I'd put all the weights, all 150 pounds, onto the bar and brought the dumbbell handles too—which I had taken from dad's trunk when he dropped me off. I put the barbell across the back of my neck, had someone hand me the dumbbell handles, and began the hike. People passed by on the trail. Some laughed. One guy asked why I didn't leave the whole mess back at the lodge and use it there—I didn't have an answer for that—and I had to stop every hundred yards to rest, since I began to get light-headed after I had crossed the dam at the near end of the lake. Two hours later I got to our campsite. My legs were like melting jelly. All through that week I did my workouts, as an extremely religious man would say his prayers. And when the week was over, a couple of the other guys who had halfheartedly fiddled around with the weights while we were there volunteered to help carry part of the load back to the parking lot.

All summer I didn't miss one workout. By the time I reported for the first football practice in late August, I had gained another fifteen pounds, going that summer from 165 to 200 pounds, and considering that the majority of my diet was as much junk food as I could possibly eat, there wasn't much fat on me either. The assistant coaches, who hadn't seen me through the summer, asked Mr. McCaa if a new kid had moved to town; I had changed that much.

But my season was mediocre. I had lost interest in football. Body-building was my sport now. I stayed on the team, though. Football players rated. And the coaches constantly said that if we ever encountered in the school halls any guys who had dropped off the team, we should spit on the losers; nobody likes a quitter.

I have no idea how far down the other parts of my life may have spiraled if I had not found this one unique thing to throw myself at so wholeheartedly. I was so lost and didn't care whether I lived or died.

Junior year. My friends and I put together a plan for ways to skip out of school. We developed an elaborate scheme for stealing and forging excused-absence passes from the dean's office. We'd sneak off campus to party the school day away. When we returned to class the next day, we'd have a forged pass stating that the absence had been due to illness. We got away with it.

It would have been better for me if we were caught; then I might simply have taken whatever punishment would come, gotten scared, and snapped out of it. But our success made us bolder each day. It began infrequently, but by the middle of the second semester I was skipping 60 percent of my classes and getting decent grades—in all but chemistry.

I still worked my job at the pizza parlor, but began calling in sick more and more, moving swiftly from being a trusted kid on his way to greater responsibility to being viewed with suspicion.

Teachers became concerned about my health. One was cynical, asking me, if I was ill so much, shouldn't I be attending classes in a hospital ward for desperately sick teenagers.

But even in the heart of so much turmoil, I still hung on to a singular dream. I had so many times where I would allow this dream to carry me away, far past the mess I was making.

*   *   *

I sat in my bedroom one night poring over all my *Muscle Builder* magazines for the two hundredth time. I decided that if I could wake up the next morning looking like anyone, it would be the new surprise Mr. Universe from Egypt, Mohammed Makkawy. He was so perfectly built, every muscle fitting without great exaggeration in its proper place. His abdominals were the best I'd seen in the time I had been looking at the magazines, and he had the face of a pharaoh.

So I cast my wish to the gods. Make it easy on me; let me open my eyes to the sound of the alarm clock, look down, and see toffee-colored skin wrapped tightly over four perfectly aligned rows of chiseled stomach muscles.

I'd stand up, look in the full-length mirror on the back of my bedroom door, and have every grove, line, joint, and bulge match his. Only it would be me. I'd run my hand through the close-cropped Afro and flex my chest watching every fiber jump to life, then get dressed in the tightest shirt I could wedge myself into and head off to school. I smiled to myself, lying there staring up at the bright yellow ceiling above my bed. What a dream that would be. Teetering in the dark spot between awake and asleep, I recalled reading that he was only five foot two. You couldn't tell it from his pictures in the magazines. I wasn't so sure I was willing to give up ten inches in height, even for such a magic transformation. It never occurred to me that if the gods could transform my body into an extremely muscular black man's, they could probably adjust the height to suit my whims as well. Logic never fogged the windows of such irrational wishes, and I fell asleep.

The class skipping, drugs, drinking, and all that grew more intense. My understanding that I was gay grew with each passing hour. I hadn't come even remotely close to doing anything about this, and I would push the thoughts I was having more frequently—of what it might be like to kiss another man, to be held by him—as far back in my mind as possible, but the feelings wouldn't go away. This one thing alone contributed to my twisted confidence that I would never be normal, would never fit in, and probably didn't deserve to live. After all, I'd been taught that people like me were the worst sort of perverts, miserable sinners who'd deliberately chosen to turn their backs on God and were headed straight toward the hottest fires of hell. When my prayers and hopeful pleadings for God to change me—to make me be normal—didn't work, I started doing everything I could to destroy my life. If I had no reason to live, I rationalized, I might just as well go out making a fuss. I had considered suicide many times; the scenarios would play themselves out in my imagination, especially whenever the black clouds would take over my head. I'd write long, emotional notes to my family, telling them why I'd done it, that I couldn't take life anymore. Every time, though, I'd wad these notes up, take them out to the trash barrel, and burn them.

I was dangerously close to losing my job because I was calling in sick so much. Teachers grew more suspicious each time I would return to class from a missed day.

I came up with an imaginary illness; I discreetly told people at work or teachers at school that I had leukemia, but pleaded with them not to tell anyone, knowing, of course, that human nature being what it is, they would tell everyone. I was setting my escape route.

I still wasn't missing any workouts, though. I would dream of building my own complete gym, similar to the ones I saw in the magazines that I continued to buy each month, right in the large storage shed attached to the carport of Dad's house. But I began to carry enough clothes and other belongings—as well as my shotgun—around in the trunk of my car, in case everything went wrong.

It did. On a Thursday afternoon, a few of us were partying hard at one of the guys' houses. We were all wasted, with the stereo blasting, when in walks the kid's father. He pitched us out of the house and called the school. The dean searched our classes and found that the six of us, who the kid's father had reported were at his house, were indeed missing from class. And how was Bobby Paris's leukemia treatment going? my German teacher asked the dean.

We drove to another kid's house and continued to party. I was due at work at four, but decided to call in sick once again. When I got the manager on the phone, he said never to bother coming in again—I was fired. I hung up the phone, kept my best "fuck him" face on, and told everyone what had happened. They said it was just as well, who needed that miserable place anyway, and we lit another joint.

I spent the night at another friend's house, since Dad was out of town on business and wouldn't be back until the next evening. We stayed wasted.

Friday afternoon I took off by myself to drive around, trying to figure a way out of the mess that was careening to a dramatic head. I drove around the countryside for hours, until after dark, then headed back to a lake house where there was supposed to be a big party that night. When I pulled up, cars were everywhere, music crashing through the trees, loud voices, laughter, a hundred or more people around. I walked down the hillside to the side of the house; it was dark out. I looked through one of the side windows; inside were all the hardest partyers from school and some other people I didn't know.

"I'm never gonna make it," I said quietly. I went back up the hill, got in my car, and sped away. I ended up back at the cornfield behind the store where I would from time to time steal bottles to cash in for the deposit, and I parked my car with the lights off on a dirt road beside the field. I had a fifth of Jack Daniel's with me and kept taking hits off the bottle as I sat there for an hour.

"Fuck it," I finally said, and threw the door open, popped the trunk, pulled out the shotgun, slid two shells into their chambers, and crashed through the young, low corn sprouts, across to the middle of the field, to a spot next to a lone maple tree. I found a sturdy stick with a forked end, since I knew I couldn't to pull the trigger without rigging a device to reach it, and sat down under the tree, taking gulps from the whiskey bottle that I'd brought with me. Tears poured down my cheeks; I sat with my back against the tree, the shotgun between my knees, the safety off, trying carefully to break the stick to the right length. I finished the last of the bottle.

The one thought that kept racing through my drunken mind was, how would I ever get to California and become a champion if I blew my brains out?

"Yeah, right, some fucking champion. Champion fuckup, you faggot," I yelled. "Fuck it. Fuck it, fuuuuccckk ittt." I wrapped my bare feet around the butt of the gun.

"Oh, Jesus, please forgive me," I whispered, then put the barrels into my mouth. I sat still, tasting the metal and gun oil of the barrel, listening to the wind and crickets, and the cars out on the highway. And then a miracle happened. I must have passed out, because the next thing I saw was the sun burning hard down on me.

"Am I dead?" I whispered. I heard the cars off on the highway and knew that I wasn't. I had fallen over sideways from where I was leaning against the tree; next to my head was a pool of orange vomit, and the shotgun was lying diagonally across my left leg. I thought about picking up the gun and finishing what I'd started, but decided not to, so I got up, picked up the empty Jack Daniel's bottle (I couldn't litter, now could I?), staggered back to the car, unloaded the shotgun and put it back in the trunk, and drove home. When I got home, I crawled into bed, pulled the covers up so that I was wrapped like a mummy, and lay there with a pillow over my face, wishing the drums would stop beating.

5

GETTING OUT OF THE HOUSE A BIT

July 1995
On the West Coast

A month after I began working out again, I decided to drive down to
L.A. and see some of my old friends from the sport; ask them if they
thought I could make a comeback, or if I was being foolish. I'd already
talked on the phone with two men whose opinions on this thing I
trusted. First I called Chris Aceto at his house in Maine. Chris was
considered a contest-preparation guru by a number of top pros, and in
my training during the last year that I'd competed, he'd helped me pull
my body together after I'd made the insane decision to compete in
twenty-two shows during a two-and-a-half-year stretch. When we first
started working together, my body was exhausted—so was I—and my
placements toward the end of those two and a half years had begun
slipping into the cellar. I needed to come up with a dramatic change to
turn my competitive fortunes around.

Chris's wife was Laura Creavelle, one of the top female pros in the
world. Before they met, she had been doing well in competition, but
after they began working together, she shot to the top of the women's
sport as if being fired from a cannon. The guy knew what he was doing.
He had an instinct for what worked for each individual athlete, and his
diet advice helped me get back into great shape the year before I
stopped competing. I figured that if I did decide to compete again, I
should get his opinion. He said that it was a great idea, if I could find
the focus. He asked me how my body looked right then and I told him
honestly. He reminded me about muscle memory and how I could be
right back in top shape in a matter of a few months, especially with my
genetics. He would be happy to help me get back into the kind of shape
I needed to be in to win shows. I told him that I still needed to think

it over and that as soon as I decided, I'd let him know. He said to give him a call as soon as I was ready to go.

A couple of days later I called John Balik. John was publisher of *Ironman*. When I met him in the early eighties, he was a great physique photographer. He ended up buying, with another master physique photographer, Mike Neveaux, what had been a respected but shabby publication, and the two of them turned it into a slick, high-quality magazine, with a large circulation. John set aside his photography to run *Ironman*, and every time I spoke with him I asked him if he missed taking pictures; he said that he didn't.

John said to give the thing careful consideration because those young pros out there were ravenously hungry, and if I couldn't do it at 100 percent, I shouldn't bother. I thanked him for his feedback, told him that I valued his opinion. Before I hung up, I asked him please not to tell anyone that I was mulling over competing again, since I hadn't made up my mind yet and I didn't want the gossip mill to start churning. He agreed that was a good idea.

I headed off to L.A. to check out the scene and decide whether I was going to do this thing or not. I needed some time alone to think, so I decided to drive down from Seattle. I took off on a rainy Monday—pulled out of the driveway at eight in the evening—after wrapping up all my work that couldn't be done from the road, and drove 350 miles down into southern Oregon, where, at some godforsaken hour of the morning, I decided to stop at a cheap roadside motel and get a couple of hours' sleep.

In the morning I decided that I wanted to take the slow way to L.A., so instead of getting back on I-5, I turned onto U.S. 199, the highway that led diagonally southwest toward the Redwoods National Park and the winding, mostly two-lane Coast Highway. It is a magnificent drive, and I seem to think best when I'm driving on a long trip. I crawled down through the mountains out to that amazing coastline, going through the redwoods, past Eureka, and on into San Francisco, all the time absorbing the air, thinking just below the surface—in that place where it doesn't feel like actual thinking so much as restlessness—about where my life was.

I stopped in San Francisco to have dinner with some friends, asking them what they thought of my competing again. They asked me why I would want to go back to that when it seemed as if I had so many other ("other" sort of came out sounding as if it meant "better") things going on in my life now. I certainly valued these two people's opinions, otherwise I would never have brought the subject up, so I stored that away for the next day's mulling and, after dinner, drove another couple of hours down the coast. I got up the next morning and drove the rest of the way into L.A., passing through Monterey, whizzing past Hearst Castle, San Simeon, and all the other coast towns and cities, until I got to the Santa Monica Freeway in the midafternoon. I got a room at the little hotel where I usually stayed, a couple of miles back from the beach—when I was here on my own dime—went straight to bed, and slept for fourteen hours, as if I had died.

When I finally dragged my ass out of bed the next morning, I called my friend Artie Zeller to see what he was up to for the day. I had let him know, a couple of days before I left, that I was coming down, but that I was planning on taking the slow way and didn't know exactly when I would arrive.

He answered the phone, clearing his throat—as the phone came closer to his mouth—like a train chugging progressively closer through a tunnel. "Hello," he said when the receiver reached his ear.

"Hi, Artie, it's Bob."

"Roberto," he said, rolling the R out in a dramatic gesture. "Where are you? You sound so close. It's either a terrific connection or you're right across the street." The clinging remnants of his New York childhood shaped every word.

"Well, I'm here all right—although not right across the street—unless you mean that as a metaphor."

"Whaat's wrong with the guy, ehh?" he asked. It wasn't his question really. It was one of our most familiar exchanges. He was imitating Joe Weider, a man both of us had known for years—Artie for probably thirty-five, me for thirteen. Everyone in bodybuilding had his take on the Joe Weider voice; Artie's was one of the best, and we would usually pepper our conversations with some of Joe's most frequent sayings.

"I'm at my hotel," I said, knowing that he knew where I meant. "Wanna get some breakfast?"

"Of course, Bob. Why don't we meet at the Rose Cafe at nine. They have terrific oatmeal there. I like it with the fresh fruit."

"Is it instant?" I asked, already beginning the teasing banter that we often used when speaking to each other.

"Of course not. They make it fresh each morning."

"I'll see you there at nine, Artie."

"Okay, Bob."

When we met for breakfast, we talked about how my latest book was coming along, and if I had seen any of the photos done into prints yet. Artie had, for years, been considered one of the foremost physique and workout photographers in the world; he had done all these fantastic black-and-white pictures of Arnold Schwarzenegger—and all the other guys at the gym in the seventies—that had become famous and were still being published all over the world. He'd done the photography for the three workout books I'd written. After catching up for a while, I asked him what he thought about my making a competitive comeback. His eyes lit up—it had always been clear to me that Artie felt I'd never fully achieved my potential as a bodybuilder—and he said that he thought it was a great idea, but that I should make sure I could do it to the best of my ability, or not waste my time.

"I'm planning to give the matter careful consideration," I told him, pronouncing the c's in *careful* and *consideration* with a deliberate hardness, being both smart-assed and serious.

"Yes, you should definitely give it careful consideration," he replied.

We spent the rest of the day together; I took the negatives of the photos he'd taken for my book into a lab I used up in Hollywood, to get the prints done, and he went along. And then we went to Gold's Gym in Venice to check out the scene, see who was around.

"There aren't too many of the top guys around anymore, Bob. It's not like it used to be. Remember? A big gang of guys would all train together and then go take some breakfast and hang out at the beach. Now everyone's moved away, mostly—like you did," he said as we walked through the gym, which was practically the size of a football stadium and packed with every conceivable piece of equipment and every style of body, from totally buffed to wimpy. He was right; many of the pros had figured out that they could live anywhere, as long as a good gym was around and a major airport nearby, so if they didn't care for L.A., they could leave and make a life elsewhere. "And everybody had personality then," he added, after a few seconds of silence, as we went farther into the gym. "Now, well, it's just changed. I guess the world moves on."

"No, you're right, Artie, it has changed. But, you know, take me for example—I love where I live. It's my favorite place on earth. But I still love it here too—I don't know. Know what I mean?"

"I know," he said, again in the Joe Weider voice.

I stayed in town a week, training at World Gym—two blocks from Gold's in Venice, eating breakfast at the Firehouse on Main Street in Santa Monica, a consistent hangout for the serious gym crowd. I watched all the people, especially the guys who looked as if they had just moved here from another part of the planet to live the dream. I saw Artie and his wife, Josie, all through the week, and we had fun, joking, catching up, talking politics.

I saw all the old gang at the gym: Joe Gold, Eddie Giuliani, Zabo, Ira. I spent a few sunsets at Palisades Park and at Will Rogers Beach.

It felt good; this place had been home for a lot of years. It was as if I'd never moved away.

When I left, I once again took the slow way back to Seattle, driving all the way north on the coast route, only cutting over to I-5 when I was less than a hundred miles from the city. I still wasn't sure what I was going to do. Careful consideration—that's exactly what this needed; I was feeling only the positives at the moment and it's easy to be swept away by nostalgia and forget the bad stuff, so I'd give it plenty more careful consideration.

The Late 1970s
Southern Indiana

While lying in bed, I heard Dad pull into the driveway. He didn't come inside for several minutes, so I got up and watched him through the front window of my room as he went through the trunk of my car, throwing things in all directions. My shotgun lay across the roof of the car. He pulled out a black ceramic bong that I had wrapped in a towel behind the spare tire, held it at arm's length, sniffed it, and marched toward the back door.

"Where the hell are you?" he yelled.

"In my room."

"Get your sorry ass out here. Let's get this thing goin'."

I stood in the doorway of my bedroom for a couple of seconds, watching him pace back and forth in the kitchen. His face was squinched, and I couldn't tell if he was crying, but something about the way he walked made me think that he was. Finally, I went over.

"First, keep your goddamn mouth shut," he growled, and then turned, drew his right arm all the way back, and let fly with a roundhouse that landed right below my left eye and knocked me to my knees. I shot immediately to my feet, the uncontrollable animal impulse overtaking me. He looked into my eyes as I stood there rubbing my cheek and looking straight at him, trying to keep from knocking him through the plateglass window behind him. He backed up a few steps, then seemed to realize that he was showing fear, went hard again, and shifted his feet to a surer stance. I slid to the floor and began to cry.

It all poured out. The class skipping, the suicide attempt, getting fired, the lies. Both the school and my boss had called him, he said. The dean had asked him if I did indeed have leukemia, then filled him in on the other details. Dad said that on Monday he had an appointment with my teachers, my guidance counselor, and the dean; he'd do his best to try to make everything right.

On Monday I went sheepishly back to school. My teachers were all amazingly forgiving; probably heard about my trying to blow my brains out. They all made arrangements for me to make up as much as possible of the work I'd missed. I was ordered to see a shrink.

The psychiatrist I began seeing was an asshole. I don't say that because I was a kid in trouble, but because it should have been obvious to any mental health professional that I was in grave trouble. I had come within inches of killing myself, and he approached our sessions with the aggression of a middle linebacker chasing an opposing quarterback, determined to tackle me and beat my problems out of me, and I wasn't about to get in the way of his success. I began to clam up during our fourth or fifth session, especially as he began to grill me on whether or not I was gay, asking the questions as if he would turn the answers over to the FBI. After six sessions I stopped going.

In the end I only failed chemistry, but my teacher was a good-hearted man and tried extremely hard to help me pass. The rest of my grades were low, but well above passing. And the school year ended.

July 1995
Southern California

When I drove from Seattle down to L.A., hoping that the trip would help me make up my mind, I decided that it was also time to go out to Woodland Hills and meet with Joe Weider again, for the first time in a couple of years. I don't know exactly what I expected to come of the visit, but I hated leaving things on bad terms, and that's where dealings between us had been left when I stopped competing. A big part of my decision to stop was directly tied to a severe chasm in our relationship, a rift that I felt he had created.

For good or for bad, Joe and his brother Ben control bodybuilding. The company they both privately own publishes magazines (*Muscle and Fitness, Shape, Flex,* and *Men's Fitness*), makes vitamins and other supplements, training equipment, and fitness clothing. Joe is publisher of the magazines and oversees operations of the empire. His brother Ben keeps a low public profile as far as all the companies are concerned, but is president of the International Federation of Bodybuilders (IFBB), an organization with 160 or more member nations that for all intents and purposes is the only legitimate international bodybuilding organization. It's made up of both an amateur and a professional division.

They helped build this sport from nothing. Oh, the sport existed before, but it was small-time stuff. The typical contest was an afterthought, attached to AAU weight-lifting meets, with the physique contest typically starting at around one in the morning, after all the weight classes of the Olympic lifters had finished; and the shows were sometimes done under a naked lightbulb, hung from the basketball hoop in a high school gymnasium.

Ben's persistence and drive had brought the amateur side of the sport right to the edge of becoming a part of the Olympic Games, and an entire professional division had been created for top amateurs who'd moved up the ranks and were looking for a competitive way to make money from the sport. He got bodybuilding and the IFBB recognized by the International Federation of Sports and a slew of other legitimate governing athletic bodies, including dozens of national Olympic committees around the world. In fact the IFBB was reportedly the second-largest sports federation in the International Federation of Sports. Amazing fact, considering that those who don't understand bodybuilding—including most sports journalists—usually question whether it's a legitimate sport at all.

Now the other side of that coin is that the Weider brothers claim that the IFBB and the Weider companies are separate and completely unrelated. Only the most naive fool would believe that. They should simply say that, yes, they are completely linked and quit the shenanigans of trying to pretend otherwise. It would be a hell of a lot healthier for everyone concerned and far more honest on their part; but of course if they did that, then nasty words like *monopoly* or *conflict of interest* would start getting thrown around—which already happens. But what do I know? I'm just an athlete, and if there is one thing that the brothers have made sure of, it is that the athletes—the people that the entire sport and a large portion of their business are based upon—have no real power or say in how the sport is run.

The athlete's participation in all of this is that Weider signs the ones who are great, or highly marketable, to product endorsement contracts. These contract relationships operate sort of like the old studio system did for actors. Just as a contract actor would only do pictures for the studio holding his contract, all the work in the sport a contract athlete does is for Weider and the IFBB. He or she cannot compete in any contests that aren't IFBB, and all guest appearances must be for IFBB-sanctioned organizations—or one of the sister organizations in whatever country the appearance is in. (In the United States, the National Physique Committee [NPC] is the IFBB's national organizing body, and each other member nation has theirs as well.)

Contract athletes can only do articles in Weider magazines and can only appear in places that have the IFBB stamp of approval. If an athlete were to do a guest appearance at an unsanctioned contest, he could realistically face a lifetime suspension from the IFBB and lose his means of making a large part of his living. And they put a clause in the IFBB rule book that says an athlete can be suspended just for publicly criticizing or questioning any of the policies of the IFBB or its officers. Pretty good little deal for the brothers; a capitalist's dream come true; and these guys do big business, as in the hundreds-of-million-of-dollars-a-year kind of big business.

So I decided to go in and meet with Joe and see if we couldn't work out our differences, because business aside, I liked the guy, and I hated how everything had degenerated into hard feelings. And, after talking for a while in his cavernous office, with phones ringing and secretaries and editors rushing in and out, we agreed that if I decided to compete again, we could almost certainly work out a new contract and be back in business together. I put that in the old think tank for my drive up the coast to Seattle; that would definitely play a major part in my final decision. Of course, I was setting aside the fact that Joe and I still had a major up-and-down history that could easily turn bad again. At that moment, though, I only wanted to dwell on the positives of the situation—the sweet nostalgia for simpler times.

The Late 1970s
Southern Indiana

The summer after my junior year I got a full-time job working at a cardboard-box factory, out on the edge of town. The man who owned the place was a client of Dad's CPA firm, and I went out, applied for the job, and started the first week school was out. I was determined not to screw up my life anymore, so I worked hard all day and in the evenings went to school to work out. Every month I bought my muscle magazines, and I now seemed to know the bodybuilding world as much as one could know it from reading about it.

So I settled into the summer, breaking my back at the factory during the day and pushing myself on the weight machine, or my barbells at home, each night. I saw my friends only on the weekends, still got high with them and rowdied around, but stayed comparatively tame.

Late-summer football practice was two weeks away, and I planned to stop working so that I could have those last two weeks as some semblance of a vacation. On my last day at the factory, all the guys who worked there decided that they were fed up with what they felt were the low wages the boss paid and decided to have a walkout in protest. I decided that, since it was my last day, what the hell, I'd go with them. They all went to a bar next door and got plastered. When we came back at the end of the day, the boss was there waiting and fired everyone—including me. When I expressed concern to the other guys over their jobs, they told me to relax—this exact scenario played out every couple of years. The boss would hire them all back a day or two later and grudgingly give everyone a raise—it was a tradition. So I went home.

When Dad got home, it was late. I had already gone to bed, after driving around with my friends some. I heard him pull up, slam the back door, stomp across the house; he threw my bedroom door open and came straight at me. I sat up, but he grabbed me around the throat and pushed me back down on the bed, squeezing tighter, until I couldn't breathe. I could easily have pushed him off, but felt myself slide into the fear of a five-year-old and just lay shaking trying to get a breath. He drew his right fist back, and with all my strength I rolled out from underneath him, just as his fist slammed into the wall in back of where I had just been. I stood shaking, not understanding what was going on.

"You stupid son of a bitch," he yelled at me, shooting up off the bed and pinning me against the door of my closet. "You really fucked up this time! Got fired, didn't ya? I got the call today. If I lose this account because of you, I will kill you, do you hear me? I am tired of your fuckups—your craziness—your psychiatrists—all of it. I want you out of my house by morning. Understand? Leave your car. Try to take it and I'll have you arrested."

I was in shock. "Where am I supposed to go?" I asked weakly.

"I don't give a flying fuck where you go." He slammed out of the room, went out to his car, and peeled away.

I tried to think. What was I going to do? And then it hit me. I'd go to California. I'd take the bus out to L.A. and start training at Gold's Gym and get on with my dreams. I could go to school out there; I'd show him; I'd become rich and famous. Who did he think he was, throwing his seventeen-year-old son out in the street? I got out my backpack and carefully began to sort through my things, trying to determine what

I really needed, and after a couple of hours I had the pack full. I even had my best blue suit carefully strapped to the outside of the pack, because I might need it for job interviews or something. *Now how will I get to the bus station?* I wondered. Even though I had technically paid Dad back for the car he'd bought me (a midnight mountain blue '67 Mustang fastback) when he'd bought a house ten miles out of town, and the title was registered under Robert Paris—so a cop wouldn't know if that was me or my father—I wasn't going to take the chance that he would tell the police I'd stolen it. I didn't think about if the police might also wonder why a minor had been put out on the street and if Dad might find himself in more hot water than me.

I called one of my friends, Kurt, who lived on the lake next to ours. He said that he'd be happy to take me into town and showed up twenty minutes later. I put my pack in his trunk, and on the way to the bus station he asked me if I didn't want to spend the night at his house, maybe cool off a bit, and see if I still wanted to leave in the morning. I said that was probably a good idea, so we turned around and went to his place. Kurt's dad traveled for work, and we would have parties out at his house from time to time; I knew my way around and crashed in my sleeping bag on the living room floor. The next morning a couple of other friends came out to Kurt's house, and they tried to convince me that while it might be cool to split for the West Coast, maybe I should stick around a few days to see what happened.

"Besides, Bobby, I talked to my dad this morning," Kurt said, "and he told me if you couldn't work things out, you could stay here. Think about it. What about football this year, and senior year and all?"

"No, you guys are probably right," I said. "I guess I can stay for a couple of days."

A week went by. Kurt and I would go into town on his motorcycle, and I had him take me by the bus station so that I could get a price for a one-way ticket to L.A. One night, after I'd been gone from Dad's a week, I asked Kurt to drop me off at Dad's house, so I could maybe go talk to Dad and see if things had cooled off any. Kurt dropped me off after dark, and Dad's car was in the drive, and after Kurt took off— telling me that he'd be at his girlfriend's house in town—I remembered that I had left my house key behind the night Dad threw me out. I tried all the doors, but they were locked; rang the bell on the front door, but Dad didn't or wouldn't answer. I pounded; no answer. Eventually I got discouraged and started walking the ten miles back to Kurt's girlfriend's house. I walked down the lonely country roads; it took hours to get into town, but I finally made it and on the way decided that I would never speak to my father again.

A few days later friends began telling me that Dad was calling all over town trying to find me. *Let him stew,* I thought. In the meantime I went in and told Coach McCaa my situation, and that I'd pretty much decided not to go west—even though it was tempting and I might still change my mind—but I had the complication of needing a permission slip and physical signed by a parent before I could play ball that year. He said that he'd try to work something out. Dad's calls around town grew more persistent. Finally, the day before football practice started, he called Kurt's house.

"When are you coming home?" he asked, his voice sounding small, tentative.

"I don't know," I said back, trying to sound tough.

"Well, I'd like for you to—please."

"Okay."

Kurt took me back to the house. Dad was standing out on the back patio, nursing a drink and smoking a Lucky.

"Hi."

"Hi."

"How long were you going to stay away?"

"You told me to never come back again."

"I'm sorry."

"I was gonna go to California."

"Well, I would have come looking for you."

After we stood silently for a few seconds, he held out his arms and we hugged, and he said that he loved me.

"Remind me to never play poker against you," he said as I took my backpack inside to my room, and then he began to laugh.

The next day I started football practice. My senior year began a week later.

The year flew by. Football was over before I knew it, and even though I had improved significantly over the year before and I was known as a good hitter who made a lot of tackles and sacked the opposing quarterback every now and then, I had realized that my athletic future was in bodybuilding. I got some inquiries from colleges about playing football and even met with the recruiter from Indiana State, but I already knew that it wasn't for me.

In school I worked hard, skipped classes only occasionally; I threw myself into my art and the speech team and drama club with relish. I was still just pretending, though, and I couldn't wait to escape. I carried my newest muscle magazines to school, and every once in a while someone would make fun of that, but I didn't care if people thought it was weird. I knew better.

One day in late spring, my friend Mac came to me and said that he had decided to join the Marine Corps Reserves and asked if I wanted to go to boot camp with him. I asked him how he was going to go to college if he was in the Marines, and he said that even though it was regular boot camp, he would graduate in time for the beginning of school. Mac and I had both decided to go to Indiana State and room together.

"So about this Marine Corps thing—what's the deal?" I asked him.

"Hell, BP, to hear the recruiter tell it, it's a pretty sweet deal."

"Are you serious?"

"Yeah, man, after boot camp you just have to go to meetings once a month. You get paid. It's seriously cool. You oughta go with me. Recruiter said that if I bring another guy along, I'll get my first stripe, just like that."

I went into the recruiter's office, and the next thing I knew I was signed up. Everybody, including my dad (and he'd been a Marine), told me I was crazy, and didn't I realize that Mac would never follow through? Sure enough, the day before Mac and I were to go in and sign our final commitment papers, he told me that he'd changed his mind. He was lying on the couch at his girlfriend's house with his head on her lap and said, "You know, BP, you can change your mind too. It ain't too late."

"No way. I said I'm goin', I'm goin'."

He just laughed and said to send him a postcard, and that he'd think of me every time he cracked open a cold one.

Going that summer to Marine Corps Recruit Depot, Parris Island, South Carolina, may have been, up to that point in my life, the hardest thing I'd ever done. It changed me in ways that would serve my life long after I left that miserable swampy island. They take away your clothes, then your hair, then your individuality and dignity; and replace them with a kind of discipline that you never dreamed you possessed. I was only enlisted in the Reserves, but that didn't mean I had things easier. All the platoons were made up of guys both in the regulars and Reserves. The guys who were there as reservists and then headed off to college after graduation were probably treated harsher, expected to do more, because the drill instructors were determined to show these college boys a thing or two. After thirteen weeks, I graduated as a Marine. I was due for registration at college two days later.

Dad picked me up at the airport when I flew in from South Carolina; I was in my uniform with my buzz-cut hairdo. He hugged me at the gate and told me how proud he was. When we got to the car, he had a cooler full of ice-cold Millers waiting; when we got back to his house, most of my friends popped out from behind trees and yelled, "Surprise, jarhead!"

We partied the night away. The guys bragged about their wild summer—all the parties and troublemaking—but something had shifted. They all teased me about my haircut, checked out my uniform, and I tried to tell them all about boot camp, but the words were hard to pull together. It was like trying to explain skydiving to people who've never been off the ground. Mac looked at me, and I could sense, as I was telling my stories—about monsterish drill instructors, and being physically exercised until you dropped from exhaustion—that he had jumbled emotions, wishing he'd gone too, but glad he didn't.

6

NEXT TO DEATH

August 1995
Seattle

My body was breaking back in with remarkable speed. I thought that it would take three months to get back into full-bore training, but after a month the poundages I was handling shot up and the muscles began to grow. I was sore all the time and starving most of the time, and I considered these to be positive developments. You can't be a world-class athlete without being on friendly terms with pain, so the soreness I felt in each body part the day after I'd trained it was like sleeping in a childhood bedroom again—familiar and pleasant territory.

I took my increasing appetite as a good sign. I'd whittled my eating habits down to two meals a day of fairly normal food, and if I could swing this increase in hunger in the direction of clean food—such as broiled, skinless chicken and plain rice and steamed vegetables—and not toward the junk food I always craved before, when I was bodybuilding, then I could get bigger and into lean shape at the same time.

I love to eat, but when I wasn't training seriously, I had almost no hard-core, kill-for-a-burrito cravings, probably because when I could eat anything I wanted and not have my career on the line every time I strayed toward junk, there was no point in dying over a piece of food that I could pop down to the corner and get anytime I wanted. Throughout the time I'd been competing I always had to battle my cravings, and I hoped that this time I would have grown up enough to let that self-destructive instinct go.

Food and diet are two of the things that make bodybuilding different from any other sport. Sure there are other sports where eating right is valued as a means to an edge, but they aren't dependent on the look that's achieved through proper diet as a criterion for success or failure. The competitive side of bodybuilding revolves around appearance; it's not a side effect, it's the purpose, the desired result of the training and dieting. The competitive bodybuilder attempts to go in two seemingly contradictory directions. First, he is trying to build up the size of his muscles, and in addition to hard training, that usually means eating a lot of food. Second, in preparing for competition, he tries to get his body fat down to the lowest point it can possibly go, and most times that means cutting back on the amount of food. Sometimes these two goals are chased simultaneously. That's one tricky balancing act. I was hoping that I'd be able to stay lean and get bigger at the same time. But there were far more serious issues to think about than whether I'd be craving salt and vinegar potato chips when I should be eating dry baked potatoes.

I actually think that I'm going to do it," I told Tommy when I called him at work in L.A., to see how he was doing with his new job at one of the major movie studios.

"But . . . ," he said back.

"But what?"

"That's what I'm asking you. Your 'I actually think that I'm going to do it' came out with a *but* attached to it. I heard it."

"Nonsense."

"I heard it, even if you didn't say it. What's your hesitation about? C'mon, spill it."

"Nothin' to spill. Training's going great. Bod's responding like I was still twenty."

"In your dreams, you're still twenty."

"I said it's responding like I was twenty, not that I am twenty."

He laughed, then said, "So what are you hesitating over? I hear it in your voice. There's something still bothering you."

"I don't know. Everybody I talk to seems supportive of me coming back. It's just, well . . . oh, never mind."

"It's the drugs, isn't it?"

"Yeah."

"Let me tell you exactly where you're coming from. You don't know if you can justify what it takes. And that, 'what it takes' includes the drugs, right?"

"Possibly."

"Possibly? Come on, Bob. We both know that the sport still hasn't cleaned up its act, and you don't know if you want to go back down that road. That much has been obvious to me for years."

"Oh, I don't know, Tommy, I mean, look at Michael Jordan this year, making his comeback. Do you think he had to think about drugs when he decided to play again? He wants to play again, he just plays—it's pure."

"I don't know. You know as well as I do that there's drugs in most every sport. Look at pro football. You think those NFL players get that way by eating their Wheaties?"

"Yeah, but those guys don't have to deal with the public thinking that they're nothing but a bunch of steroid heads. They might still have the drugs, but at least their sport gets respect."

"Now, why would you go worrying about what the public thinks of your sport?"

"Because I want it to grow. When it grows, there's more money, and when there's more money, there's more respect. You know how that cycle works."

"This whole drug thing is all blown out of proportion. It's your body—you should be able to do whatever you want with it, you know. I mean it's not like anyone's ever died doing this—have they?"

"Well, there was Mohamed Benaziza." I could hear his other line ringing. "You know he . . ." It kept ringing.

"Sorry—hang on, let me see who this is."

He put me on hold. When he came back, he asked, "Can I call you back later? The big cheese is on the warpath—gotta go do a little butt-kissin'."

"Sure, Tommy. Talk to you later."

Tommy had nailed it. The biggest hesitation I had left about this comeback revolved not just around the drugs, but also the perception of drugs in the sport. The public perception about steroids in sports, particularly bodybuilding, was one thing, but the idea that you could maybe die doing this thing was a whole other can of tuna, and I could clearly remember the night I heard the news about the death of one of my fellow pros.

October 1991
Seattle

I answered on the third ring. Sunday night; I had considered letting the machine pick it up.

"Bob, it's Artie." My friend Art Zeller sounding small and far away.

"Hi, Artie. What's up?" I sat on the edge of the bed.

"I've got some bad news, Bob. Momo Benaziza died last night after the Dutch Grand Prix." The sadness was unguarded in his voice.

"What do you mean died?"

"They say his heart stopped a couple of hours after the show."

My mind ran backward as my voice finished two or three more minutes of "What a waste" and "What about his family?" Artie and I didn't talk long; we didn't have much more to say to each other, given the news he'd just passed along. Both of us were thrown by what anyone with eyes could see had been coming for years. A professional body-builder had died from what he did to himself to meet the standards of modern competition.

Because of my work schedule I had decided not to compete on that year's European tour. I had done two of them in one year, and they were grueling tests of endurance for the athletes. Seven or eight contests spread over a few weeks, each one in a different country. When you were on the road like that, you had to worry, in each new city and culture, about finding your food and a gym to train in, and being on a precontest diet made the travel and the foreignness all the more intensely wearying. In all my life I'd never feared hard work, but those Grand Prix tours were some of the hardest things I'd ever done; every athlete who'd ever done one felt the same way.

It all came pushing down; same old arguments. My mind rolled back in waves. The voices of judges and fans filled with good advice and wisdom:

"You just need to be a little harder."

"Looks like you're holdin' a bit of water."

"Man, he's so fucking ripped you can see his heart beat."

They always wanted us to look a certain way and didn't care what we did to get there.

When was the first time I knew it could happen? Probably driving home from World Gym in the red Jeep on a night so perfect it belonged in a picture.

Spring, 1988. I was competing in two days in the Niagara Falls Grand Prix and had already started cutting back on my liquid intake; four cups of black coffee were my only rations that day. The day before I'd started on Aldactazide, a potent combination of diuretic and aldosterone inhibitor, and in addition to having to pee every five minutes, my skin was beginning to wrap like cellophane around already fat-free muscles. I had just gone to the gym to do a final thirty minutes on the stationary bike. I did it more to burn nervous energy than phantom fat.

While driving home along the Santa Monica Freeway, a bolt of lightning hit me as my abdominal muscles suddenly and unexpectedly cramped up so hard they turned inside out on themselves. It seemed that the muscles were going to rip away from the bone. Unbearable pain volted through me as I straightened up to stretch my abs, only to have my lower back seize up just as tight. Rod, my boyfriend, had gone with me to the gym so that he could do his workout, and as this was all happening, he started to cry because I was in such obviously intense pain and he didn't know what to do.

"Water and salt," I tried to tell him through clenched teeth. "I gotta get some water and salt."

I knew the formula. I was, like all my fellow professionals, a chemistry specialist without a degree. I had to be. If I wanted to stay competitive, I needed to keep up with the standards the judges were demanding from us. The judges and the fans.

I had never been able to escape from the imploding moral dilemma of wrapping my dreams around a sport with an unofficial rule that you had to use drugs to be remotely competitive. It was all about the drugs. That is the hardest thing for me to say about the sport that has occupied my life since before I graduated from high school.

The IFBB loved to let people think that the professional division was drug tested, and—except for a few nasty cheaters (but who can truly root out all the rotten apples?)—drug free. There is not one person that I know of in the sport who truly believes that. We all know it's a crock, a manipulation of perception surrounding a complicated issue that won't go away.

I had been the first male professional athlete to write the IFBB president, Ben Weider, demanding drug testing on the pro circuit. That was in 1985. He wrote me back saying that it would happen, but by evolution, not revolution. In 1990, after a few years of testing for steroids at the amateur World Championships and most of the women's contests, the federation decided to make the leap and test the male pros first at the Arnold Schwarzenegger Classic in the spring and then at the Mr. Olympia in the fall. The whole year leading up to those shows was thrown into turmoil for the guys who took this notion of testing seriously, and I was one of them. A number of guys were searching desperately for chemical masking agents and other ways to get around the urine test the day before the competition.

Supposedly some women had found various ways to circumvent detection. In one legendary story, a female athlete used a catheter and small squeeze bottle containing another person's drug-free urine, and when she went into the rest room—accompanied by a testing official to witness the passing of fluids—the athlete pressed her legs a certain way and filled the cup with this steroid-free pee-pee, letting it flow, seemingly naturally, from the device stuffed up inside her vagina, and she passed the test. Most men agreed that this would be far more difficult, not to mention painful, for a man to pull off and kept searching for better solutions. Many guys turned to their friends in other drug-tested sports to find out how they got around the tests. But some of us took the notion of drug testing seriously, knowing that, whether we agreed with drug use or not, taking the whole question out of the sport would help it grow by leaps and bounds—and everyone involved would benefit. So some of us began training drug free. That was a mistake.

In 1990, I needed to qualify for the Mr. Olympia by placing in the top three in one of the smaller shows during the year. Because I'd decided to take the whole supposed shift over to a drug-free sport seriously, I placed low in the qualifying contests and didn't get a spot in the Olympia lineup. Probably just as well, though, since the contest was a dismal failure.

For years the fans had been saying to clean up the drug use in the sport, most of them demanding some form of testing be used. When the Mr. Olympia was staged that year in Chicago and the athletes, who didn't test positive for steroids, were clean—at least clean enough to pass the test—they weren't in the kind of freaky condition that the fans had come to expect. And many of those same people who had pushed for testing complained loudly that the show had stunk and something needed to be done to get the level of conditioning back up to where it used to be. It was clear to the IFBB officials that this could not go on, since ticket sales would eventually suffer and fan support would dwindle, so they opted to drop the on-site testing the day of a show and instead instituted a random test, supposedly by way of a computer-generated lottery to pick those who would be tested at any time throughout the year. Ironically, random testing was also the new procedure of the International Olympic Committee, which was clearly having its own difficulties in keeping performance levels high and drug perception low. No one I knew of was ever selected in that random lottery, and after about a year, the tests, random or otherwise, were never mentioned again. For a while they continued to write in the magazines as if testing were still on track, often saying that random testing was a superior system for catching drug users, but then even that faded away.

But in this world, illusion meant a great deal more than reality. Ben was working hard to get bodybuilding accepted as an Olympic sport and knew that the reputation for drug use in this sport—even if the burden fell unfairly on bodybuilding and ignored all the other sports where the use of strength drugs was common, and perhaps even more abusive—posed a major obstacle in the minds of the International Olympic Committee.

Now a pro athlete was dead and I didn't even know the details yet, but I would've bet on severe dehydration or insulin-induced coma enhanced by heavy anabolic-steroid and growth-hormone use.

The next day, as I got more details, I tried to put myself inside Momo's head on the day he died and to separate the false rumors I was hearing from the truth. This much I could deduce to be true: Momo, who had already won most of the shows on a seven-city European Grand Prix tour, woke up the day of the last contest complaining of being gravely ill and exhausted. His color was gray with a greenish tint, most likely enhanced by the skin dye athletes used to boost their tans because dark skin looked better under the lights on stage. He asked Wayne DeMilia, the IFBB vice president in charge of coordinating the tour, if he could skip the contest that day, but then just before prejudging, Momo changed his mind and decided to compete.

When Momo complained to Wayne about being ill, most likely all Wayne had to do was say to him that he had a responsibility to his competition contract, which all athletes signed, guaranteeing that they would compete where and when they promised to and not back out of a show at the last minute. I imagined that Momo instantly told Wayne— through his interpreter, since Momo spoke only a few words of English and Wayne spoke no French—that he would be fine and that he'd compete, and then through the rest of the day proceeded to keep to himself how severely he was suffering.

If Wayne had known just how sick Benaziza was, not only would he have allowed him to drop out that day, but most likely he would have insisted on it. I felt that this would have been the case because I had watched Wayne deal with these situations on the tours I'd been on. Wayne DeMilia had been a friend of mine for a number of years, and although I'd always had difficulty agreeing with the way he ran the pro division, I knew from my own experiences on these contest tours that he had a great deal of responsibility: keeping all the athletes in line, taking care of last-minute problems with each contest promoter, and other general troubleshooting; and it was no surprise that on a complicated tour like this there was a bunch of trouble to shoot along the way, including illness. An athlete would complain about being ill, and then he and Wayne would talk (or maybe argue) it out, and they would decide if this guy really was too sick to compete, but if he wasn't, Wayne would make sure that the man lived up to his agreement.

My personal experience with this happened at the 1989 Mr. Olympia in Rimini, Italy. The week before the show I came down with a severe flu, with daily vomiting and diarrhea, and began dropping weight rapidly. I did the show, twenty pounds under my best weight. As the weekend wore on, I got progressively more ill and needed bed rest. I was contracted to do the contest tour which began on the day after the Olympia, but there was no way I could make it. So I went to Wayne and told him what was happening; he reminded me of my contract. I said that I was too sick and not joking, and that in my condition I could easily get a doctor to agree with my decision not to go on. He let me pass on the tour without any further fight.

When Momo came to Wayne to say that he was too sick to compete, and Wayne tried to establish exactly how ill he was, something must have gotten lost in the translation. Momo may have thought that if he didn't compete, he wouldn't get his prize money from the previous shows. Now, many times Wayne did hold on to the prize money until the end of a contest tour. Perhaps to keep the ponies in line.

If Momo thought that by not competing that day, he might lose the money he'd already won, then his decision to go ahead seemed a forgone conclusion. Momo had a wife and three children in France, and, like anyone else, had bills to pay. It was also not uncommon to hear of some top pros and plenty of wanna-bes spending between fifty and a hundred thousand bucks a year on anabolics and growth hormones. If this was the case, then the solution to his dilemma was obvious.

Because Momo was a superstar in the sport and had been on a hot streak for a couple of years, the promise of him competing in this contest had helped sell tickets. Momo wouldn't have been happy at the thought of the crowd and contest promoter being disappointed with him for dropping out. So the show went on.

During prejudging Momo left the stage frequently to vomit blood and wobbled just this side of collapse. Later it was determined that he had suffered at least one heart attack during the grueling morning competition. As the day went on, his condition grew worse, but he was winning. Again, Momo asked to drop out, but for some unexplained reason he decided to continue, performed at the night show, and thrilled a capacity crowd of zealous fans with the illusion of spectacular condition. He didn't disappoint those who had paid to see him at this freaky best.

*   *   *

Next to death." It was a phrase reported in the magazines to have been coined by Swedish pro Andreas Cahling when he saw the condition Frank Zane was in, as Frank walked toward the stage to compete in the 1979 Mr. Olympia. At that time the phrase didn't mean actual death. It was a way of expressing that the man was in a condition so fat-free that it was inconceivable that the edge could be pushed any further. Frank won his third Mr. Olympia that night and it marked the start of a turning point. It was the beginning of the end for reasonable bodybuilding. "Next to death" in '79 wouldn't get you into the top twenty in the nineties.

Momo wanted to get back to his hotel and sleep, but he had an obligation to attend the postcontest VIP banquet. People had paid extra on their tickets to get to meet all the pros in person. So he went; skin ice-cold; eyes sunken in his head; barely moving. All the athletes who saw him worried and saw themselves.

We had started down this road before when we experienced the scare of nearly losing an athlete during a tour.

Fall of 1988. Spring of 1989. Both times in Germany on a multicity contest tour. I had been there myself those times. In 1988, Harold Struthers, a popular veteran athlete, had collapsed in complete and un-relievable head-to-toe body cramps at a VIP banquet after the night show in Munich. He was rushed to a German intensive care unit, where doctors were baffled by the severe lack of water and minerals in such a healthy-looking man. How was he still alive in such a state? they wondered. And what had he done to get this way?

Six months later while self-administering insulin in his hotel bathroom the day before the German Grand Prix in Cologne, Harold fell into a convulsive coma. He wasn't a diabetic, he was pushing the edge. It was rumored throughout the four weeks of that tour that some of the top guys got harder-looking by using insulin to manipulate blood sugar and metabolism. In this world, new chemical notions swept quickly from rumor to practice. By the time of the German show at the end of the spring tour of 1989, guys who were willing to do anything to move up in the placements and prize money were convinced that insulin was the secret.

The morning of the prejudging, an exhausted Wayne DeMilia entered the backstage area where the athletes were scattered around sitting on folding chairs or on the floor leaning against walls. Only whispered voices broke the quiet. We were all waiting for some news.

Wayne had just come from the hospital where he'd spent the night, after going in the ambulance with Harold. The doctors told him that Harold would most likely be dead by the end of the day. The most any of us could do was cry. And of course, the show went on.

Then the most amazing thing happened. After the prejudging was over, we got word from the hospital that Harold had made a miraculous recovery. All of his problems stemmed from his having overmanipulated his insulin levels, and he had gone into severe diabetic shock, but even though his condition had been critical, his recovery was quick and spectacular. He was going to be checked out of the hospital and wanted to attend the night show later that same evening. The doctors tried to convince him that he should stay in the hospital for a few days of observation—they probably wanted to figure out how he had made such an amazing turnaround—but Harold insisted on being released. Since all his systems had returned to normal, the doctors could do nothing to prevent him from not only leaving but also attending the show that night as a spectator.

The year before, Harold had recovered from the edge of death after being overly dehydrated from diuretics, which was what had sent him into those massive, severe cramps. The doctors replenished his fluids and minerals and he rejoined the tour, since the German contest had been right at the start of it. After giving a posing exhibition (instead of competing) at the next show, he competed in the last five Grand Prix contests, and placed well too.

The Harold Incidents, as they became known, had all of us—anyone in the sport with more than an ounce of sense—wondering if the time would come when someone would go out to that edge and not come back.

Two years later, in Holland, it happened. Everyone stood, panicking, over Mohammed's body as it went cool and stiff. Porter Cottrell, one of the pros on the tour, who was also a fireman, tried every paramedic's technique to bring him back, but nothing would. By the time a doctor arrived, he was dead.

Everyone in the game was affected differently by the death of this man. Some of the younger pros and amateurs trying to get their pro cards said that it was the risk you took, and that, hey, people get hit by buses too, so what the hell. It pushed me one step closer to quitting the sport, adding another brick to the wall of hatred I was beginning to feel. It seemed, after all, a silly thing to die for.

*   *   *

In all the articles written about Mohamed's death, I can't recall if it was ever mentioned that it was time to revisit strict drug testing—and really make it work. Some articles might have led in that direction, but I can't remember them. The general tone was of the shame in losing such a fine athlete and man in the prime of his life, and how his heavy drug use had been no secret, but there was no collective cry to reexamine the root of the issue.

Anabolic steroids did not directly kill Momo Benaziza. It would be easy to jump to that conclusion in a society where the media, in a vastly ill-informed hysteria, paints steroids as both magical and evil. It would have been a false leap. His autopsy showed that the overuse of diuretics caused his death. Some bodybuilders use diuretics in the week prior to a contest to get rid of the water under the skin that can hide muscle definition. A diuretic causes the user to pee a lot and flush excess water out of the system. For the bodybuilder, this water release can add a visual finishing touch to an already in-shape physique. Under most circumstances, conservative, occasional diuretic use posed no threat to the user. These drugs are regularly used by people with high blood pressure and other ailments. The problems with the diuretics seemed to come either with using too much at one time—causing severe cramps from the loss of minerals in the excreted fluids—or with using them too frequently, as one who depended on them might on a Grand Prix contest tour where peak condition must be achieved contest after contest, for several weeks. If severely misused, diuretics can cause a heart attack and death.

If any real effort is ever to be made to eradicate drugs from bodybuilding, all the drugs that athletes use will have to be included in the test. It's not enough just to test for steroids, you have to get at the diuretics, the insulin, the growth hormone, the clenbuterol, and any of the other new additions that pop into use. And you will have to do both year-round surprise random testing and testing on the contest day as well. You have to make sure that no one finds a way to cheat the system, to be fair to those playing by the rules. It's got to be that, which could get into some sticky civil liberties issues, or let the whole thing go, be honest about the situation, and figure that every once in a while someone will push too far and pay with his life.

Tommy called back that evening. He wanted to know why, if I was having such a dilemma over the drugs, I was even considering making a comeback. I told him that was exactly what my whole hang-up was all about—this dilemma, and whether or not I was making something out of nothing. I loved the sport, but hated this element of it. I hated the hypocrisy of some of the athletes who tried to pretend they'd never used drugs. I hated how the whole drug question got so twisted in the media—the same media that glorified great athletic endeavors, in more acceptable sports, as if the athletes they celebrated had found the cure for world hunger. And I wasn't really sure exactly how I felt about the drug issue. It was easy to say that I was against drugs in my sport, but was that a moral feeling or a desire for more mainstream acceptance of bodybuilding?

"What's so fucked up about them dropping the testing is that without drugs it would still be the same guys succeeding. The fans would have eventually adjusted. The IFBB guys weren't patient enough to see it through. They caved too soon."

"I know all this, Bob," Tommy said, seeming a bit impatient, but trying to hide it. "But other than trying to create a cleaner perception, what is the point? Prohibition never works. It's your body; no one has any right to tell you what you can put into it."

"I agree—I'm as libertarian as you are on the prohibition thing. But, I don't like the idea that I need to take drugs in order to succeed in this sport. That's my bottom line. I'm not necessarily against the drugs, per se, it's just that if I don't use them, I don't win—period. That pisses me off."

"Then don't compete."

"That's not good enough. Maybe I wanna compete, and maybe when I do it, I don't wanna beat my head against a brick wall and place last in the shows."

"Rock and a hard place, Bobby boy."

"Exactly," I said, frustrated, ignoring his not-so-subtle pun.

"So you think you can create more change inside the sport than on the outside ranting about how it needs to clean up its act—right?"

"Right. Say I do this right and win the Olympia—when I'm doing press after the win, I start saying, as the top guy in the sport, that it is time to make a choice between drug testing—real, honest drug testing—and just letting nature take its course and maybe seeing more dangerous chemicals come into vogue—and making that into a strong platform. . . . Oh, I don't know, it sounds so stupid now that I say it out loud."

"Face some facts, Bob. Bodybuilding might get more popular, but it's probably never going to be the next tennis or golf. People are still too fucked up about the body. Nearly naked athletes onstage, flexing their muscles, showing off their bodies, turns a lot of people off."

"Well, it's not burlesque. There's a reason those guys are onstage. The audience can be built up to ten times the size it is now. That's what I want. And the athletes who go into this should get the respect they deserve for the hard work they put into their sport."

"Oh, you wide-eyed dreamer, you."

"Maybe, but honestly, that's why I even consider busting my ass in the gym again. This thing could be a lot bigger than it is right now, and I think that I want to be a part of that—even if it means that, at the moment, I have ignore some of the things about it that I don't like. I'm not alone in feeling that way either. There's two kinds of guys in this sport. The first kind doesn't give the drugs a second thought. They do what it takes, never questioning whether or not it could ever be different or better. The other guys think about the moral dilemma of the thing and wanna work toward a time when there's no decision to be made. In a strange way, I'm kind of envious of the first guys—it's simple for them. They just say fuck it, do it, and get on with it."

"So suppose they institute the testing again, what then?"

"If they did it like the last time—where it was more of a test of which athletes could find a way around it, or go off-cycle in time to test clean—and they didn't do the thing right, so that no one could get past the thing . . . well, I might consider that a violation of my rights. Know what I'm saying?"

"Kind of—not really."

"Okay, if they take my urine, knowing that most of the people being tested have scammed on some way to mask the fact that they are still on drugs, or have found some other esoteric thing that doesn't show up on the test that's being done, and I've legitimately trained natural for the show, I'm going to feel like my privacy has been invaded without being guaranteed that the invasion is for an airtight reason. Unless they can come up with an uncheatable system, the test is a violation of my right to privacy."

"Well, hallelujah, Perry Mason. Makes sense to me. Let's see you get it past the officials though. Seems like the kind of testing you're talking about would cost a bloody fortune. And there's still the fans. Sounds like a bunch of them wanna say that there's no drugs, but still have the drug bodies up onstage."

"Some—not all. See why I'm so damned frustrated and indecisive? I mean, the politically correct thing to do would be to just make my comeback and pretend that this issue doesn't even exist."

"And . . . ?"

"Not possible."

Tommy sighed. "Look, you wanna do this and close out some chapter in your life, then do it and do it right. If you wanna push for drug testing from there, then I guess that's admirable—do what's in your heart, what you think is right."

"You know, that's the problem. My heart, as you call it, is telling me one thing one day and the complete opposite the next. I don't think I've ever been this indecisive about anything."

7

I GET EDUCATED

Late Summer, 1979
Indiana

Two days after boot camp I was at Indiana State in Terre Haute. Six or seven of my high school friends had decided to go there too. All of us lived in the same dorm building. Mac and I roomed together. The university campus was composed of drab, post–World War II buildings that looked as if the planners had bought the 1950s reject blueprints from the dictator of a small Communist country.

My first weeks at ISU were consumed both with going to class and falling back into the trap of partying with all my friends.

When I left boot camp at Parris Island, I weighed about 175 pounds, without a single ounce of fat on my entire body. We did no weight training in boot camp, but did so much running and hard-core calisthenics that I had trimmed down into a physique that I still remember as being the best I ever looked or felt (in a body style so completely different from the best I ever looked as a competitive bodybuilder). All that went the way of the dodo bird within weeks of starting college. I didn't do a lick of exercise, except pulling up a chair to a dorm cafeteria table or tipping a beer bottle.

Mac and I didn't exactly hit it off as roommates. I had just come from boot camp, and in spite of all the partying and general letting myself go, I was in a mode of discipline regarding such things as bed making, dirty-clothes throwing, getting up at five in the morning, and so forth. I had also been changed by my summer experience in other ways that didn't make me the best roomie for someone thinking he was getting the old laid-back me. My attitude was still gung ho; things were rigid and intense. I had a strange haircut consisting of, well, no hair at all, at least not longer than a quarter of an inch—and that may be a trendy style now, but it definitely wasn't then. Mac moved out of the room after a few weeks, claiming that he just couldn't take my hard-ass, weird ways anymore. I started distancing myself from all my friends.

I had completely forgotten about bodybuilding. As I sat at my desk one night, though, drinking the last of a six-pack and coughing up some green stuff from the chain-smoking I'd been doing, I pulled one of my old magazines out of the bottom desk drawer and flipped through it wondering if they had a weight room on campus.

The next day after classes and dinner, I went over to the recreation building and asked the woman sitting in the reception booth where the weight room was (figuring that if I acted as if I knew there in fact was one, my chances of finding it were better). She said that it was in the basement of the building, and that I needed to leave my school ID at her desk if I wanted to go down there. I did.

I went past the gymnastics room, and whom should I see in there but Kurt Thomas, spinning around on the pommel horse. I recognized him from TV. I knew he went to school here and I supposed that he was getting ready for the Olympics, but I had more important things to attend to than watching a stranger spin around in the air—famous world champion or not—so I kept going to the stairs.

I could hear the groaning and clanging from the top of the stairs, and it got louder as I went down; now voices could be heard, laughing, buzzing, growing louder with each step. And then there it was. Inside an indoor running track, a tall chain-link fence encircling, were dozens of people moving about in a huge room full of gym equipment. When I got to the gate, a young man who had a body that resembled those of the guys in the magazines was hanging by his hands, doing chin-ups on the top crosspiece of the fence gate. Another guy in a sweat-drenched, gray T-shirt was standing behind him yelling at him to pull his fat ass up: "Come on, two more," and so on. I stood watching until the guy dropped down from the bar and sat straight down on the concrete floor, taking a white towel and mopping off the sweat that was making his shirtless upper body shimmer under the fluorescent lights. I went inside. A heavy man who looked like a football lineman was on the bench press, doing reps with what looked like over four hundred pounds. Another guy was jogging in place, holding twenty-pound dumbbells, and shadowboxing with the weights in his hands, making it look as if he were only holding on to feathers. There were people everywhere, and equipment that I'd only seen in the magazines, although it did look a bit rusty around the edges, but that was just fine; I knew where I would be spending my evenings. I stayed for about five more minutes, watching a man do squats until he eventually put the bar back and fell to the ground exhausted and panting for air.

"How late is the gym open?" I asked the woman at reception.

"Two more hours, baby," she said, looking at her watch. "Hey, what's your hurry?" she called after me as I ran out the front glass doors.

I ran the whole way back to my room, about three blocks, and was completely winded by the time I unlocked the door. All I could think was that I had gotten out of shape fast, since only a month and a half earlier I'd been running five miles—in combat boots no less—as if it were a stroll around the block. I quickly changed into some gym clothes and ran all the way back to the rec building, again totally out of breath by the time I got to reception.

"Oh, damnit," I muttered. "Sorry, but I forgot my ID."

"No, you didn't, sugar," the woman there said, smiling and holding it up. "You ran out and left it right here—Robert Clark Paris. Mm-mm, that's a fine name you got. You come back again to see me?"

I felt myself blush and go shy. "Well, actually, I came back for a workout."

"Yeah—you look like you work out. Go on ahead; I can see you're a shy one."

"Thanks," I said, and rushed off to the basement gym.

The gym was even more crowded now. I took my time and walked around the entire place, checking out where each piece of equipment was, mentally putting together routines that I'd never been able to do because I'd never had this many toys to play with before. I decided to start with my chest and do some bench presses. I'd never done them with a barbell before, only with the station on the Universal machine. I was shaky at first, but my instinct kicked in and I got the rhythm of the thing down by the third set. A guy came over and asked if he could work in, and we gave each other a hand on the sets, then he asked me what I was doing next. I said I wasn't sure, so he asked me if I wanted to train the rest of my chest with him and I did.

The next day I had a 7 A.M. class and woke up nearly as sore as I'd been the first time I worked out in the high school weight room, but I went to my economics class, smiling the whole way, anxious to get the day over so I could get back to the gym.

I fell right back into the groove of regular training, scouring my old muscle magazines for new routines to try for each body part. I got friendly with guys in the gym after seeing them every night for several weeks, and we would all talk about the day when each of us would compete. A poster went up in the gym, saying a Mr. ISU physique contest would be held in three weeks. I thought, *What the hell, I'll enter.* By this point I had almost no contact with my old friends from high school, other than seeing some of them in the cafeteria. I had my room all to myself; Mac had decided not to move back in. I wasn't partying anymore; I'd stopped smoking cigarettes cold turkey. I went to the pharmacy section of the school bookstore and bought my first bottles of vitamins, which I put on a shelf—kind of a place of honor—looking at them all the time, making a big production when I would take one each day, as if making a conscious event out of swallowing them would improve their magical qualities. One of the guys in the gym who was also going to do the Mr. ISU—even though I was never sure if he was even a student or part of the faculty, or just some guy from around town—asked me, with a completely straight face, if I had ever shaved my body before. I said I hadn't, but knew that I would have to before the show. He said to be sure not to do it too long before the show, in case the skin were to break out with razor rash or ingrown hairs. He said that different people did it in a variety of ways, but he preferred to use a bar of Ivory soap and a razor in the shower: work up a soap lather on each area and sort of push the razor back and forth, making sure to allow for bends in the limbs and other sensitive areas, such as behind the knees, where it was easy to slice yourself open without realizing it. I thanked him for the advice, since I'd never even thought about how to get the hair off my body.

When I first began reading the muscle magazines, I assumed that all the guys weren't hairy. In time, of course, I realized that shaving was simply an accepted part of the sport, since one famous athlete talked in an article about how much he hated doing it before contests, but how it was necessary in order to let all the definition of the muscles show; the ridges and grooves couldn't be hidden, as if behind a curtain.

When I learned this, I wasn't shocked. I had friends on the swim team and they shaved their arms and legs and chests—if they had hair there—for competition, supposedly to help them glide through the water faster. I quickly accepted that when it came time for me to step onstage, I was going to have to find some way to make my body as slick and bald as those of all the guys in the magazines; fair enough.

The Mr. ISU was on a Saturday. On Friday, as many people in the dorms were headed home for the weekend, I got myself ready for the show. Since all the showers in the dorm were communal, I decided that I couldn't stand the embarrassment of shaving my body in such a public place, so instead of using soap and water, I bought six cans of shaving cream and a couple of packs of razors and butchered myself in my room. When Mac came by to ask if I wanted to go to Columbus with him for the weekend, I was in the middle of doing my left leg. Foam and cutoff hairs were everywhere surrounding where I was standing, naked and three-quarters bald-bodied, with my foot up on a chair. He laughed and asked me what I was doing and I told him. I hadn't told any of my friends that I intended to do the contest because I was afraid that they would all tease me. He said that was pretty cool, good luck, and, hey, don't cut myself anymore. I had trickles of blood on my chest, forearms, and elsewhere. I laughed, knowing how ridiculous I must have looked— standing there bloody, covered with bits of hairy lather, naked—and told him to have a good weekend. I finished shaving at around six o'clock, showered off all the funky lather, cleaned up my room, and went to the cafeteria for dinner.

I don't know what I expected to happen the next day. I had never been to a physique contest, and I'd only been training seriously for a few weeks. I believe I thought I would win, that the judges would see how dedicated to bodybuilding I was and give me the title. I wasn't sure what to wear, so I got out a pair of baby blue bikini underwear that I thought looked the most like the posing trunks I'd seen in the magazines.

My magazine hero was Robby Robinson, a man whose ebony skin looked as if it had been polished with a floor waxer and who had a reputation as being totally focused, quiet, introspective. One of the most inspiring physique photos I had seen was of Robby standing with his back to the camera, the photographer having snapped the picture during a break between sets of a workout. Robby's back looked quite literally like a cartoon superhero's, flaring up from a tiny waist to shoulders that appeared two yards wide. He was wearing a torn rag of a shirt that looked as if it were made more of the knots holding it together than the fabric itself.

Articles told how Robby would warn new training partners not to talk to him while they were working out, and he was considered the hardest-working, most consistent athlete in the sport. He was said to be so focused that he would often go for days at a time without speaking; in competition he was supposed to be intense backstage, not mingling with any of the other guys, keeping totally to himself and burning up the competition. He was a Mr. America, Mr. Universe, and had taken second in the Mr. Olympia; it was predicted that it was only a matter of time until he won that ultimate professional title. I decided that my personality during the competition should be like Robby's: quiet and introverted.

The prejudging for the contest was held where some wrestling mats—which were used for stretching and the intramural wrestling team—were rolled out on the concrete floor next to the gym, just outside the chain-link fence.

When I arrived at 9 A.M., I pictured I was Arnold or Robby showing up backstage at the Mr. Olympia. I found a secluded spot near the end of the fence, while all around were clusters of gawkers and other guys in the contest stripping off clothes, pumping up their muscles, flexing, joking, putting on baby oil. The whole place smelled as if a tanker ship of baby oil had smashed upon a nearby wall. As I stripped off my clothes, I immediately felt cold, naked, small, and foolish; but I clung hard to the notion that later that night I would be—naturally—crowned Mr. ISU. The room seemed enormous and I felt as if all my muscles had been stripped off with my jeans and sweatshirt. I had on those blue underpants; I noticed a few others were wearing nearly the same thing. Indiana wasn't a place where you could pop down to the store and buy posing trunks. The one guy whose physique I most admired in the gym, Will, came over and asked how I was doing. I said fine—not wanting to break my isolated concentration too much, but curious, nonetheless, where he had gotten the maroon posing trunks he was wearing. He said that he'd sent away to Frank Zane's mail order company for them. I was amazed by his planning. He asked me to give him a hand with the oil on his back, and when I'd carefully spread a layer, making sure not to miss any spots, he said to turn around and covered my back with a coat of oil as well. He was in perfect shape; not quite to magazine level, but defined, and every muscle looked perfectly trained. I knew that his hero was Frank Zane—that was no big stretch of imagination, since Frank was the current Mr. Olympia and the muscle hero of fans who preferred his sleek-looking physique to more exaggerated ones—and I thought Will had done his hero proud.

A dozen or more guys were in the prejudging. All of us pumped with the weights, trying to gorge the showy muscles of the chest, arms, and shoulders with blood, to make them look larger and more explosive than they were, until we were called by the head judge to line up under the lights rigged over a row of wrestling mats. I hadn't thought about this whole thing enough before I entered this contest to realize that I didn't know how to pose. The only mirror I had was a small one in my dorm room to let you comb your hair, and mirrors no larger than that one over the sinks in the dorm bathroom. I hadn't even seen my whole body in a full-length mirror lately so that I could rationally decide if I was developed enough to do even this show. When the judges asked for the first pose, I just did what I thought would look the most like the poses I'd seen in the magazines. Front double biceps, the judge called for; I held up my arms and flexed them; and so on. I glanced down the lineup and noticed that most of the other competitors didn't seem to know how to pose either; most were guessing as I was, so I didn't think that would count against me. The judging lasted about half an hour, each guy getting called out from the lineup to show all the compulsory poses, then everyone being compared to everyone else. I didn't get compared much. I figured that was a sign that I'd won—being so superior to everyone else that few comparisons were necessary.

During the break between the prejudging and the main show—slated for seven o'clock that night—I went back to my dorm and pulled out the training journal that I'd started keeping the month before. On the inside cover I wrote "Bobby Paris, Mr. ISU." Then I let my mind wander to where all this could potentially lead and, after a few minutes' consideration, wrote beneath the first inscription a list of the titles I thought I would win, bim, bam, boom. I figured that from this point it would take about five years to win the Mr. America, and that I was sure to become a Mr. Universe that same year, so I wrote "1983 Mr. America" and below that "1983 Mr. Universe." At that moment, the mid-eighties seemed like a different century, and I was sure, if I got the breaks I needed and trained real hard, that my prediction would come true.

I set my journal aside and flipped through my magazines, trying to decide what I would do for my posing routine for the night show. I went down to get some dinner, then half an hour before the show, walked over to the small auditorium where it was to be held. The evening passed like a dream: once again stripping off clothing, pumping up the muscles, putting on a smooth coat of oil, listening to the music coming from onstage and the applause and hoots of the audience— probably two hundred people—waiting my turn to go on and do my routine (I still didn't know what I was going to do once I got up there, but was sure some streak of improvisation would overtake me), and finally it was my turn to go on.

When each competitor was finished, the ones who did well were complimented and backslapped by people hanging around in the small room we were using as a backstage. You could tell that there were definite favorites, including Will, in his Frank Zane posing trunks, who everyone said was a marvelous poser after he'd finished onstage. He went six guys ahead of me and came over breathless (those who have never done a bodybuilding contest don't realize how incredibly taxing a well-executed posing routine is. It's like doing a full ballet, aerobics class, and isometric session all at the same time), panting, trying to catch his breath.

"Good job, Willy," I said, "sounds like they loved ya." The cheers and screams had echoed loudly as he came offstage and back into our room. "How'd ya come up with such a great routine?"

"I . . . uh"—sucking for air—"I . . . uh . . . just took Frank Zane's . . . routine . . . from last . . . year's Mr. O . . . This friend of mine . . . video-recorded it . . . and I just did the same . . . routine." And then Will walked away to more compliments and, slowly, as he got his wind back,

broke into wider and greater smiles, walking around, occasionally picking up a barbell and doing a few curls, or flexing in the full-length mirror
that was propped up in the corner of the room.

The announcer called my name; smattered applause. I walked up the
steps to the elevated stage and moved into the glare of the overhead
lights. The light enclosed me and some music snapped to life from the
speakers on both sides of the stage. I began to move from one unsure
pose to another. *Oh, yeah,* I thought after a couple of seconds, *I haven't
shown my back.* A few polite claps—no more. I could see a bit through
the light now; in the second row were two women from my science
class. They spoke to each other behind cupped hands—did I just see
them laugh? I suddenly noticed, for some reason, my baby blue underwear. I did a couple of more awkward attempts at poses I could remember, bowed a little, and walked quickly offstage, and into the backroom
area. No one congratulated me and no wave of cheers followed me off
the stage. I went and sat down in the corner with all my clothes and
wiped the sweat off myself. I looked down at my legs and noticed for
the first time patches of hair, around both kneecaps, that I'd missed while
shaving. I felt like packing my gym bag, putting on my clothes, and
fleeing back to my room, but I stayed there silently watching everything
unfold as each guy went onstage and either came off looking as I imagined I had looked, or just the opposite, gloriously confident.

The show didn't last long. The announcer brought all of the competitors up onstage and asked the audience to give us all a hand,
which they did. Then the announcer asked six guys to stay onstage
and thanked the rest of us for competing, asking us to kindly leave
the stage. I went back, toweled off the wretched baby oil, and got
dressed. They were announcing all the placements. Will won the Best
Poser award. *Good for him,* I thought sincerely. The guy who eventually
won the contest was the man who had been doing the chin-ups on
the gate in the gym the first night I went down there. I stuck around,
sitting in the same place, watching everyone, holding back the urge to
cry.

After all the audience cleared out, I took my gym bag and walked
around in front of the stage. The guy who had organized the contest,
who was said to be a Mr. Idaho (or one of those small Western states)
and was bulging out of a too-tight white dress shirt, was standing there
talking with another man, who was wearing a blue suit. The man that
Mr. Idaho was talking with had a twitch in his eye that made him look
as if he were constantly winking at the whole world. I excused myself
and asked Mr. Idaho if I could please bother him for a moment of his
time. He said sure and asked the winker to hang on a second.

"Do you mind if I ask you what you think I need to do to improve?" I asked, truly wanting to know.

Mr. Idaho looked at me for a second, squinting, racking his brain, trying to figure out where he'd seen me before.

"Um, I was just in the show," I said quickly, getting a little embarrassed that he didn't even remember me from a show that had finished just fifteen minutes earlier.

"Oh . . . um . . . sure. Of course I remember. Listen, you just keep training hard." He gave me a distant pat on the shoulder, as one might give to a slightly retarded stray dog. I stood there for a few seconds because maybe he had more to say. The guy in the blue suit, who winked in every direction he turned his head, winked straight at me, then snapped away to wink at a wall. Thirty seconds passed. "So if you'll excuse me . . . I, uh . . . ," Mr. Idaho said.

"Oh, yeah . . . yeah . . . hey—thanks for the advice." I smiled a "you asshole" grin, turned, and walked out of the lecture hall and back down to the locker room outside the gym area.

Will was standing there, still wearing his Frank Zane posing trunks, talking with one of the other guys from the show, telling him the same story he'd told me earlier, about the friend who'd taped the *Wide World of Sports* Mr. Olympia segment so that Will could copy Frank Zane's routine.

"Hey, Willy, congratulations, man," I said, not sure if these guys were going to blow me off, as Mr. Idaho had.

"Hey, Bobby, thanks. Hey, you did real good too. Sorry you didn't place, man," Will said, as I looked at the Best Poser medal hanging from a red, white, and blue ribbon around his neck.

"Ah, you know . . . ," I said.

"No, really, Bobby, you only been trainin'—what?—a couple months, right? I mean, you did great for that much time in the gym."

"Yeah, I guess."

"Hey, man, you just gotta keep poundin' the weights. You'll get it in no time," the other guy said.

"Um, thanks," I said, still wanting to cry or shrink down into the size of a mouse so that I could crawl away under some floorboard.

"Hey, why don't you meet me here six o'clock Monday. It's chest, shoulders, and triceps. We'll train together," Will said, smiling, seeing that I was feeling pretty dejected.

"You treatin' me like a charity case?"

"No way. I've seen you train. You work hard—it's like, let's train some together—that's all."

"All right, see you guys Monday." And I headed back to my dorm, not smiling, but not wanting to break into sobs anymore either.

When I got back to the dorm, most of the building seemed empty. Everyone was either home for the weekend or out partying. I took a long shower, trying to scrub off the smell of the baby oil, and I kept scrubbing long after the odor was gone. In the mirror over the row of sinks I could see that my chest was beginning to break out from the shaving, and all my skin appeared raw from the hard scrubbing. My eyes looked red and empty in the steamy mirror. I went back to my room and pulled out my training journal again, and where I'd written "Mr. ISU," I scrawled it out with a ballpoint pen—drawing back and forth until the pen went through the cardboard cover of the notebook. I looked at the rest of it, where I'd written "1983 Mr. America" and then "1983 Mr. Universe," thought about scratching those out too, but hesitated.

"It's just a fucking college contest," I said, then wondered if that sounded like sour grapes. It did. I put the notebook back in the drawer without having crossed out the other predictions, got dressed, and went down to my car to go out and get something to eat. Whether or not I was humiliated in the contest, and regardless of whether I really did have a future in bodybuilding, I was determined not to turn to drinking or getting high as I might have in the past. However, I was starving. This competition business was hard work, and it certainly made a boy crank up an appetite.

I met Will in the gym on Monday, and we had a pretty good workout together. I was kind of intimidated because he was obviously a better bodybuilder than I, given his success in the contest over the weekend. After that night we didn't train together all the time, maybe once or twice a week. One night, right after we'd both finished working out, he asked me if I'd ever heard of Dianabol. I told him that I hadn't. He was surprised, asking again if I was sure that I hadn't ever heard of it—maybe I'd heard it called D-bol. I said, no, I hadn't. He said that it would help you get bigger and stronger, and that he knew of a doctor in town who would prescribe it if you asked him in just the right way.

"What do you mean by that?" I asked.

"Well, you know, you gotta tell him that you're real serious about your training, and that you're thinkin' about doin' D-bol anyway and felt like you should probably go through a doctor instead of buyin' it off some guy in the locker room—you know, go at it that way . . . real concerned that you make all the right moves as far as your health's concerned."

"You can get it in the locker room?" I asked, and even though I was totally drug-savvy in all the recreational substances, this was news to me, and I was sounding like a dweeb.

"Heck, I don't know. I just meant that it was something to say—kinda, you know, to grease the wheel."

"So, is this stuff bad for ya?"

"Nah—all the top guys do it. Just what you do if you wanna be good. I never tried it, but I was thinkin' maybe one of us could go to this doctor, and then we could split a bottle of the stuff."

"Well, how's it come? Is it, what, like a cough syrup or somethin'?"

"Little pills."

I had goose bumps, standing there in my sweaty gym clothes, thinking that there was a secret I'd been missing out on. But I was intrigued, and if all the top guys were on to this, then it was definitely something I needed to try too. I said that since I had a car, I'd go to this doctor and see about getting some; we could split whatever I got and then compare results.

That night I started thinking about how I was starting to find out all the secrets of this sport, and as I was finishing up a short story for my English class, I decided to go into the university infirmary and talk to a doctor there and see if I couldn't save a trip out to this other doctor's office.

The next morning, I went into the infirmary, which looked like a small hospital, and asked the nurse if I could see a doctor. She asked why, and I said that it was personal, so she put me in a small office and told me a doctor would be along directly. After fifteen minutes a graying, heavyset man came into the room.

"Hello, I'm Dr. Clemson," he said as he came around the desk and sat down behind it, then leaned his chair back to put a stack of manila folders on a shelf behind him. "The nurse said that you had something of a private nature to discuss with me."

"Yes, sir." My voice cracked and I cleared my throat and looked down at the ground, getting nervous.

"Well? What is it, son?"

"I um . . ." I stalled, feeling some numb shaking begin in my legs.

"Is this something of a sexual nature?"

"Oh—no, sir."

"Because if it is, I can assure you that anything you tell me is in the strictest confidence."

"It's nothing like that. You see, Doctor, I've been working out with weights and I, uh . . ."

"Yes, I can see that, go on."

"Well, this guy in the gym told me about this stuff and I was wondering if maybe you could prescribe me some."

"Excuse me?"

"Um, I think it's called Diabanol."

"You mean Di-ana-bol," he said, correcting me calmly, and he looked away at the clock on his desk. When he turned back around, the look on his face was angry. "Do you even know what you're asking for, young man?" I shrugged my shoulders. I didn't know what to say. "How dare you come in here asking for steroids!" His voice got louder. "Do you understand the incredible danger involved in what you are asking me for? No, I should think not. Otherwise you wouldn't be here wasting my time. Now get out of my office, and if you ever come around with such a stupid request again, I will personally see to it that you are kicked out of this university. Get out—now."

I sat there for a couple of seconds, sinking, wondering what I had done wrong. He snapped his arm toward the door, pointing a fat finger at it, then burned a stare right through me until I got up and quietly went out the door, closing it gently behind me. The nurse who had taken me into the office was standing behind the reception desk and frowned a question—like, are you finished already?—straight at me, and I walked quickly past and out of the building.

When I got back to my room, I picked up the piece of notebook paper I'd written the other doctor's name on, took it down the hall to the pay phone, called the office, and made an appointment for the next afternoon. After I spoke with the receptionist, who had a squeaky little voice and a French accent, I went back to my room, got my books and the short story I'd written, and headed off to English class, still wondering what exactly I'd done that had upset that school doctor so much.

That night in the gym I reported my progress—or lack thereof—to Will and told him that I was going to see the other doctor the next day. He told me I was stupid for going to the school doctor—and besides, he had already tried it a month before and gotten the same reaction.

"Thanks for warning me," I said.

He just smiled one of those smiles that guys like him always use to get past anything, and it worked.

*   *   *

The doctor's office was in an old house. A classic Craftsman bungalow allowed to get run-down into little more than a shack. The office was on the ground floor, and I wondered, as I sat on one of the mismatched chairs in the lightless, dusty waiting room, if the doctor lived upstairs. I also wondered if the original woodwork was under the cheap paneling that covered the walls. The squeaky French nurse finally said that the doctor would see me now, and I went into his office, which had probably been the dining room. It looked like a laboratory for a mad scientist; he looked like one too: Albert Einstein hair, wild white mustache, food-stained off-white smock. He smelled like a Tiparillo, or some other cheap cigar, and walked with a right-legged limp.

"How may I help you, young man?" he asked.

"Well, sir, I'll come right to the point."

"I wish you would."

"I have been training with weights now—with a great deal of seri-ousness—for some time." I felt my attempt at mock boldness was sound-ing like a bad late-late-show movie actor. "And I have heard about some pills called Dianabol." I looked up at him. He nodded for me to continue. "To be frank, sir, I have considered simply buying some of these pills from a man in the weight room. On careful consideration, however, I have decided that it is probably safer if I seek medical assistance on this matter."

"You want a prescription for Dianabol, is that it?"

"In short . . . yes, sir, it is."

"Why didn't you just say so. Hop up here on the scale, let's get some vital statistics." He headed toward an ancient-looking scale.

He took my height and weight, blood pressure, tapped around on my back making it sound like a ripe melon, then went to his desk, pulled out a pad, and wrote out a prescription for one hundred Dianabol.

"You can have that filled at most any pharmacy," he said as he handed me the slip of paper. "Take three a day, and come back to see me in one month. If you begin to feel the least bit odd, stop taking them and come back and see me. You can pay the nurse on your way out. Oh, and one more thing, young man. In spite of what you may have heard, I don't give these pills to everyone who comes in here. You seem like a sincere young fellow. Just be careful."

I went to the nearest pharmacy and had the prescription filled. The pharmacist looked at me funny and shook his head, almost impercep-tibly, after he took the paper. Ten minutes later, he handed me the little sack.

"Do you know what you're doing?"

"Yeah," I said as I took the bag from him. I turned around quickly and headed to the checkout stand, feeling as if I'd just scored a bag of dope and had barely escaped getting caught by the cops.

When I got back to my room, I poured the little robin's-egg-blue pills out on my bed. They contrasted sharply against the bright yellow spread. I scooped them up, let them cascade through my fingers, then put them back in the bottle. I thought for a second, then emptied out a small vitamin bottle, poured the pills back out, counted fifty of them and put those into the brown, plastic vitamin C bottle, and put the rest back into their pharmacy container. I sat there looking at both bottles, looking especially at my name printed on the pill bottle from the pharmacy. I opened that one and pulled out one pill. I got a water glass, ran down the hall to fill it from the drinking fountain, and came back to the room and bolted the door.

I wonder how they work. Will I get high? Am I going to feel it right away? I thought. I put it on my tongue and held it there—no real taste, maybe a little sweet—and swallowed it, chasing it with a full glass of cold water. And then I sat there. Nothing. Sat a bit longer. Still nothing.

Must take a while, I thought.

That night I gave Will his fifty pills, and he gave me my money. He only thanked me halfheartedly, and I couldn't help but feel as if I'd been used, but that was okay because he'd let me in on this secret.

I took my three little pills a day, making a ritual out of each one as I had done with the first vitamins I'd bought, only with more wishful intensity. I didn't notice anything much for a few days, although it did seem that my workouts became more intense right off the bat, but I figured that was just enthusiasm making me push harder. After ten days I began to notice that all the weights, on all the exercises, began to creep up, and my muscles felt extra springy and as if they'd been shot full of some kind of firm jelly. My body began to look rounder, in the way the guys in the magazines seemed to have a sweeping roundness to each body part. I felt more like an animal in the gym, able to lift more, more often, and to push myself harder than ever before. I saw nothing negative at all about these changes, and they continued to keep coming until my fifty pills ran out. Will told me that he was experiencing the same thing, and as he trained sometimes with his shirt off, I could see he seemed to have sprouted extra fibers and grooves all over his physique.

And then the end of the semester was suddenly upon us. I never went back to that doctor to get more of that prescription, and Will never mentioned it to me again either (I don't know whether he went on his own or found another guy to go for him or also decided not to get more). I felt as if the whole fifty-pill experiment had been some vacation into a strange land that I could always go back to later, and my instinct was telling me that I needed to train awhile longer without Dianabol to learn how my body worked naturally. It was a fairly mature decision for me and in the end a good one, because I did learn things about how my body worked that I probably never would have if I'd kept on taking drugs and only experiencing their artificial jet-pack qualities.

A week before the semester ended I decided not to return to ISU. It was a snooze, I told myself. What was actually happening was that I wanted to begin to break away from my old high school friends and start to create my life without a bunch of guys around to remind me of my history—good, bad, or otherwise. In between the semesters I decided to enroll at Indiana University, which was only thirty-some-odd miles from home. The campus was beautiful—with its tree-lined paths and old limestone buildings set among the rolling hills—but incredibly intimidating. When I went over to register for classes, I got lost so many times that eventually I had to get a map of the campus. It was winter, the trees withdrawn and skeletal sidewalks icy, and I walked around feeling for the first time as if I were away at college.

Before classes began I looked in the yellow pages to see if there was a real gym in Bloomington; there had to be I figured, since it was such a sports town. I found one. It was the only one in town, and it was new, out away from campus in a racquetball club—one of those huge buildings where the interior smelled like cedar siding and chlorinated spa chemicals. The trim around the rough-hewn walls was painted with yellow, brown, and orange accents, and there were row after row of glassed-in courts, with sweaty businessmen coming to and from thrilling games. The place was virtually identical to ones that sprang up all over the country in the late seventies, when racquetball was the new major recreation trend and people were joining these clubs in buzzing hordes. In the back corner of this building was a small gym, with brand-new equipment, all shiny and expectant, wanting badly for someone serious to put it through its paces. I immediately joined and had a tremendous leg workout that bone-crackingly January day.

Until classes started, I drove from Dad's house over to Bloomington each day to train and soon became friendly with the owner of the gym and the guys who worked there. One guy had won the Mr. IU contest that year, and in a fit of stupidity I claimed that I had won the Mr. ISU. I don't know what I could have been thinking; I guess I felt that nobody would ever be the wiser, but I left the gym that day feeling like an ass. Soon word spread to the people in the gym that the new Mr. ISU was training there, and they greeted me like a champion. After a couple of weeks I decided that it would be great to work at this gym too, so I asked if I could get a part-time job once school got going and I'd settled into classes, and I got hired.

I moved into a dorm and almost immediately knew that I'd made a mistake in changing schools. The restlessness I had been feeling at the end of the last semester wasn't over that school, but over school itself. I attended classes for the first three weeks, then gradually began to stop going. At the same time I was getting my hours increased at my new job because I was so good with teaching new members their exercises, and everybody there seemed to like me. Before I knew it I was working fifty hours a week, still living in the dorm. I was rooming with a musician—in one of the great roommate mismatches of the year—who insisted on practicing his trumpet late at night and lamenting for his roommate from the semester before, who had also been a musician, and I suspected was responsible for what appeared to be dried boogers, wiped within arm's reach, all over the wall next to my bed. One day I came back to my room from work; roomie was there with one of his friends, and they were looking at things on my desk, which included a calendar illustrated with photographs of Arnold Schwarzenegger.

"Maybe he's gay," the friend said, referring to me, having not yet heard me come through the open door.

"I don't know—probably—he's just weird, that's all I know," roommate responded.

"Excuse me," I said, pushing in between them toward my desk. They both went pale. I simply sat down in my chair and said nothing, figuring that would intimidate them far more than if I made a stink. They slinked quietly out of the room. I pulled out my suitcases and boxes, packed them with everything that belonged to me, put them in my car, and drove through the darkness to Dad's house, where I spent the night in my old bedroom, sleeping deeper than I had in a month.

What do you mean, you left? You just snuck out in the night?" Dad asked me the next morning when he came in from spending the night at his new girlfriend's house.

"I couldn't handle it. I gotta job, I wanna work there—maybe I'll go back to school next semester."

"Not on my dime, you won't."

"I guess I can look for an apartment in Bloomington."

"As long as you have a job, you can stay here. I'm never here anyway."

"Oh, so things are getting serious between you and Ellen?"

"She's a fine lady," he said, and chuckled, not snidely, but happily.

He must be in love, I thought. I said, "I'm happy for you guys. You know, Dad, I won't stay long—just long enough to get on my feet."

At the Get Fit Gym in Bloomington, the owner would tease me because I held such a romantic notion of what life would be like out in California as a pro bodybuilder. He loved to tell me that he had heard that Joe Weider was totally corrupt and lived only to suck the life out of the bodybuilders, whom, this guy claimed, Joe would use to advertise Weider products, then toss aside like so much trash once their usefulness was finished. I told him that he didn't know what he was talking about. All one had to do was read a magazine to see that all the pros loved Joe and came to him in droves to get training advice. They said so in all their articles. I would soon be one of them too, I'd tell him, and he'd just smile and look at me as if I were someone who still believed that the world is flat. He told me that the real athletes stayed where they were and won state championships, never worrying about going to the scene out West, where all the kooks lived. A true bodybuilder didn't care about winning the Mr. Olympia and trained for the love of the iron, period. Now this was a man who, as best as I could tell, had never touched a weight in his life and only opened the gym to supplement his salary at the fire department.

What the hell does he know? I used to think every time we got into one of these conversations about bodybuilding and his supposed inside track on politics in a sport that he knew next to nothing about.

I talked him into carrying Weider supplements to sell at the gym, mainly because I was convinced that they were the best made (the magazine ads said so, after all) and they were the ones I wanted to take.

When I first bought my magazines from Cummin's Book Store in Columbus, I saw that all the top guys were in the ads for the Weider protein powders and liver tablets and vitamins and every other potion they had going in those days. A guide in the magazines told you where you could get these products near where you lived, and I was surprised to see a health food store in Columbus listed among those places. I didn't even know that we had a health food store in town. I decided that I would make superior progress if I could get my hands on some of the superduper, new, and improved weight-gain powder shown in the full-page ad that had Arnold Schwarzenegger—looking tanned beyond Caucasian capacity—standing, with his shirt off, behind stacked cans of the stuff. And if it was good enough for Arnold . . .

I ventured down to this health food shop one day, after calling first to make sure that they did indeed carry Weider products and then putting together enough money to buy a case of the magical powder. They had one case of the weight-gain powder, all in small cans. The elderly man working in the store, who looked like an aging hippie, with long, tangled, gray hair and layers of colored beads around his neck, tried to tell me that he had another product that was better. He said that he only carried the Weider stuff because he got constant requests for it, probably, he speculated, because it was heavily advertised in the Weider magazine. The products were known in health food circles as crap, he added, and the one I wanted to buy had been analyzed by a laboratory back East and found to be mostly sugar and fillers—you gained weight because the stuff was like powdered Hershey bars in a can. He figured that I'd be better off drinking milk shakes from the Dairy Queen—at least they didn't taste like dead skunk, as this garbage did. He shook his head, the hair swinging back and forth (I expected a bat, or at least some moths, to come flying out of the thick tangles), and said that it was a mystery to him why something so filled with sugar would also taste so lousy, adding that it was probably a crass marketing ploy—making it taste bad—to throw the drinker off the trail of its being of inferior quality.

I thanked him for his advice and said that I'd take the case anyway. He rang it up, took my money, asked me if I wanted any other vitamins to go along with it—he could recommend some good ones—and I told him no thanks, this was all for now (I couldn't afford anything more, and besides, this guy's advice was at best suspicious and at worst slanderous of Joe Weider and the great champions who depended on Joe's products).

As the weeks went by at the Get Fit Gym, I believed that I was on the fast track to becoming not only a star employee, but maybe even a manager. The owner wanted to organize a local competition, and I asked him if I could be responsible for most of the details; he told me to, yeah, go for it. I met with hotel managers and got prices for blocks of rooms for out-of-town fans. I met with the managers of a couple of auditoriums where the contest could be held. I tried to find a guest star to come and do a guest posing during the show. I knew that I wouldn't have the budget for a major star, so I got the phone numbers for a few top amateurs whose names I knew from the magazines. I wanted to have Richard Baldwin, who lived in Florida and had done well in several national competitions. He had a Frank Zane type of symmetrical physique that I knew would appeal to a broad audience. I contacted Richard at the gym he owned, got his price for the appearance (which I thought was reasonably inexpensive), and I put together a list of all the expenses (I had negotiated substantial discounts for both the hotel and the auditorium I thought best suited for the show) and presented them to my boss. I had worked for two weeks—unpaid—putting all this together, and he took one look at my proposal and said that he was real sorry but he'd decided not to do the show. Just like that. It was never mentioned again.

Two weeks later he said that he was thinking about opening another gym somewhere and asked me if I knew of any towns around where one might be successful. I told him that I felt that Terre Haute could use a gym—there was both a university there and a reasonable-size town— and if it was done right, it could be a hit. He asked me if I would look into it for him. So I did. I drove over to Terre Haute a couple of times a week, scouring the downtown area for a suitable site. I found three that would work. I advised him on what equipment to order; he decided to go cheaper and bought some out of an ad in *Ironman* magazine that I tried to tell him would never hold up to commercial use. I went around to all the local high schools and met first with their athletic directors and coaches and then with all the teams, trying to drum up interest in this new gym, knowing that having the top athletes in the area train there would quickly build a good word-of-mouth reputation for the place. The equipment wasn't great—the gym in Bloomington had much better stuff—but Will, the guy from the college gym who had won Best Poser in the Mr. ISU contest and had been in on my Dianabol adventure, and I trained together at the new gym a couple of times before it opened, and I knew that it would be a good basic hard-iron gym.

Finally, right before the gym opened, after I'd worked my ass off getting it ready, I was informed that an older man who managed the Bloomington gym would not only have this new place named after him—it would be called Red's Gym, since his nickname was Red—but he'd also manage this place as well, traveling back and forth between the two towns. They hired a couple of the guys who'd been in the Mr. ISU contest to work there part-time.

I should have seen the writing on the wall, but didn't because I was loving what I was doing so much. I came into the Bloomington gym one Sunday night after hours to work out and, when I tried the door, found it locked. My boss was inside, and he opened the door, keeping it held partially closed as he looked at me standing there holding my gym bag. Some other guy who looked as if he were being interviewed for a job was standing at the counter.

"I'd rather you didn't come in tonight, Bobby," my boss said.

"Oh, sorry, Jim, I just wanted to get a quick workout. I won't get in you guys' way. Who is that anyway?" I asked, nodding toward the other young man inside.

"Never you mind. I really don't want you in here tonight. Can you come in first thing tomorrow morning, though, say, nine? I have something I want to talk to you about."

"Um, sure, Jim. You can tell me now if you want," I said nervously, not knowing—or not wanting to know—if this was good or bad.

"It'll keep."

"Okay, Jim. See you tomorrow. Night."

"Yeah, sure."

As I drove through the growing twilight back to Dad's lake house, I couldn't help wondering what the hell was up with my boss and had the sinking feeling that whatever it was it couldn't be good. Although I did hold out hope that Jim was just acting mysterious because he wanted to surprise me with a raise or a promotion the next morning.

I kept thinking about all the great workouts I'd had at the Bloomington gym, coming in sometimes late at night so that I could allow my imagination to soar as I pushed against the weights. One of my favorite games was to pretend that Arnold Schwarzenegger and Joe Weider were standing right there rooting me on through a particularly difficult set.

I had learned from the guy who won the Mr. IU contest about wrapping my knees while I did heavy squats. The wraps gave the knee joint extra support, and the first time I'd tried using them my weights shot up by at least 50 percent.

So as I'd be in the empty gym late at night, I would imagine that Arnold and Joe were there giving me tips as I wrapped each knee, preparing for a set that I would take till I couldn't take any more. I'd hear them scream at me to do one more rep, then another, and another— and I always did them, as if they were truly standing right there (or I were truly in California at Gold's Gym), fully expecting me not to fail them. I never did fail to do what these imaginary training partners asked me to do.

* * *

The next morning I arrived at the gym at just before nine. The door was closed and locked. I could hear Jim—and it sounded like Red too—through the door; their voices were muffled. I knocked and Red opened the door, but wouldn't look me in the eyes. Jim was behind the counter shuffling a small stack of papers.

"Morning, guys," I said, being taken over the falls by a woozy feeling.

"I'll come straight to the point, Bobby," Jim said as Red nervously looked at his fingernails. "I'm gonna have to let you go."

"Wha . . . ," was all I could get out.

"You have those time cards, Red?" Jim asked as Red seemed to flush literally bright crimson.

"Yeah, they're right here, Jim. Bobby, you know I like you a whole lot and—"

"Anyway," Jim cut Red off, "it looks to me like you've been paddin' your time cards for the past couple of weeks. You got hours down here that definitely weren't authorized by me."

I tried to break in. "But, Jim, what about all my—"

He cut me off too. "Hear me out now and let's get this done. There's more. We did an inventory of all the Weider supplements last night, and there are several cans of protein powder missing. You're the only one who could've taken them. You're the one who wanted the crap to begin with."

"I didn't steal any protein, Jim. And all those hours on my time cards are legit," I said, feeling as if I were going to pass out. These guys began to look as if they were mirages twenty feet away. "All those hours are for me going over to Terre Haute to open that gym for you. If anything, I didn't put enough hours down."

"Now who told you that you were getting paid to go over to Terre Haute?"

"You did."

"Not all those hours I didn't. And you're lyin' to me about those cans of protein too. I'm not going to press any charges if you'll just leave."

"I'm not lying to you, Jim. I paid for all the protein I took, honest."

"You haven't been honest since the first day you came in here. Now please leave before I change my mind about pressin' charges."

He went back to his papers, and Red still wouldn't look at me, so I turned around and went out the door. Red followed me out.

"You shouldn't have told us that you won the Mr. ISU, Bobby," Red said as he walked beside me out the back door of the building. "You must have known that we'd find out sooner or later, especially after we opened a gym over there."

"I know, Red. It was stupid to do that. I'm sorry. Is that what this is all about? I worked real hard here. I never deserved to be fired. I didn't steal nothin'—those hours were legit."

"I really don't know what it's about, but Jim gets something in his head and that's all it takes. I'd better get back inside. See ya around, kid."

"No, you won't." I turned around, got in my car, and left.

The drive back toward Dad's house flew by in a blind dream, and I was at Brown County State Park before I even realized I'd left Bloomington. I pulled into the park entrance. Right inside the entrance, off Highway 46, there's an old wooden covered bridge that one of my great-great-grandpas—I couldn't remember which one at that moment, even as I tried my damnedest to recall family history—had helped build when he was a young man; it crossed the black water of Salt Creek. I came from a long line of builders and growers and fixers and hardworking people who didn't get fired from jobs. I'd had jobs ever since I was eleven years old—I'd been a paperboy for the *Louisville Courier Journal*, mowed lawns, caddied golf—because Mom and Dad required it; I tried to work hard and get ahead.

I drove across the bridge and into the forested park and headed up to one of my favorite spots—a clearing way up a hill, where I could see half the county spread out like a lumpy old rug.

If I don't get out of this fucking state, I'm gonna die, I thought after I'd sat there for an hour. Finally I got back on the road to Columbus thinking about what I would do now that I wasn't in school anymore and didn't have a job.

I went to Dad's office and he sat behind his desk, leaning at an angle in a high-back leather chair, smoking a cigarette, the fingers of his right hand gently stroking the keys of his adding machine—which he could work at lightning speed—as I told him what had happened. He listened intently, never interrupting, until I'd finished.

"You're telling me the truth?"

I nodded yes.

"Welcome to the school of hard knocks, Son. You try and try and hit that brick wall no matter what you do. So what are you going to do now?" He blew out a cloud of smoke that looked blue-yellow in the office light.

"Be damned if I know. If I had the money, I'd go to California, and I'd leave right now. I mean, that's what all this seems to be tellin' me to do."

"But you don't have the money, right?"

"No shit, Sherlock. What was your first clue?"

"My first clue, smart-ass, was that you're still here and not on a west-bound interstate. Adjust your tone, Son. I didn't do this to you."

"Sorry. Just pisses me off's all. I'm not goin' to work in some factory, Dad. I wanna bodybuild. Ah, hell, I gotta get outta here—that's all I know," I said, pacing back and forth in front of his huge, cluttered desk.

"Why don't you sleep on it. Things might be clearer in the morning," he said, but then seemed to catch himself, thought a few seconds, and added, "Sorry, that probably came out sounding condescending. Looks to me like you've reached one of those points in life where you're going to have to make some tough decisions. You already had your chance at college on my dime, but you could stick around and work—get back in school next fall."

"School bored the crap out of me. I wanna get out and see the world. Right now I know if I don't try my hand at bodybuilding, I'll get too caught up in some dog-dull life and never do this thing."

"Robert, I'm not going to lie to you. These wild schemes you have about becoming a muscleman are . . . well . . . I won't say stupid, because it's your thing, but . . . well . . ." He stopped, sighed, and squinted out the window, rubbing his wrinkled forehead between his fingers and thumb.

I tried to ignore this. No matter what I did or what he thought about it, I was on my own; that much was crystal clear.

"Well, I thought about it all the way into town," I told him as he looked back from the window to me and lit another cigarette from the one he'd just finished, "and I think I might go down to Florida. I've got enough money socked away to at least make it that far. It ain't California, but there's probably good gyms down there, and at least it's warm. I'll call Mam-ma and Pap-pa Clark and see if I can't stay with them a few days, once I get down there, just till I get set up with my own place."

My mom's parents had moved to central Florida full-time a few years earlier, after going down part-time during the winter for as long as I could remember. Florida was their idea of paradise. I was sure that they wouldn't mind if I came down.

Later that night, after I'd spoken with Mam-ma on the phone, and she'd said that they'd love to have me for a few days, I packed all the stuff that I needed, said good-bye to Dad, gassed up right before the on-ramp to I-65, and headed into the night, south toward Louisville and beyond.

8

SOUTHERN EXCURSION

I cannot say what brings others to bodybuilding. I can only tell what drew me. Like a priest pulled to the altar, the spirit of hope directed me to it. Bodybuilding became my religion because it was at hand. It was immediate and sure and risky and guided by my own efforts intertwined with a quirky poker hand of ancestral gifts. There was no cheating it; all results were in exact proportion to the invested effort. Its influence ran deep—like an underground river that spreads out from vast torrents into minuscule tributaries—and its waters became my life.

In so many parts of my life I was split in two. I was both a good and bad boy. Cripplingly shy and a ham. Driven for success and lazy. A wide-hearted dreamer and crushingly pessimistic. An artist and an athlete.

The depth of my belief in the power of bodybuilding grew out of my desires as an artist. I pretended that I wanted grand success as an athlete in some traditional sport, but only because that was what I believed was the right thing to feel. Great athletes were the good guys and were rewarded with adulation and wealth. Artists generally struggled. When I discovered bodybuilding, I knew—with the sort of instinct that reveals itself in rare moments—that I could have both. I could be the artist I'd always dreamed of being and I could be a jock and exert my physical presence in a way that would demonstrate to all the world that I was truly a man. I could have taken no other sport as far as I did this one. It is misunderstood, underappreciated, corrupted by petty greed, and considered to be the realm of freaks, but it is also beautiful and can be graceful and thrilling and lifted high above the dull thud of conformity.

In bodybuilding propaganda, the idea of the physique as a living, breathing sculpture is a cliché that many of those in the sport feel obligated to repeat as a means of defending the sport from unrelenting criticism. Most of the people saying it don't really believe it, otherwise bodybuilding would be much different from what it now is. But I do believe it. It was my strongest guiding principle during all the years I did this thing. I believed that through athletic effort, I could build a work of art; I would carry that work around with me—I couldn't leave it in the studio, as a traditional artist might. And that was never the most comfortable thing in the world for me because, even though I was proud of the work, it got old having to constantly explain it. But attempting to perfect this work-in-progress was what kept me going into the gym each day, and it's a big part of why I consider getting serious about training again.

Years ago, as I got more successful, I couldn't help but feel that I was walking around town in a gorilla suit, like a little boy living inside this exaggerated costume that in many respects strongly resembled something human, but was definitely away from the normal human form—a walking freak.

A lot of the guys I know in the sport want to be freaky; that is their driving principle—to be the biggest physical freak possible, crushing the competition through sheer brute size. It doesn't matter to them if the whole physical package looks exaggerated beyond recognition; in fact that's part of the point. The guy who works toward being a freak doesn't care that such an extreme distortion of the human form repels far more people than it attracts. They work toward brutal size, with no regard for whether it's in proportion to height, bone structure, or any other physical trait. They torture themselves, with high levels of esoteric drugs and obsessively strict diets, toward muscular definition that makes the body appear to have had the skin peeled away with a scalpel. Gigantic veins crisscross every exposed, exaggerated inch of meat; these bodies don't look as if they could walk around the block, much less run an athletic mile. Onstage, they clank through gruesome contortions that are supposed to pass for professional-level posing. They have followed the path of their own creation (or at least their willing participation), purposely turning themselves into monsters whose muscles serve one introverted purpose: battling to the top of a hierarchy based on who can out-grotesque the other competitors. And especially during the last ten years, bodybuilding has continued to push even further toward freakiness as a guiding principle. It's a cycle that has become less of a trend and more of an established standard. With each passing year more of the judges, fans, and athletes (especially the ones who like the current fashion) seem blinded to the fact that they are preventing the sport from achieving more respect and in turn attracting more money and prestige.

My goal, on the other hand, was to build—finessing the weights as a sculptor might use hammers and chisels—the most perfect human sculpture that I could, using my body. And, like many conscientious artists, I have rarely been completely satisfied. I could always have done something to make the sculpture better. That is what kept me going. And that is why I even contemplate doing it again, to attempt to get closer to my ideal—this picture I carry in my mind of what that would mean—to feel just one time as if I have gotten as close to perfection at this one thing as humanly possible.

Was I simply a little boy walking around in a gorilla suit? Maybe. But as long as I didn't let the little boy believe too strongly that the suit was really him, he was okay.

Each day I go down into the gym and feel the old passion return, bit by bit. Today I trained my back. I had a severe pain in the left side of my neck that shot down into my shoulder. I'm probably doing too much, too soon, but I can't help it. It's as if I have returned to childhood and am intensely playing with all my old toys, trying to touch them and run around the room with them as much as I can before the dream, or whatever magic brought me back here, breaks and I'm back to my regular life again.

I stuck the Eagles' *Hell Freezes Over* in the CD player and moved the selector to the sixth track, where the older songs begin. I cranked up the volume, and even though I'm feeling tired and sore and my neck hurts, I start in on the first exercise.

Today I started with bent-over barbell rows because I know there is no better exercise for making my back as thickly muscled as Arnold's was in those *Rolling Stone* pictures I saw of him when I was a teenager. I have to be careful since my lower back isn't as strong as it used to be and is given to fits of going out of whack, irritating a sixteen-year-old injury if I do this exercise the wrong way. So I warm up slowly, using a light weight, making sure that I keep all the stress on my legs, and begin to pull the bar up toward my rib cage. The muscles of my back spring to attention; I can picture them, hundreds, no, thousands of fibers lighting up, cranking their electric charges into life, pulling against the dread enemy, gravity. At the end of the set I stretch my back muscles and especially my lower back (none of this work will do any good if I get hurt), stand up, and flex the muscles that run down the side of my body I can't see, from the top of my butt all the way up to my ears. I flex them just to feel the tension as they leap further into life, like a dog jumping at the door when you hold up its leash.

I put more weight on the bar and begin to do rep after rep, until I can't do any more. My breath comes hard now, chugging uphill against the dizziness. I stretch some more, rest a few seconds, add more weight, and launch into another set, pushing even harder this time. I imagine I am rowing a racing scull down a sunlit river; each time I pull the bar up it puts me one stroke closer to the finish line. The last three reps are hard. I really have to focus in to keep from swinging my upper body up and down, putting my lower back in danger.

The workout keeps going from there. I move from one exercise to the next with the smooth efficiency of someone who can find his way in the dark. I stretch and pull and flex and pant—and smile at the beauty of it all—and before I know it, it's finished, and my back feels as if it has been pumped full of helium; the pain in my neck and shoulder is now gone. And the CD is finished as well, so I turn off the stereo and head into the shower.

When I strip off my training clothes, I check out my body in the bathroom mirror. It has changed so much in the last couple of months; the slight fatty bulge is almost gone from my waist, and my shoulders are looking round again, my chest taking on some sense of trained shape.

"I could really make this work," I say quietly, and hold up a handheld mirror to look at my back, which is beginning to V once more, a few details of the individual muscles standing out underneath the sweat. "Maybe this isn't so crazy after all."

In my mind I was convinced that I could still train seriously, that I still had the stuff mentally and physically, but in my heart I knew that I'd have to get into the gym for a while to see if it was going to ignite and take hold. Now I knew that it would not only catch fire, but that it was entirely possible that flame could burn hotter than ever.

Summer, 1979
Florida

_____

I passed through Louisville an hour after I left, crossing the Ohio River on the John F. Kennedy Bridge, a bridge that had always marked the beginning of the adventure whenever, as a family, we'd drive down to Florida on vacation. I'd gone to Florida twice on my own—or rather with some of my friends—on spring break during my junior and senior years of high school. We had partied all the way down, and both times—going down in my car—had come back with only fumes in the gas tank because we'd all run out of money.

I was by myself and it was already dark as I crossed the bridge that had seemed to go on forever, across the black muddiness of the river, when I was a boy, but now flew by in a few seconds. I drove through the night, only stopping for gas and coffee; I'd pop a No Doz every couple of hours, and the sun came up through the window on my side of the Monte Carlo, turning the red clay cliffs orange as I was flying down a secluded stretch of interstate in southern Georgia.

By the time I got on the two-lane highways that led to the town where Mam-ma and Pap-pa lived, the landscape had turned flat and dismal. Bony cattle stood on the other side of falling-down wire fences, and the towns I'd pass through were heavily sprinkled with tar-paper and corrugated-metal shacks and rusty cars up on cement blocks. The Florida of spring breaks felt like a distant planet, and I began to ask myself what the hell I was doing down here, and why I hadn't just taken the chance that my couple of hundred dollars would hold out and headed off to southern California, where I'd wanted to go in the first place. This was beginning to feel like an extremely cheap substitute, a detour away from my dream.

I finally headed into an area where the towns began to look more substantial, and I started to let myself grow optimistic as I crossed into Lakeland—the sign at the edge of town said that it was "an all-American city." This was the town where my grandparents lived.

They were both sincerely happy to see me, although neither one could understand why I wasn't in college.

"Bobby, now you know that chances are if you don't get yourself back in school again, you'll never go back," Mam-ma said, pulling the baking pan full of chicken breasts out of the oven as I sat at the kitchen table drinking ice tea.

"I know. Maybe I'll go back soon. I've always worked to educate myself, Mam-ma. I've promised myself that even though I'm not in school, I'm gonna read at least a book a week. I figure I'll learn a lot more that way than if I was sittin' bored stiff in a bunch of classes. School was—well, all I know is that I need to try my hand at bodybuilding for a while ."

"Well, how are you plannin' to make a livin'?" Pap-pa asked, looking straight at me.

"Well, sir, that's a good question. Come Monday I'm going to start lookin' for a job. And I need to get a place to live if I decide to stay down here."

"Don't you worry about that right now. Is this how you like your chicken done, Bobby?" Mam-ma asked. "It's a whole lot better fried, but every since Don had his heart attack, the doctors have said to start broiling his chicken with the skin off—so I've done it that'a way, but I don't like it one bit."

"That's perfect—exactly how I eat it. Can you pass the corn, Pap-pa." He didn't look up.

"You're going to have to speak up, Bobby. He still won't wear his hearing aid."

"Please pass the corn, Pap-pa," I said, surprising myself with how loud my voice came out.

"I ain't deef," he said, passing the bowl of corn on the cob. Mam-ma and I exchanged slight smiles.

"I saw that," he added.

"Maybe I should buy you an ear trumpet for Christmas, Pap—get one in solid brass."

He smiled back at me with his crooked grin. "Anybody ever make any money at this muscle-buildin' thing?"

"Remember that summer, couple a years ago, when I came over and you took me and my friend John out to Nebo and dropped us off—out to the fire tower?" I asked, speaking up but being careful not to yell again.

"Yeah, it was out by the old Fleetwood place. Old man Fleetwood kept a still out in those woods."

"Now how would you know about a still?" I asked him.

"I wasn't blind—everybody knew about it."

"Oh, Don," Mam-ma put in as she got up to start the coffeepot.

"Anyway, when I came over that summer I brought a magazine with me. Remember? It was the music magazine *Rolling Stone.*"

"Gathers no moss," Pap-pa said, smiling.

"What?" I asked.

"Rolling stone gathers no moss."

"Uh . . . right. So, I don't know if you remember or not, but that magazine had an article about bodybuilding. That was why I carried it around. I told you all that I was going to look like that in six months."

"I remember," Mam-ma said as she sat back down.

"Well, there was the main guy in that article—guy who came over here from Austria. Arnold Schwarzenegger's his name. He and this pal of his, Franco Columbu—according to this article—they both make good money. It said that Arnold was makin' a hundred thousand a year. Franco was makin' fifty." I looked at them both and could tell that they thought I was full of beans.

"How much was it, Connie, I was makin' when we first got married?"

"Eleven dollars a week, and doggone happy to get it too."

"That's about where I am right now," I said, laughing.

*   *   *

I stayed with them for a couple of weeks. At first I felt miserable because I would wake up at eight-thirty or so in the morning and they had been up for hours, going about their business, even though they were retired. Feeling as if I were sleeping the day away compared to them and not having a job yet made me feel guilty and young—not young in a good way, but in a spoiled way. I couldn't seem to make a move where I wasn't feeling guilty. I'd lie on a towel in the backyard to get a suntan, and Pap-pa would begin to mow his grass, and he said no thanks, didn't need my help, when I'd offer it. I decided to shave down one day because I'd let all my body hair grow out again. (Like many novice bodybuilders, I was always trying to stay shaved, as if that would speed along my progress.) Pap-pa let me borrow his electric razor, and I stood in my bathing suit on newspapers in the garage—while Mam-ma squeezed orange juice from the fruit off a tree in their yard—buzzing the black hair off in patches. Later that night she asked me if, in the future, I could clean out the razor after I'd used it. I didn't know any better and had left it crammed full of the stumps of my body hair, and Pap-pa'd had to clean it out. I got embarrassed and promised that I would.

I'd go out searching for jobs as far away as Tampa, but no one wanted to hire me. What were my skills? they would ask, and I couldn't come up with any—besides showing people how to exercise. And I couldn't find a gym. Lakeland had one health spa–type place, filled with light chrome dumbbells and glitzy, nearly worthless machines, but there was no hard-core gym around, and I began to feel myself getting out of shape. Finally I went to the library and pulled out the phone books for all the surrounding towns and located a gym in Solar Grove, a little spot several miles from Lakeland. I drove over that day and checked the place out.

Hard-iron gym; that's what this place in Solar Grove was, a pure and simple hard-iron gym. I got goose bumps when I went through the front door, even though it was nearly ninety out. It was basic, in the way Red's Gym in Terre Haute had been, but all the equipment looked more solid and worn by years of heavy use. I'd found my place to train. A guy was working out as I came through the door, the biggest body-builder I'd ever seen; thick slabs of muscle hung out of the tank top he had on, and his legs looked like sequoia trunks.

His quads have got to be as big as Platz's, I thought. Tom Platz was the reigning king of legs in the California bodybuilding world, and he was constantly in all the magazines as he worked his way toward the pro ranks. His legs were what most bodybuilders dreamed of having theirs look like.

I stood by the front desk and watched this guy finish training his arms and couldn't believe that there were actually people this big walking around. He looked, to my naive eyes, as if he were ready to enter the Mr. Olympia.

"Help ya?" he asked me when he'd finished the last sets on his triceps. He came up to the front of the gym and pulled a pitcher of ice tea from a refrigerator behind the desk and drank huge gulps, letting tea roll out of his mouth and down his sweaty shirt. He stopped drinking and resumed panting for air.

"Yeah . . . I was wonderin' if you sold memberships?" I felt like a little kid shyly approaching Santa Claus.

"Wadda you think?" he shot back, and took another big sloppy gulp of ice tea. Not exactly a service-oriented place, that was for sure.

"Sorry, maybe I can come back and talk to whoever works here."

"You're talkin' to him now."

"Oh . . . well, I was lookin' for a place to train."

"Try the spa on First Street."

Must have been a new cutting-edge sales technique. Tell people to fuck off and get them begging to give you money.

"Um, did I do somethin' to offend you?"

He just stood there staring at me for at least two minutes, which seemed more like two hours.

Then he laughed. "Shit, sorry, man. Ya caught me in a fuckin' test rush."

"Oh. I don't understand."

"It's just ever once in a while—specially when I'm dietin' my ass off—I get these rushes of test, and, well, it's like, 'Get the fuck outta my way,' ya know."

"Wadda ya testin' for?"

He laughed and ice tea shot out his nose, and he wiped it away.

"You live on another planet or somethin'? You look like you train."

"Yeah."

"So you never heard of testosterone . . . you know—test."

"Ohhh," I said, feeling like a rube.

"So it makes me an asshole sometimes. Satisfied? Now that I'm bein' all sensitive and that kinda shit? So you wanna train here?"

"Yeah, that'd be nice. I just moved down here, you know, and this is the first real gym I've come across."

"Uh-huh—only one tween here and Orlando."

"So what's it gonna cost me to work out here?"

"How much you have?"

"Oh, it's gonna be that way, is it? Tell ya what. I'll give you all the money I have on me right now for a year's membership—how's'at?" I smiled at him in a look that I was sure appeared both sincere—like a little, innocent boy—and completely smart-assed.

Once again he looked at me for what seemed like an eternity, sizing me up, trying to gauge whether I was severely inbred or a con man trying to rip him off. He took another big slug of ice tea, wiped the sweat and tea off his face with a dingy towel that had been hanging on the back of the desk chair, looked straight at me, and smiled. "Gonna cost you two hundred bucks for a year," he finally said.

"What about just a couple of months?"

"You compete?"

"Want to. You?" I wasn't about to bring up my disastrous Mr. ISU outing or start out on the wrong foot with any more lies about having won it.

"Doin' the Florida in two months. That's why I'm dietin' my ass off."

"Oh. Looks to me like you'll do real good."

"I'm gonna blow 'em all away and then go out to California—get myself a Weider contract and live on the beach in Venice."

"Cool. You know Joe Weider?"

"Well . . . I, um . . . I got this friend, used to train at the same gym over in Orlando before he moved out West. You probably seen him in the magazines—Pete Grymkowski."

Of course I knew the name. The guy was in the Weider magazines all the time. Huge shoulders; they always compared his deltoid muscles to cantaloupes.

"Oh, you know him? Didn't he buy Gold's Gym not too long ago?" I knew this, of course, because I'd read it in a magazine, but I tried to say it as if I were some sort of insider, spouting information that nobody else had the privilege to know.

"Yeah. He'll help me get a fuckin' contract. You ever get out to California—before I do—you oughta tell him hi from T.J." He laughed, as if he thought the idea of me in California was a great joke. "How old are you?"

"Nineteen. Why?"

"You oughta do the Teenage Florida."

"In May, right? Think I have enough time?"

"Fuck, I don't know. I don't even know what your body looks like. Hell, I just thought you'd wanna jump into competition."

"I do, but I wanna do it right, that's all."

"So what's stoppin' ya?"

"Well, I haven't got a place to train yet for one thing."

"Look . . . What'd you say your name was?"

"I didn't—but it's Bobby, Bobby Paris."

"I'm Terry Gerard—people call me T.J."

"You spell Gerard with a J?"

"No, man, just what people call me—'s'at okay with you?"

"Yeah, I'm cool." I didn't want him going off on me again.

"Anyway, look—if you train here for the show, just gimme fifty bucks and you can work out all the way up to it."

"Um, okay, but can I give you twenty-five now and the rest in a couple of weeks? It's all I got on me now."

"Yeah, whatever. So you were gonna try to get a year for twenty-five bucks?" he asked, smiling and shaking his head. I just shrugged and then pulled out two tens and five ones and gave them to him, saving out enough to get five dollars of gas for my drive back to Lakeland.

"Oh—you gonna be needin' any juice?" he asked, his voice slightly lowered, as he counted the money and then stuck it in a locking drawer on the desk.

"Nah—thanks, I had some this morning."

"Oh, wadda ya on?"

"'Scuse me?"

"What juice are ya on—deca, test, Anadrol—what?"

"I meant orange juice. My mam-ma squeezed it fresh this morning for breakfast."

"Ah, fuck, man—you gotta lot to learn." He shook his head as if he'd just met the world's biggest idiot. When he turned around to put his ice tea pitcher back in the refrigerator, I noticed that his shoulders, and as much of his back as I could see around the edges of his tank top, were covered with dozens of boiling zits, which hadn't been apparent at first because he had such a deep tan.

August 1995
Seattle

Good afternoon, Weider," the front-desk receptionist answered.

"Joe Weider's office, please," I said, and was immediately connected to another ringing line.

"Joe Weider's office, Annalise speaking," Joe's head assistant answered in her slightly German accent.

"Hi, Annalise. This is Bob Paris."

"Hello, Bob, how are you?"

"Well, thanks, and you?"

"Good, thank you."

"Is Joe in by any chance?"

"He is, Bob, but he's in a meeting, and he's got three other people waiting outside his door, and two other calls on hold."

"Okay. Um, Annalise, could you help me with something please? Joe keeps telling me that he's going to get back to me on a proposal, and he keeps saying next week, next week, every week—and it's been three months now. Is there any way you can give me a time when he'll be free, so I can speak with him and pin this down?"

"Well, Bob, is there any way you can maybe write something in a memo and fax it to him?"

"Um, not really. The ball's pretty much in his court at this point."

"Well, this is really the worst day you could have possibly called. You can't believe what he's doing to himself, working so hard."

"I know, a man his age should be retired and off enjoying life."

"That's true," she said, then paused a couple of seconds as if thinking what to do. "Oh, hang on a second, Bob, let me see if he can spare a moment, although it doesn't look good, so I can't promise anything."

"Thanks, Annalise." And she put me on hold.

I was getting frustrated, that was for sure. He kept promising a new endorsement contract every time I called, and I believed that in spite of our problems in the past he was sincere. But here he was somewhere between seventy and eighty years old (nobody was quite sure of the exact age) and working long days, buying new companies, expanding into new countries, overseeing operations of the magazines, working weekends. The guy supposedly had more money than God and still wanted to approve every photo that went into *Muscle and Fitness*, staring for hours at transparencies on a light board to select just the right one, then moving on the next minute to buying out another vitamin company.

"Hello, Baab." Joe suddenly came on the line.

"Hey, Joe, how's life?"

"Ahh, you couldn't believe how busy I been."

"I know, Joe. Why don't you slow down some? Enjoy life a bit."

"I know. . . . Did I ever tell you what a therapist once said to me? He said, I got no pleasure principle [Joe saying each *p* as if he were beating a bongo]. I got my first job when I was eleven years old, and I haven't stopped since." I'd heard this little speech a hundred times before. "All I can do is work."

"I can certainly relate to that. But you oughta slow down."

"I know. Listen, Bob, you're gonna hate me, but I haven't had time to put your proposal together yet. Give me another week. I'll have an answer next Tuesday."

"I know, but, Joe, you've been telling me that for almost three months now. I mean, like I said when I was in your office a few months ago, I just want to know if we have a future together. I think it'd be great if we did—if we could put the past behind us—but if there's nothing here, Joe, all I'm asking is that you please just let me know." I tried to stay calm because I kept promising myself that I wouldn't let my temper flare up. Our past relationship generally revolved around him pushing my buttons by saying stupid things that he knew would make me mad, me getting angry, and him responding by telling me that I was neurotic, and of course once someone declares you neurotic, your every action that follows will only serve to prove his point. If he called me neurotic, I'd probably lose it no matter how hard I tried not to.

"You're so impatient, Bob. You gotta learn to relax. You're so high-strung. I'll call you next week. Okay?" The line went dead.

I knew that if any business between us was ever going to get done, I'd have to continue calling every week until our signatures were on the dotted lines.

What am I doing? I thought.

"Oh, well," I said, and waved the phone away, as if I were a magician trying to make it disappear. I changed my clothes and went downstairs to take my frustrations out on the weights. It worked too. I had the most intense arm workout I'd had in years; the weights seemed to have wings and flew wherever I wanted them to, defying their natural desire to lie there and pout, motionless and cold. I caught second and third winds, and it truly felt like the old days. I had to look at my face in one of the gym mirrors to make sure that I hadn't accidentally stepped into a time machine and been transported back ten years. No, there was that thirty-five-year-old man looking back at me still; no miracles; I grew ten seconds older and went back to finish my workout.

Summer, 1979
Florida

I paid my additional twenty-five dollars and started working out at the gym in Solar Grove, which was just called the gym. For the first week I still lived at Mam-ma and Pap-pa's house, but then I got a job—if you could call it that—as a bouncer at a tacky nightclub attached to a liquor store in the same town where the gym was.

My first night working there a man was beaten half to death in the parking lot by another ball-bat-wielding patron, who thought that the guy he busted up had scratched the side of his pickup with a car key. The next night a guy stuck a .22 pistol in my face because I'd let into the club a woman whom he had broken up with the week before. I talked my way out of that one, and when I went back to my grandparents' house that night after work Mam-ma asked me how things had gone at work, and I told her, "Swell."

I asked her what she was doing up at three in the morning and she said that she couldn't sleep. She had been sitting in the family room reading her Bible.

A few days later, Mam-ma, Pap-pa, and I went to look at an apartment in Solar Grove that I'd seen advertised in the paper, and they helped me pay the first month's rent on it. The folks who were renting it out had converted their detached one-car garage into a small studio apartment, and I moved in the next day.

In the gym I would train at the same time as T.J., but I trained alone. That first day I'd come to the place he was training by himself, but only because he'd thrown a tantrum at the guys who were there with him and tossed them all out of the gym. I soon discovered that T.J. trained with a small entourage. More like slaves actually. Two guys—whom I understood he'd known since high school—would follow him around as he trained and hand him all his barbells, load and unload weights from the machines, fetch him something to drink, or do any other menial thing that crept into the dim passageways of this guy's mind. It was both sad and hilarious to watch grown men voluntarily subject themselves to the kinds of abuse this man would unleash on them. If they didn't have their hands ready and waiting to catch a dumbbell he was going to drop at the end of a set, he exploded. If his beloved ice-tea pitcher wasn't waiting for him at just the right minute, a tantrum would rock the building. His little group effort didn't stop there either.

One day, after I'd been training at the gym for three or four days, I was showering after my workout. This typical locker room shower area had six or seven showerheads distributed throughout a small tile room. T.J. had finished his workout at about the same time I did. After he'd had his ice tea, he came into the locker room followed by two young women I'd never seen before. He stood there as they pulled off his sweaty gym clothes, and then, still wearing their own clothes, they followed him into the shower area, where I was standing under the running water, a bit dumbfounded. They began to scrub him from head to toe; they washed his hair and every orifice and appendage, including his little pee-pee. (Lest anyone get the wrong idea, this was not a sexy scenario playing itself out. I found it as erotic as watching vultures pick at the carcass of a dead cat.) They scrubbed and scrubbed, and he would scold them both when he felt they'd missed any key areas. I finished my shower as this was all unfolding and went back into the locker room to dry off and get dressed for work. I wasn't uncomfortable being seen naked. I'd never been shy about nudity. In high school I used to go with my friends, every summer, out to a nude beach at a lake near where we lived, and there were dozens of naked men and women there—everyone completely comfortable. The sheer weirdness of this situation was what got me out of that shower; but it didn't end. After these women had bathed him, they toweled him dry, slathered him in moisturizer, and dressed him too. I decided that I was going to have to train at a different time of the day.

I loved to train alone. I would venture deep inside my head and use my mind to push my body so hard that every workout ended with my feeling as if I were going to be sick. Every day T.J. would offer me advice on my contest preparations. At first I listened intently as he sat behind his desk holding court. One day he'd tell me that I needed to be eating low-fat; a couple of days later he'd tell me that I should be eating high-fat; one day I should only eat egg yolks, the next, only egg whites; and so on. I eventually began to simply nod and ignore his advice. I followed a diet out of one of the magazines.

He kept trying to talk me into buying steroids from him. I told him that I didn't want to do them—that I wanted to train natural for the Teen Florida—but the reality was that I couldn't afford them. I was making, maybe, a hundred bucks a week at the disco, and every week I'd worry how I was going to make so little money stretch so far. I also worried about how long I could even keep this job. It was a violent place; everybody was always talking about shooting each other or cutting somebody up, and I had no relish for fighting—a hundred bucks a week was nothing to die over.

The weeks tumbled by as I got ready to do the Teenage Mr. Florida. I'd go over and visit my grandparents a couple of times a week, and Mam-ma would always make me the meals that were on my diet, all the time asking me if I wouldn't rather have something more normal to eat instead. They both asked me if I'd given any more thought to going back to college, and I always told them that I was still thinking about it, but that all my energies were going toward my upcoming contest. I complained one evening after supper that I couldn't find any posing trunks to wear for the show, and Mam-ma said that if I could get her a pair, she'd make a pattern and sew me some. She was a wizard with a sewing machine. I knew that T.J. had gotten a pair of Frank Zane trunks in the mail, and so the next day I asked him—being careful not to arouse one of his "test rushes"—if I could borrow them for a couple of hours to get a pattern made. I didn't expect that he would let me borrow them, but was pleasantly surprised when he did. I rushed them immediately over to Mam-ma, she quickly traced out a pattern (I explained to her that the guy I'd borrowed them from had a wicked temper and had only let me use them for as hour—which was all true), and I ran them back to the gym. Later that evening I went with her to a fabric store, and we bought the right sort of stretchy material and some elastic for the waistband, and later that same night she sewed my first pair of posing trunks. They fit perfectly and I told her she should go into business. She laughed as I modeled them for her and Pap-pa in the family room.

"What's going to happen to all your big muscles once you stop this thing, Bobby?" she asked as I did mock, shaky poses.

"Hell, Connie, they're just gonna go to saggy blubber, that's what," Pap-pa interjected.

"Oh, Pap, that's not true. Besides I don't ever plan to stop. I'm just gonna keep gettin' bigger and bigger. I'll be the best in the world one day," I told them, snapping the elastic on the trunks, then doing a strange little spinning pirouette, with a sort of—ta-da—vaudevillian ending.

"You just make sure you don't get too big for your britches. Remember, the folks who really know you still remember changin' your diapers," Mam-ma said.

"Hey—how's your horse? Remember?" Pap-pa asked me, smiling.

"Why, he's just fine, sir. I keep him in that little studio apartment of mine over there. Ride him to work every night. Speaking of which, I've gotta get to work so I can put some food in my hungry mouth. Can't become a famous Mr. Universe without packin' the old gut." I stuck my stomach out as far as it would go and patted it with both hands. We all laughed. A few minor quibbles aside—like poverty, for instance—I was completely happy right then; going after everything I'd dreamed about; and I had my first pair of posing trunks—made by hand by that famous designer Madame Mam-ma.

9

MR. OLYMPIA CALLS ME
BY NAME

August 1995
Seattle

I am once again deeply in love with training. Not simply training, but the barn-burning, all-out effort of pushing and pulling against extreme gravity that I had only ever experienced during times of uncluttered, iron-willed focus; the kind of focus that, as a young man, I directed toward turning myself into the greatest physique star in the world.

Years ago, I got off track somewhere, lost my bearings, began to care more about what other people thought about my chosen sport than what I thought about it. That was a mistake. I can say that now—knowing that I still have many strong disagreements with the direction the sport has taken in recent years. But despite those disagreements I should have been deciding whether pursuing my dreams in bodybuilding was worthwhile, not listening to other people—friends and total strangers—tell me that something they didn't understand was beneath my potential. I know now that no matter what I decide, as far as competition is concerned, it will only be my own opinion that I weigh. Everyone else's is, while maybe not irrelevant, at least beside the point.

Some in bodybuilding would say that my career as a professional was unsuccessful. Of course it would all depend on how someone defines success. I now have mixed feelings about my success as a pro, but in many regards I can see how those years were, for me, something of a failure.

When I got to a certain level of success, after I'd earned professional status, I slowly began to move toward seeing my success in bodybuilding as a stepping-stone to bigger and better things—as if this thing in and of itself weren't enough. In an ambitious quest for my ultimate destiny,

I began to ask myself if I shouldn't be doing something grander, if there weren't higher, better mountains to climb. That was when I began to stop thinking that this thing could simply be done for its own merits; that it didn't need to be a stepping-stone, but was the goal itself, and that I could stand on that rock proudly, never thinking that I had to leap onto the next one. I began to worry that I would never be taken seriously as a man if I was only defined as a Mr. Universe—a mere muscleman—and not as Joe movie star or a senator or corporate president or whatever. I feared that I would always be seen only as a stupid piece of meat—as if being well built were an automatic indication of my low intelligence or inability to do anything else—if I didn't move on. It's taken me a lot of hard years to understand that being automatically seen as stupid because I'm a bodybuilder says more about the person holding that opinion than it could ever say about me.

If I were to decide to return to competition, I know now that I would do it right. And it would be a tangible success that would be apparent to me and anyone in the sport. This isn't empty bragging either. This understanding comes instead from a deep-seated instinct, cultivated by years of living with my own need to be the best in the world at something. But aside from the fact that I now know that I could come back, I also realize that simply getting to this point is a major personal victory. Maybe that sounds like a bunch of hyper-positive, New-Agey, feel-good drivel. I don't think it does, and that's what counts when it comes to dreams.

Now when I go down into my gym each day there is a freedom that I haven't felt for years and it shows in my workouts. I haven't decided if I'll compete again. Also, Joe Weider hasn't gotten back to me to say if we'll be able to do business together again, and I haven't decided what I'll do about the drug question yet—I'm still extremely conflicted over the notion of having to use bodybuilding drugs again—but I go downstairs and face all that equipment and feel as if I have been given another chance; not by Joe, or any of the judges, or even any of the fans, but by me.

Summer, 1979
Florida

The weeks passed quickly, and before I knew it the Saturday of the Mr. Florida contest was only a few days away. I thought that, given my limited experience, I had gotten myself into pretty good shape, and that since it was only a teenage contest I'd be entering, I was sure to win, or at least place well. T.J. would check out my progress as I practiced my posing routine in front of the full-length locker room mirror and would give me grudging compliments.

"Not bad for a teenager," he'd say, or, "You look pretty good for trainin' natural. Sure you don't wanna get somethin' from me for these last weeks—it's not too late ya know."

I took his compliments in stride, knowing that, with the foul moods he'd been in from his dieting (and I suspected from all those drugs he kept shooting himself full of), his faint praise was actually stronger than it sounded.

He had been impressed with Mam-ma's job on my posing trunks and told me that I should have her make him some too—a comment that I pretended to ignore, since I knew that he would never pay her, even for the material. According to one of T.J.'s friends, the guy squirreled away every nickel as if they were going to stop making them the next week. We'd gone out to lunch together twice, and I was barely able to afford groceries, but he would disappear to the rest room the minute before the check arrived and not reappear until it was paid. And I'd been sucker enough to pay it both times, even though he ate twice what I did.

The contests were in Miami, at some big-time auditorium, and T.J.'s best friend asked me if I wanted to drive down with them; we could all get a hotel room together. I said that, yeah, that'd be cool. As we drove down, all we got to hear the whole way was T.J. going on and on about how he was going to blow everybody away at this show, and how he was sure that Joe Weider would have talent scouts in the audience, and he figured that the weekend would end with him being Mr. Florida and signing a fat Weider contract, so that he could move to California and do nothing all day but work out and lie on the beach. He also thought that it was a foregone conclusion that, with his body, he'd win the America and Universe that year too and be getting ready for his first Olympia by this time the next year.

We found a cheap motel several miles from the auditorium and spent the last three days before the show either going to a gym we'd found, where several other of the out-of-town contestants were also training, or going to Miami Beach to lie out and get some last-minute tan.

T.J. said that we needed to carb up by slowly increasing the amount of carbohydrate foods we ate for the last two days before the show. This sounded great to me since I'd decided to cut my daily food intake, during the last two weeks, down to three cans of tuna fish—in water— and a few vegetables. I was starving.

The night we got to Miami we went into a health food store down by the beach, and T.J. bought some chewable vitamin C tablets that he said tasted great and didn't have any calories. I bought some too and ate two immediately, which was a mistake because then I couldn't stop eating them and had gone through a bottle of 250 in less than an hour. They tasted so good—so orangy and delicious—it was hard to believe that they didn't have calories as TJ said. (Of course they did have calories; outside of the vitamin C, they were pure sugar. I just didn't know any better at the time and obviously neither did he.) Two hours later I had massive, unstoppable diarrhea and spent that first night in Miami lashed to a toilet.

The next evening we both started carbing up—after T.J.'s friend jabbed him with three different syringes full of some different things. They both refused to tell me what they were, especially when I asked if any of them were things that would help me for Saturday.

Carbing up, I learned from my sage companions, consisted of eating a bunch of starchy foods throughout that evening and the next day. What I didn't know was that, because I had been severely restricting my carbohydrates for a couple of weeks, the minute I started eating them, I would trigger cravings that made a glutton seem like an anorexic. I ate bread and pasta and pastries and pretty much anything I could get my hands on and that fit into the confines of my minuscule budget—but I ate and kept on going, but, I guess luckily, I still had major diarrhea from all that vitamin C or I would have blown up like a hippopotamus. Instead all that food went straight through me, and I ended up with . . . well, let me simply say that I became in dire need of Preparation H. This carbing-up business was definitely not for the delicate or faint of heart.

In one of those strokes of blind luck that any competitive bodybuilder can reminisce about having been surprised by during inexperienced times, the combination of all that rich food and my diarrhea conspired into a bit of a miracle. I actually got in better shape, even if it was along a painful path—one that should have been the undoing of months of my hard work.

It was obvious from the start of the judging of the teenage heavyweight class that I was one of the favorites to win. It would either be me or this other guy, against whom the judges kept comparing me throughout the prejudging.

And this prejudging stuff was hard. If anyone wanted to say that bodybuilding competitions were nothing more than glorified beauty contests, with nothing athletic about them, they should've been required to go through a full competition prejudging. That would have given them a different perspective.

You stand onstage, supposedly relaxed, but actually totally flexed while standing there *looking* relaxed. Every fiber is tensed, as if you're doing a full-body isometric contraction, for half an hour or more, without letting up. When the judges call two or three athletes out of the lineup to compare them, if you are one of those guys, you go through and hold the poses that they call for, while they compare every detail of your physique and condition against those of the other guys who've been called out with you. Holding a pose is, again, like an extended full-body contraction, and you go through one pose after the other, all the while with your heart pounding at coronary pace, because you are in the heat of competition and in front of a critical, seen-it-all audience—with all those things adding up to increase the intensity of the flexing. When the judges finish taking you through the mandatory poses, you return to the lineup feeling as if you have just run twenty wind sprints while carrying an anvil. And you go back to that lineup and once again stand looking as if you're just standing there, but with every cell, from the neck down, tightly crunched. And then they call you out again for more comparisons, usually right when you have almost, but not quite, caught your breath from the last time around, until all the athletes in the running have been totally scrutinized by every judge. The judges make their placements, first place through last. That half an hour—or up to an hour if lots of people are in your weight class—onstage during prejudging seems like ten days, and you wonder what it ever felt like not to stand there straining against the exhaustion of your well-trained body. You are an athlete who can push himself through torturous hours in the gym, but you'll leave the stage at the end of prejudging looking for a place to collapse. If your mind isn't ready for this process, your body won't follow.

Two guys dropped out during the prejudging, one complaining of severe cramps, the other needing to vomit and possibly faint—and maybe both simultaneously. After everyone in the class had been compared, the judges called out this other guy (whom I was being compared against the most) and me. They ran us through all the compulsory poses three times, and we looked at each other—in between a front double biceps and a front lat spread, on the second time through—as if we were both thinking, *What the hell are they doing, trying to kill us?* And then it was over, until the night show.

In the backstage dressing room, T.J.'s friend Tony started telling me how superior my physique was to that other guy's—while the other guy got dressed right next to me. Tony asked us to both stand up—and for some reason we both did—and began to compare us body part by body part, all the time running this other guy down and talking up my superiority. I could tell that the other guy (I didn't even know his name because the judges had called us out of the lineup according to the numbers we wore pinned to the front of our posing trunks) was beginning to feel a little intimidated, especially when Tony said that he might be in slightly better condition, but I had, by far, the superior physique and would go much further in the sport. I was flattered by what Tony said, but thought that it was unnecessary to make this guy feel bad. I told Tony so too, after the other guy left (before he'd left the dressing room, he said that his name was Billy, and we shook hands and said that we'd see each other back there later), but Tony told me not to get mad because he was only trying to help me by psyching Billy out.

Frank Zane was the guest star at the contest. He'd already won two Mr. Olympias and was going to guest-pose at the night show. I was excited to meet him, having read all about him in the magazines—about his famous Olympia battle against Robby Robinson the year before, how he used to be a math teacher, was an archery expert, and was into meditation and yoga. I could probably tell him more about his life than he knew. I wanted to tell him about Will, back at Indiana State; how he had been such a big fan and had used Frank's Olympia posing routine and bought trunks from his mail order company; and how my Mam-ma had made trunks for me off a pattern from his brand—and on and on.

I'd like to spend some time just talkin' with him—pick his brain some, I thought, feeling that I still needed to learn so much more about this sport. I still felt like a three-year-old who'd just done his first coloring-book drawing and had it hanging in an art gallery.

I gathered up my belongings and headed out to the lobby, to see if I couldn't run across Frank Zane. He was there, all right, sitting behind a card table autographing posters and photos he was selling. His wife, Christine—whom I immediately recognized because she was also a celebrity from the magazines—was sitting beside him, next to a man in a red sport coat, who was taking people's money for the pictures. This was exciting; I'd get to meet them both. The only complication was the line. At least fifty people were waiting to meet them too. I was going to have to think about this. I wanted to watch T.J.'s prejudging, so I poked my head inside the auditorium and asked a woman standing there what was going on. She said that they were just getting started on the over-forty men's contest, but that there seemed to be some unexplained delay—maybe it was the stage lights, she speculated. I thanked her and went back out, knowing that I had probably at least another hour before T.J. would be up, and I was more interested in meeting a living legend than watching the old-timers; I got on the back of the line.

Wow, this is moving fast, I thought. After only twenty minutes or so I was up near the front. I pulled money out of my gym bag and tried to calculate how much I'd need before I got home, and I seemed to have enough for the poster (a magnificent shot of Zane doing a double biceps pose) if I ate really light all the way back to Solar Grove. Then I realized that I'd better formulate my questions; I was only two people back from the table.

"Hello, Mrs. Zane, Mr. Zane. How are you both doing?" I was all nervous smile when I got up to the table.

"Fine, thank you," they both answered at the same time.

"Uh, son, which one did you want?" the man in the red sport coat asked.

"Oh . . . uh, sorry, the poster please, sir." I handed him the money, in bills that I had worked from their former crumpled state into being flat, if still wrinkled. I just stood there smiling, frozen—every thought had flown south for the winter.

"Who did you want this signed to?" Frank Zane asked me, looking up over the top of his wire-rim glasses. I could see the muscles of his forearms move as he rolled the pen between his fingers.

"Oh . . . uh . . . whoa . . . I . . . uh . . . um . . . just sign it to me . . . to . . . um, Bobby, please, Mr. Zane."

"There you are, Bobby." It was the first time a professional body-builder had said my name, and it was a two-time Mr. Olympia to boot—*yeeow.* He stuck out his right hand, I looked at it for a couple of seconds, snapped out of it, and shook it.

"Thanks very much."

Christine smiled at me and said quietly, "Thank you."

I didn't move, but then the guy in the red coat said, "Sorry, son, but it's a long line."

"Oh. Sorry—I . . . um . . . well . . . good luck in this, um, this year's Olympia, Mr. Zane."

"Thank you," he said, then turned his attention to the person behind me, who was nudging me to one side. I rolled up my poster, picked up my gym bag, and started to leave.

Before I got five feet away I turned around and said, "It was an honor, sir."

He nodded at me, smiled again, and went back to autographing pictures. I went over and sat on one of the velvet-covered benches that were scattered throughout the lobby and unrolled the poster to look at how it was signed. In curving, black ink it read, "To Bobby, Train Hard, Frank Zane, Mr. Olympia." I looked at it for several minutes, all the time thinking that he had overcome such tremendous odds to become a Mr. Olympia. He wasn't huge, like so many of the other pros. He competed well under two hundred pounds, in a field of much larger men. But everything was in its proper place, and all the muscles popped out like the features on a stone cliff, or some element of nature that looked beautiful and all one piece when you first looked at it, but separated into millions of intricate details once you really focused in on what you were seeing—that was him. He was infinitely detailed, and that's what allowed him to win against bigger men. I carefully rolled up the poster again and went back into the auditorium.

I found a seat six or seven rows back from the stage and watched the start of the men's middleweight division. It was fascinating to see these guys under the lights; they all looked terrific, but I began to be able to separate out the ones who were going to do the best. Since this was the first contest I'd seen, I'd never had the chance to do that before, and to be honest, I'd never really considered what a thoughtful bodybuilding judge must have to go through to place the athletes in a just order.

To many people, all bodybuilders—or anyone who has above average muscular development—look, for the most part, completely alike. As humans, when we are dealing with the unfamiliar, sometimes the distinctions of individuality manage to escape, or are never pursued at all, in a quest for psychological simplicity and comfort. The physiques in a bodybuilding contest are, however, as unique as fingerprints; anyone who gets even casually absorbed by the sport quickly learns to discern a great physique—or condition—from a good, average, or poor one.

It must be comical for the person attending his, or her, first physique contest to hear some of the more vocal audience members give their critiques.

"Ah, he's got no calves," the old salt might exclaim about a contestant. The novice spectator overhearing this begins to look at the stage for a man with his feet attached to his knees.

"He's fat as a pig," the seen-it-all fan pronounces, and again the newcomer searches the stage, this time for the obese person, only to see someone who looks as if they haven't got an ounce of fat on their entire body.

Overstatement is highly common among the aficionados of muscle. That fan most likely thought that the athlete's calves were less than impressive or underdeveloped compared to the rest of the muscles. Also, a bodybuilding fan calling a contestant fat doesn't mean the same thing as it does in everyday life. "He's fat as a pig," in bodybuilding speak, means that the contestant's muscle definition isn't showing through as much as the current muscle-world fashion demands; it lacks an extreme, almost inhumanly low level of body fat. Mr. Fat-as-a-Pig would still probably be seen, if he were, say, walking down the beach, as completely fat-free.

When it comes to bodybuilding, unless someone knows the sport, the distinctions that fans take for granted can be elusive. I've had entire conversations with total strangers that went something like this:

"What do you do for a living?" someone asks.

"I'm a professional bodybuilder," I used to reply when I was still on the pro circuit.

"Oh, yeah, you look like you work out. How much can you bench?"

"I'm not really concerned with that. I work out with heavy weights, but heavy single bench presses are more the concern of powerlifters. That's not really what bodybuilding is about."

"Oh."

Sometimes I lose them at this point, but chances are that the conversation continues:

"So you're a professional, huh? I got a cousin [or neighbor or whatever] who's a professional bodybuilder too. Maybe you know him."

"Oh, yeah, what's his name?" I ask sincerely (well, sincerely the first several times I had this conversation, anyway). "Maybe I do know him."

Clem Cadidlehopper, he might say, or some other name I've never heard.

"Know him?" he asks.

"Sorry—don't know the name."

"You sure?"

"I know all the pros. He won any shows?"

"Well, last year he was thinking about entering himself in the Mr. Cheddar Cheese Festival contest, back in Bumpkisville. You should see him though, big guy—not your size—well, maybe he's about your size. No, now that I think about it, he's even a little bigger—strong as an ox—benches over eight hundred."

Yeah, right. Therein lies the problem. This guy thinking that the person he mentioned is on the pro bodybuilding circuit is roughly the same as if he thought a cousin of his who plays golf at the local public course is a top moneymaker on the PGA tour.

The distinctions are unique. According to judging standards, the athlete's body must be evenly developed among all the muscle groups. The thighs must be as fully developed as the chest or back or any other body part. The muscular development should be in proportion to the athlete's height and bone structure. The judges look for how each muscle is shaped, and in what kind of muscular condition the athlete is in. Are his muscles defined enough, compared to those he is competing against? Is his physique—in an exaggerated bodybuilding sense—aesthetic? Does everything appear to go together—does he have huge arms, but undeveloped calves? How does he present himself? It is entirely possible for a great physique to be overlooked because the athlete doesn't know how to show it to his best advantage. That's why a good athlete stands in a prejudging lineup totally flexed, while appearing to simply stand there. By keeping the muscles tensed, he gives the illusion of being more muscular than someone who may even be physically superior, but is lurking about onstage completely relaxed, with his stomach hanging out and his shoulders drooping.

The more advanced the competition, the smaller the distinctions in detail grow between the athletes. In a lower level—even up to the state championship level—amateur show, the quality of physiques may vary widely, but at a pro show everyone onstage has battled his way through the amateur ranks, having already won local, state, national, and even world championships.

By the time the middleweights had finished, I'd managed to pick out the three guys who I thought would do best in the class. Two out of three of them got called out for the last judges' comparison, which I'd already figured out from my own judging was a fair indication of whom the top placers were going to be.

Someone tapped me on the shoulder and I turned around in my seat and saw a man with a shaggy handlebar mustache smiling at me.

"You looked real good up there," he said.

"Thank you." I started to turn back around.

"My name's Cliff."

I paused and twisted around again. He had his hand sticking out over the seat next to me. I shook it.

"I'm Bobby."

"How long you been training, Bobby?" He smiled at me and winked. *My God*, I thought, *he's flirting with me.*

Now, this was distressing on two accounts. First, I hadn't fully come to grips yet with my sexuality. Even though I knew that I was gay, I had never even come close to doing anything about it—beyond getting, what I had finally figured out to be, a minor, secret puppy crush on Will, from the weight room back in college. Second, I didn't find this guy attractive in the slightest (didn't anyone ever tell him to trim his mustache, or his nose hairs?).

"Couple a years," I said, and started—again—to turn back around in my seat.

"I think you're going to win."

"Thank you," I said, over my, mostly facing forward, right shoulder.

He moved over a seat in the direction I kept turning, I suppose so that I didn't have to contort myself to talk with him. "No, really, I think you'll win. Didn't I see you walking around with some other people?"

"Yeah—I have a friend coming up in the heavyweights."

"Oh, yeah, and how do you think your—friend—will do?" He winked again.

Yeeeks, what a lizard, I thought.

"Um, you know, we just train at the same gym. He thinks he's gonna win."

"What do you think?"

"I think he looks great, but there's a bunch of great physiques in this show—you see that one guy in the middleweights?"

"Yeah—he's really hot. I know him from the gym where he trains here in town."

I was starting to get uncomfortable, but I figured that the guy probably wasn't going to leave me alone, so my best manners—which were so ingrained from my upbringing that it was useless to struggle—drew conversation out of me that I couldn't seem to help. "So you live here in Miami?"

"No, I just come out here pretty often, that's all. Actually I live in Venice—Venice Beach, California. Heard of it?"

Now that was a stupid question, I thought. Anyone in bodybuilding knew all about Venice and the town right next to it, Santa Monica—they were the center of the universe for all things muscle. The heavyweight class were beginning to file onstage and position themselves in numerical order in a line that went from one stage-wing curtain to the other. Damn, these guys were huge.

"Oh, yeah, I've heard of it," I said while watching the lineup get settled in. "My friend from the gym says that he's gonna move out there. He's friends with the guy who owns Gold's and he's got some connections to get a Joe Weider contract."

"Really? I know Pete. You do know that's who owns Gold's, don't you? Pete Grymkowski."

"Course."

"I know Joe Weider too. I've done some work for his magazines."

I wondered if this guy could be the West Coast talent scout that T.J. had talked about. I said, finding boldness that took me by surprise, "So are you out here scoutin' talent for Joe Weider?"

"I'm afraid not—that doesn't really happen. If someone's great, Joe will usually hear about it. This is a very small world."

"So you don't think T.J.—or anybody else for that matter—is gonna leave here with a Weider contract?"

"Not unless they forge it."

"Oh." There went my chances of being discovered as the next great teenage sensation, and getting signed to a big contract, by this phantom talent scout. T.J. was so full of shit.

We stopped talking for several minutes while we both watched the judging unfold. I found T.J. in the lineup. He had looked so huge and overwhelming in the gym; now he didn't look so good.

"Which one is your friend?"

"Third from the right. Number sixty-two. Whadda you think? How'll he do?"

"Well, to be honest—I'm sorry to have to say this about your friend—he has great quads, but he's got no calves, his symmetry is almost nonexistent, and he's fat as a pig. He should learn to stand better onstage too—see how he's all slouched over. Ouch . . . sorry."

He seemed to be one of those guys who enjoy giving you their unvarnished opinion, especially when it's slicing. I wanted to get mad and defend T.J., but I couldn't—the guy was right. At least ten guys in the class were better. His body had looked so good, in a monstrous sort of way, in the gym, but now nothing seemed to fit together—it was a hodgepodge of oddly shaped muscles and uneven development; and he wasn't as muscular and defined as the other guys. He needed to stand up and pull his belly in too. All those injected potions, all that asshole behavior—blamed on his hard diet and drugs—and it looked to me as if he'd be lucky to place in the top fifteen—and there were only eighteen men in the class.

As the comparisons wound down, I told the guy, Cliff, that I had to run, and he started to try to get me into conversation again, but I had already gotten halfway to the aisle. He got out of his seat and came over, wished me good luck in the contest, and said that if I ever got out to L.A., I should give him a call. He handed me a business card; it said that he was a photographer. I put it in my pocket and then, once I'd gotten out in the lobby, threw it in a trash can.

The break between the prejudging and the night show was miserable. I had to go with T.J., because I didn't have my own way around and our motel wasn't within walking distance. He had at least three temper tantrums, one of them directed at me because I'd accidentally pushed the seat too far forward when I got in the backseat of the two-door car we came down in—he had refused to get out of the front passenger seat to let me in and I had to scrunch my way past him. He alternated between icy quiet and explosions until we returned to the auditorium for the rest of the show.

The teenagers came after the over-forties and women's show. Women's bodybuilding was just getting off the ground in those days, and there was tremendous controversy over exactly how muscular ("manly" was the way I heard one judge put it backstage) the women should be. These conversations revolved mostly around one contestant in particular, Laura Combs, who was dividing all observers' opinions because she was so developed and ultraripped—defined to a level that would make most male contestants envious.

Finally my show was on, and when I came out onstage to do my posing routine, all the rehearsal I'd done seemed to vanish, and I felt—sort of as I had in the Mr. ISU contest—naked and shaky and clunky. I got a bunch of applause when I finished though, and people backstage said that I'd done a good job.

Eventually, only the final five in my class were standing onstage waiting for the places to be announced. They started at fifth, and I held my breath as each time someone else's name was announced; a perky young woman would come out and hand them a trophy and hang a medal around their necks. By the time it got past third place, I thought that I was going to win. The announcer told the audience that only one point separated the second-and first-place athletes, then he dragged out some suspense as he said, "And—in—second—place—iiiiissss—please take the second-place trophy to . . ." The audience sounded like a swarm of buzzing flies, and the lights created rainbow halos, while his voice sounded as if it were a record working its way up to full speed. "Bobby Paris."

Everything swooped back to full speed, and the woman brought me my trophy and medal, and only then did I let myself feel the disap-

pointment, as everyone crowded around to congratulate Billy on winning. I did too; I wasn't going to be a public poor-sport.

One lousy fucking point, I thought.

I'd been a competitive athlete long enough to know that few people
ever remembered who took second.

T.J. didn't place in his show and he got pissed at me because I had truly
enjoyed watching Frank Zane's guest-posing routine at the end of the
show.

"You're a selfish motherfucker," he said to me on the way back to
the motel.

I hadn't done anything more selfish than carry my trophy back to
the car. I had told him that he'd get 'em next year, and he growled that
there wouldn't be a next year, then he fired up a fat joint and kept it
all to himself. I had no intention of smoking any, but his bogarting
manners, not even offering, were atrocious.

The week after the contest, my life in Florida began to crumble.

Dad had forwarded a piece of mail from the Marine Corps about
something that I'd committed to before I left home. I had been discharged from my Reserve unit into a pre–officers candidate school,
called the Platoon Leader's Class. I was supposed to go to Quantico,
Virginia, during the summer to do another, much milder version of boot
camp, and I'd completely spaced it off.

That night, I showed up to work at the disco, and the manager took
me into his office and said that I had completely ignored his latest orders
to ask all black people coming into the club to show three picture IDs.
White people only needed one, if even that. This was his new method
that he'd told us all about a couple of weeks before. The doormen were
supposed to use this technique to keep the place purely pale, and of
course I wasn't about to get into that racist bullshit, so I ignored it and
applied my ID policy the same across the board, as I had the whole
time I'd worked there. After they saw that I wasn't going along, a couple
of the regulars had given me a hard time about it. One of them even
threatened to cut my "nigga-lovin' heart out with a sharp rock" the night
before I left for Miami.

"There's no way I'll do that," I said to the manager.

"Do it or get the fuck out."

I got up and left.

That night I went back into my apartment, opened the refrigerator, and except for a small bowl of tuna mixed with mustard and a glass jug of ice tea, it was empty.

The next morning I went into the gym to train because I thought that I might enter the teenage Mr. America, and as soon as I came in the door, T.J. told me that if I wanted to keep training there, I had to pay him two hundred dollars cash for a membership, by the next day. He said that it was all right if I worked out that day, but that I would have no more free ride at his place. I tried to remind him that I'd paid him fifty bucks and hadn't gotten anything for free, but he ran off to the back of the gym to yell at someone because they'd accidentally dropped a dumbbell too hard. T.J.'s friend Tony, who'd gone to Miami with us, was standing there and told me that T.J. was just angry about the show and taking it out on everybody. I told him that T.J. was a major asshole.

Instead of leaving, as my first instinct told me to, I got pissed off and threw myself into a heavy back workout. At the end of it I was doing four-hundred-pound dead lifts, and on the fifth rep of my last set, I felt something go—*sproing*—in my lower back. The whole back side of my body went numb, and I couldn't stand all the way up. I started to hobble out to my car, and when I got to the front door, T.J. laughed and asked, "Whatsa matter—hurt yourself?"

"Fuck you, man," was all I could say. I expected that he'd try to pound my brains in, but he stayed behind his desk with his mouth open. I got to my car and drove to Lakeland, nearly paralyzed with pain.

Two days later I was back on the interstate reversing the route that had brought me down through Louisville to central Florida.

I'd gone straight from the gym over to my grandparents' house, and after I'd hobbled inside all hunched over, I told them everything that had been happening. Mam-ma asked me if I wasn't only a couple of days away from the rent's being due on my apartment. It was. And wasn't my Marine Corps commitment pretty important? It was. And how was I going to survive without a job? I couldn't.

The next day they bought me a set of retread tires, to replace the bald ones I'd been driving around on. The day after that, they gave me enough gas money to get back to Indiana (I had insisted that I had enough money, but they told me to take it anyway, which was good, since I'd only had enough to get me about as far as Tennessee). They kissed me good-bye and stood in their front yard waving as I drove away. Before I knew it, I was driving through the dark, my back still freshly out of commission, a second-place trophy in the trunk, headed for the Georgia state line.

It seemed as if the only thing that had held my life together during my stay in Florida had been focusing on the contest. After it was over—after the buildup and discipline were finished—and the contest day had come and gone, everything suddenly fell apart.

10

A WEEK FROM NEXT TUESDAY

August 1995
Seattle

I told myself that I wasn't going to keep bugging Joe Weider about business, but I couldn't stand this characteristic of his where he'd get rid of someone by saying that it would be done next Tuesday, or whatever, and then, lo and behold, Tuesday would come and go, and there'd be nothing—no promised phone call, no new contract on the fax machine, nothing. You could call him again, just as a reminder, only to be told, once again, that it would be next Tuesday, or two weeks from Tuesday. He'd actually get insulted if you pointed out to him that he'd promised it last Tuesday, and every Tuesday before, for months on end. The guy definitely played the game by his own rules, but since he and his brother practically owned the game, everybody else who wanted to be involved had to play by those rules too.

Maybe Joe didn't want to do business with me again. But if he didn't, I wanted him to say it, not make promises and then not deliver, hoping that I'd get frustrated and go away.

I think he wanted me to beg. He wanted me to say that he'd always been right and I'd always been wrong—and that I promised to do whatever he said without question or fuss. He was used to having bodybuilders beg him for things. A lot of these guys looked like big, strong men, but they built up their muscles without ever doing anything to build up their character, and they shivered like little boys in the principal's office whenever they dealt with Joe.

One day, in the late eighties, I sat on the antique couch outside his office, waiting to talk to Joe and the president of the company about why I had refused to do what I thought was a particularly sleazy *Muscle and Fitness* cover shot the week before. Another top pro sat on the couch next to me talking big trash about how he was going to tell Joe off about something or other; he ranted for fifteen minutes, and if I had been Joe's assistant, I would have checked him for a gun before I allowed him in the office alone with Joe. Well, he went into the office eventually, and the second the door closed, I could hear this big, angry pro body-builder start kissing Joe's ass, up one side and down the other. He started begging Joe for an extension of his endorsement contract and pleading with Joe to—please, please, please—put him on a magazine cover. When this guy finally came out of the office and I started to go in, he came around the corner all cocky, as if he'd really told Joe where to get off. It was hard not to laugh.

Joe was definitely expecting me to beg. Screw that. Kissing ass has never been one of my strong suits.

I could hear myself: "Oh, please, Joe, take me back. I'll never again object when you want to make me look straight by draping me with limp bimbos on a magazine cover. Oh, no, those covers aren't degrading to me as a man, or to all women in general. I'll never again open my mouth to talk about being gay, because I know that might offend some housewife in Tennessee—who doesn't buy your magazines anyway, but might run across it accidentally in the supermarket.

"But now I'm begging you, Joe, please take me back. I'll do everything you tell me to do. I promise. I should never have tried to create my own ideals and values. I should have let you do that for me. I'll be loyal to you no matter what, because you're a god, Joe. All I have to do is read your publicity to know that. You are the master, Joe—the Master Blaster. Can you ever forgive me for not letting you do with me whatever *you* thought best?"

Yeah, right—I can just hear myself.

Summer, 1979
Southern Indiana and Beyond

By the time I crossed the Ohio River, out of Kentucky, my lower back was killing me. The drive had been torturous, but I'd pushed through the night and into the next day, taking it all in one long stretch; the pain in my back was all that kept me awake. As the last few miles to Dad's house hummed by, I felt myself sinking into one of the black holes that I hadn't felt in months. The last time I'd had this strong a sense of falling down a dark well had, in fact, been along almost the same stretch of interstate that I was on, as I was headed down to Florida.

Dad seemed happy to see me, but let me know, when he asked how

long it would be until I left for my Marine Corps obligation, that he
was hoping I wouldn't be around too long. I wasn't.

Three days later I had to fly to Virginia. I thought that, like the boot
camp at Parris Island I'd gone to a year earlier, I wouldn't need to bring
anything, not even a toothbrush, because it would all be taken away
anyway when uniforms and gear were issued within the first hours.
When I arrived at Quantico, all the other guys who'd come had brought
suitcases of clothes and toiletries. I immediately knew that I'd screwed
up, especially when I accidentally ripped out the seat of my pants, while
I was contorting against my injured back muscles to bend and tie my
shoe. I was walking around, the only former Marine in the whole bunch,
with my ass hanging out of my britches and no other pair to change
into. I didn't have to worry about that for long though. The morning
of the second day, we were given complete physicals. I went into the
examining doctor's office and he asked me to sit down.

"What seems to be the matter?" the Navy doctor asked, eyeing me
carefully as I took a seat. Since my drive back from Florida, sitting down
had become an elaborate process, as I had to shift my hips one way,
and sort of support myself by putting my hands on my knees and creak-
ing down. "You seemed to have some trouble sitting."

"It's nothing, sir." Since my only Marine experience had been under
the severest conditions, where any misstep could bring the world down
around your ears, I wondered what would happen to me if I revealed
that I was injured.

"Stand up," he said, not really barking the order as I was expecting,
but more like a normal, concerned doctor.

I reversed my elaborate sitting process, trying my best to hide it. For
some twisted, self-torturing reason, I still wasn't sure that showing up in
this condition wouldn't land me in the brig.

"Bend over please, and touch your toes."

I tried, I really did, but I couldn't get my hands below my knees. I
stood back up, embarrassed.

He picked up my file and started writing. "Have you had a recent
injury?" he asked, still writing.

"Yes, sir," I replied quietly, and added, "A minor one."

"I'd say it's not very minor. You can't even bend at the waist. I'm
sending you home, son. I see here that you were a Marine, transferred
from your Reserve unit to come here. I'm sorry to have to do this, but
with your back in the condition it appears to be in, I have no choice."

This doctor had the final word on my future there, and through his
words, my short time as a Marine ended. I sank deeper, feeling a despair
at this new failure—even though the trip had been a complete sidetrack,

I still had my pride—especially as I was transferred to a dorm full of guys who'd come for the summer but were, for one reason or another, being sent home too.

That night, sitting on the front porch of the building in my torn pants, I smoked my first cigarette since I'd started training in college. I sat there watching the world collapse inside my head, wondering what the hell I was going to do, puffing away on a Winston and hating my very existence—wishing I had a joint. I had graduated, with honors, at Parris Island, and now I saw myself as just another bum who couldn't hack it.

I was back in Indiana three days later. Dad asked pointedly, his eyes brown icebergs, what I planned to do. I couldn't give him an answer and excused myself to go to the bathroom. I stood in front of the mirror, held on to the sink, and tried not to cry. Ellen, whom he'd married while I was in Florida, told him to relax and give me time to figure things out; she said that he was being impatient for no good reason and that I was, after all, his son. She told him this in the kitchen of Dad's house, and I couldn't help but overhear it. She told him that since they had been living at her house and Dad's was sitting empty, there wasn't any reason why I couldn't stay in it until I figured out what to do. I came back into the kitchen right then and told them both that I wouldn't be around long. Dad just looked at me and then out the window, toward the lake. Ellen told me that she was proud of how I'd done in the contest and asked me how my back was feeling and if I needed to see a doctor.

I was lost. I thought about trying to find a job, but that seemed useless since I had no intention of sticking around, since there wasn't anywhere for me to train. If I could find a way to leave, I was gone. I'd been paid for a week at Quantico, even though I was discharged, but that was only a week's wages at a second lieutenant's rate and that was no fortune. It wasn't going to last long.

Later that week, after I'd mostly sulked around feeling sorry for myself, with nothing more on my mind except how I was going to get to California so I could finally get my life on track, I went into Columbus and ran into a girl I'd been casually acquainted with in high school. She told me that there would be a big party that Friday at Joey Lynch's house.

"Do you know where that is?" she asked.

"Yeah, I know where it is. I lived right next door when we were kids."

"Oh, that's right. You did, didn't ya."

"How would you know that?" I asked, smiling.

"Bobby, you seem to forget, we went to school together since you and your family moved from Brown County."

"Oh, you're right." I didn't remember that—well, maybe vaguely— but she probably knew better than I did. I couldn't seem to separate out much of my childhood from the winter fog that I remembered living so much time inside.

"See ya there?"

"What?" I'd been drifting.

"On Friday."

"Yeah, maybe I'll stop by. I'm plannin' to leave for California soon, but if I'm still around, I'll come by."

How would I get to California? I thought of nothing else all week as I hung out at Dad's house in a bleak and worsening mood. I had about three hundred dollars; I figured that would probably be enough to get out there. What would I live on, though, until I got a job? I couldn't ask Dad for money. I could be starving to death and he wouldn't loan me a dime.

Friday came and I was still trying to figure out my next move. I remembered the party at Joey Lynch's house and decided to go into town and check it out. Maybe there'd be some people there I knew.

The music was blasting. I could hear it from the street as I parked my car in front of the house where my family had lived before my parents got their second and final divorce. Once I got inside, I knew within two minutes that I had to get away.

I saw Mac Cobell come into the backyard and yelled, "Hey!"

"BP. Hey, bud, what's up?" He came over and we hugged. I hadn't seen him since college.

"So what are you going to do now?" Mac asked as we stood next to the icy keg on the back porch. A couple of dozen stoned and drunk people I had grown up with bounced around whooping and talking and dancing.

"I don't know," I said loudly above the music. "I'm thinking about goin' to California. You know—for my bodybuilding."

"Fuckin' A, how 'bout I go with you?"

"What?" I screamed at him. "You say what I think you said?"

"Hell, yeah, bud, let's do it. I got nothin' goin' on here."

"Huh," was all I could say, and I gulped the last of a kegger cup of

Miller High Life down in three big swallows. "Hold tight, man. I'll be right back."

I tossed my empty plastic cup, which I'd accidentally cracked by squeezing it too hard on my last gulp, into the garbage can on the porch, went down the four steps out to the back of the Lynches' yard, and lit a cigarette. I had only started smoking again about two weeks before, after stopping for nearly a year because it didn't mix with my training.

I sat down on the grass, smoking a Winston on the spot where Joey Lynch and I used to camp out, near a clump of bushes at the adjoining back corners of the huge lots our parents' houses sat on. We'd pitch a tent and then during the night sneak cigarettes and sometimes shed all our clothes, cutting naked out to the highway that bordered the yards behind ours, to streak up and down as traffic passed by, an occasional driver honking and waving. We hid behind bushes whenever we thought we were about to be caught, laughing, filled with adrenaline.

Up on the porch was one of my best friends, whom I had grown distant from ever since we had tried to room together—unsuccessfully— at Indiana State, and now he wanted to move to California with me. So he said.

I felt like ripping all my clothes off and streaking naked up and down the highway, except I was nineteen now and could be arrested for indecent exposure. The way my luck had been going lately that's exactly what would happen too, and they might get to throw in underage drinking and public intoxication charges to boot.

Mac came walking over right when I was finishing another smoke.

"Let me have one of those, bud. So, whadda ya say? Does it sound like a plan?" he asked, taking the cigarette I shook out of the half-empty pack.

"Okay, let's go," I answered, cupping my hands around my lighter.

"Shit, yes. Hey—wanna burn a doobie to celebrate? I can maybe scratch one up. Hang on, I'll—"

"Nah, think I'll pass. I'm kinda tired. I'm gonna book on back to Dad's house. I'll call you tomorrow and we can make our plans."

"All right, but call me. I'll be at home," he said as I started to leave. "Hey, BP, fuckin' A, man—it'll be a blast."

"Later."

I drove back to Dad's house, weaving my Monte Carlo around the familiar bends of the back roads.

What the hell am I gonna do? I wondered.

When I pulled in the driveway, my lights caught on big lumps of things in front of the house.

What the fuck? I thought. *What the hell is . . . son of a bitch . . . that son of a bitch.*

There on the driveway, right outside my old bedroom window, were all of my clothes, shoes, books, underwear, pictures, letters, and every single useless thing I had accumulated in my short life—lying strewn on the dew-wet asphalt. On top of the heap was my Teenage Mr. Florida trophy.

I tried my key in all the doors. Dad had changed all the locks and was nowhere in sight.

I opened the trunk of my car and jammed everything in. At first, I tried to fold the clothes, but I started to cry. I wondered if there wasn't a big old tree by the road somewhere that I could just run my speeding car into to end this whole mess. I began just stuffing in whatever would fit in the trunk and backseat, drove out on an empty gravel road on the other side of the lake, parked, and curled up on the front seat to get some sleep. I figured that I had another long trip ahead of me.

Were you serious last night about going with me out to California?"

"Hell, yeah, BP."

"Not gonna change your mind like the Marine Corps thing?"

"Nah, man. Come on, cut me some slack on that."

"Two questions. When can ya leave? Got any money?"

"How 'bout now—and, yes, I can lay my hands on some cash—maybe a thousand."

"Make ya a deal. I only got about three hundred bucks. So here's the deal—we go in my car and we combine our bucks and use 'em for whatever it takes to get there and get set up. The trip'll probably be the end of that car, so I'm gonna be sacrificin' it to get us out there."

"Sounds like a plan."

We were on the road within three hours, headed north toward Indianapolis and the westbound interstate. When we got to the western border between Indiana and Illinois, I did an exaggerated wave at the road sign that said something to the effect of "You are now leaving Indiana." It was a good-bye wave. Mac laughed and said that we were going to have a blast.

We pushed on through the rest of the day and into the night, but because the '79 oil crisis was unfolding right then, when the Monte

Carlo's tank got to empty, we had to pull over to the side of the road, someplace in the middle of Kansas, and crash out in the car. Every single service station was closed until morning; the guy working at the station where we'd last filled up had warned us that they would be, and this oil business was all anyone could talk about on the radio. It was just so much static and inconvenience as far as I was concerned.

We picked our way west, cutting down through the Rockies on two-lane highways and marveling at the mountain passes that felt like roller coasters as we drove through them. We went to the Grand Canyon because we both decided that missing it would be a crime.

We crossed out of Arizona and into California at the tail end of the night. I looked out the window at the WELCOME TO CALIFORNIA sign as Mac slept. I'd dreamed that Joe Weider would be waiting there to welcome me when I finally made it out; there was nothing but a bunch of desert and darkness. In spite of that, I waved hello to the sign.

August 1995
Seattle

I sound bitter when I talk about Joe Weider. I should temper that perception.

I will always be grateful to Joe for helping me become a success in the profession. His magazines made me into a star. I'm not a mainstream household name, but he helped make me a star in my world, and it wasn't too many years ago when that would have been plenty for me.

On a number of levels, I was a disappointment to Joe. One night in the late eighties—right after I'd decided to make my first comeback—on location in Tahiti, modeling for a *Muscle and Fitness* swimsuit layout, the magazine's art director, Jim Chada, told me that Joe had been deeply disappointed that I hadn't lived up to my potential in bodybuilding. Jim said that he could still remember the day, years earlier, when Joe got the first studio physique photos of me and had shown them to everyone in the office, claiming that I was going to be his next superstar. I told Jim that I figured Joe's disappointment with me began when, shortly after, he found out I was gay. I also told him that it wasn't only the fact that I was gay, but that I refused, even while I didn't talk about being gay in the media, to let Joe blatantly portray me as straight in his magazines, and we had fights about it constantly. Jim said that he didn't know about that, but what he did know was that Joe wasn't antigay.

Joe constantly told me this also—that he wasn't antigay. He always said that he had lots of gay people working at his magazines, and that he had no problem with that. I always reminded him of the big difference between having openly gay people working behind the scenes and having an openly gay Mr. Universe being one of the public faces of the sport, and that our personal history proved over and over again that he wished I wouldn't be open about who I really was.

Beyond my having turned out to be gay, Joe was disappointed in what he regarded as my stubbornness and my resistance to listening to his advice. I am stubborn. It's the only way I've survived. As to not listening to his advice, well, certainly at times listening and taking advice were not my strongest traits, but I'm always cautious whenever I hear someone infamous for not listening, or not taking advice, talk about the flaw of someone else's not being able to do the same things.

He also always told me that I needed to get in better shape—meaning that I should set aside my personal vision of how my physique looked best and turn myself freakier—and never seemed to understand when I explained to him the dilemma I was having over the drugs, or that I thought my body was far more commercial in the kind of condition I would get in than if I took it to a more extreme level.

In spite of all those things, though, I hope that I'm never too petty to admit that I will always be grateful and will always hold a place of love and respect in my heart for Joe.

I don't know Joe's brother Ben at all, beyond extremely quick interactions at contests, and the exchange of a few business letters. I don't know of any athlete in the sport who does really know him, or anything about him, beyond his public image. He is only a part of the scene either at contest time or in administering the sport. Other than that, he's always remained elusive from of everyone else in the sport, except the other administrators who work with him. However, these two brothers have spent years dedicated, for whatever reasons, to something that most of the people in their lives probably told them was stupid and weird. That dedication to building this sport into something legitimate—despite any objections I have with how they've done it—is something that I find admirable.

The world that Joe and Ben helped create was a beacon of hope to me, and definitely at one time that was more than enough.

July 1979
Southern California

The first thing I remember thinking was that the streets were so broad and clean. There didn't appear to be a cigarette butt or empty styrofoam cup anywhere in sight. It was beautiful.

Mac and I had pieced together our way toward Santa Monica, getting lost several times. The city had seemed to begin a hundred miles earlier, way out, away from the center of things, in what should have been raw desert. I wondered what the first people who'd seen it thought. When we filled up with gas, out in what ended up being outer suburbs, I paid a dollar a gallon for gas for the first time.

"Jeeezzus," I said to Mac, "things're expensive out here."

He agreed.

I had been talking the whole way about how we needed to go to Santa Monica and Venice as soon as we got in the area, so I could find Gold's Gym and maybe look up Arnold Schwarzenegger's address in the phone book and drive by his house. Mac didn't know who he was, so I explained. I also told him that maybe Arnold would meet me and want to take me under his wing, as a student or something. Mac looked at me as if I were an idiot.

We found our way to Wilshire Boulevard and got off there to ask for some directions to the beach. I pulled over and asked the first person I saw walking down the wide, clean sidewalk. He said, "Go fuck yourself, lousy tourists. Go back where you came from," and kept walking.

"Let's just keep goin' in this direction," Mac suggested.

Sure enough, after a couple of miles we both saw the ocean, as we descended over a shallow slope in the street.

"There it is," I yelled.

"Hell, yes, BP, we made it."

By the time we drove to where Wilshire Boulevard ended at Ocean Avenue, it was obvious that we were in the middle of some sort of paradise.

"Which way should I go?" I asked Mac.

"Try right. Right feels lucky."

He was smoking a celebration joint—that's what he called it—and had offered me some, but I'd already quit again, the day that we left Indiana. I had decided no more pot, no more cigs, no more booze—I was leaving to become a star and I didn't need vices to get in my way.

I turned right. A park ran along the left side of the road, with what looked like a religious statue, of some lady in a long robe.

"Says her name is Santa Monica," Mac said as he read the sign on the bottom of the white statue, looking beyond me through the window.

"Oh—imagine namin' your daughter after a city," I joked.

"Hey, BP, pull over, man. Park the car."

I did, and we got out and walked around the park. It skirted the edge of a high cliff; the park was fifty yards, or less, wide and looked miles long, filled with grass, sidewalks, benches, and palm trees. When we got to the edge and looked over the fence, there was the ocean, crashing against the beach below, just across another road. I let out a breath; it felt as if I'd been holding that chestful of air for years.

"We gotta get down there," Mac said, pointing at the beach.

"Let's go," I said, taking one more look around and noticing a mountain range in the distance that seemed to wrap its way around the bend in the beach and ended at a point several miles north. Out in the distance, miles offshore, was an island.

We finally found our way down to the beach after a polite gentleman, whom I cautiously ventured to ask, told us to take the Incline down and then gave us directions.

The first thing we both did was go running into the waves. We'd both been wearing nothing but cutoffs since the sun came up and beat through the car windows out in the desert, so we parked the car and ran straight into the ocean, diving through the foam and spray, coming up shaking—teeth rattling. The waves were enormous, and rough.

"Well, it's not at all pacific," I yelled over the crashing sounds as the water tried to pull us out farther, and the sand swooshed past my legs and through my toes in raging rivers. "But it sure puts the Atlantic to shame."

"What?" Mac yelled.

"Nothin'. I was just sayin' how great it feels to be here."

"Fuckin' A, BP."

We got a room at one of the little courtyard motels, a couple of miles inland from the beach, on Wilshire Boulevard.

The first thing I did, once we had our room, was check the phone book for Arnold Schwarzenegger's number. No luck. I called information, and the operator said that it was unlisted. I told her that was fine, but asked if she could, by any chance, give me the address. No, she most certainly could not. Drats.

The next thing I did was drive back down toward the beach to try to find Gold's Gym. I had written the address in my training journal. I had called the gym one night, from Florida, after I got the number from Santa Monica information, and I asked the guy who answered the phone for the address and he gave it to me.

The gym was on Second Street. I drove around the block twice before I finally figured out that I could park in one of the city garages across the street. When I walked up to the gym, the large picture windows facing out on the street were mostly covered in steam. I could hear the clanging and sounds of human exertion from out on the sidewalk. Two guys went past me as I stood outside trying to work up the courage to go in. When I looked up, it startled me—it was Tom Platz and Roger Callard, two of the most famous guys from the magazines. A woman in a bikini flew by on roller skates and knocked me into the door. I caught myself just in time, but in tripping, went through the door and nearly made my grand entrance facedown on the floor. The place was packed. Bodies were everywhere.

Oh, my God, that's Mike Mentzer, I thought as I spotted one of the latest Mr. Universes head into what appeared to be the locker room.

Nearly every current muscle star seemed to be training right there, right at that moment. It looked like a *Muscle Builder* magazine convention.

I bought a two-week membership, and the whole time I was signing the release form and paying my money, the owner, Pete Grymkowski, was standing a few feet down the counter, going through some files. I thought about saying hi, from T.J., but decided not to. What if he thought that T.J. was as big of a dickhead as I did? Or, given T.J.'s hot air on nearly every other subject, what if he didn't know Pete at all? I kept my mouth shut and paid my money.

The workouts I had there were not the best of my life. I'm sure eventually they might have been, but for the two weeks I trained there I was much too intimidated by all the famous musclemen I saw each day to concentrate fully.

There was also the matter of money. As in, how were Mac and I going to make some? We were already getting down there in the cash department.

Mac had an uncle in Orange County somewhere. This area fifty miles down the freeway, the manager of our motel told us, was thick with Republicans and born-agains. She said that she avoided going there at all costs. She also sipped gin out of a bottle in a paper bag all day long, so in general Mac and I didn't know what to make of her opinion.

We went to visit his uncle, getting badly lost and winding up in Pasadena somehow, before we stopped and bought a map.

Mac's uncle told us that any number of the factories in the area were always hiring. He also said that getting a week-to-week motel was going to be a lot cheaper around that area than up in Santa Monica, which he thought was infested with too many liberals and those sorts. Orange County, he offered, was a vastly superior spot.

Since our two weeks of rent had run out at the motel on Wilshire Boulevard, and I'd used up my two-week pass at Gold's Gym, and we were going to have to get jobs soon anyway, we decided—with a good deal of hesitation on my part, until Mac convinced me that it was probably only temporary—that we would relocate to Orange County.

We called around to motels in the area that advertised weekly rentals. Since this area was popular with transient types—such as us—there were plenty. The cheapest one was out by the Buena Park Airport, which we soon discovered gave those living across the street from it all the restful quiet of a life lived inside an electric blender.

To say that it was a dive would be a compliment. The old man working the desk looked us up and down and said that he was giving us his best room.

"Two weeks rent—in advance," he went on to say, wiping chicken gravy off his chin with the back of his hand.

"Oh, I thought this was a week-to-week place," I said.

"It is, but ya gotta pay two weeks in advance. Kentucky?"

"Sorry?"

"You all sound like probably Kentucky. I got people in Covington."

"Southern Indiana, actually," I said, "not too far off."

"Well—welcome to Californ-i-a, boy. No hookers—ya hear me? This ain't that kinda place." He pointed a greasy finger at me. Mac had wandered outside to look around.

"Oh, yes, sir, most decidedly yes."

"Unless you're gonna share 'em with me," he added with a phlegmy laugh. A small piece of saliva-covered biscuit flew out of his mouth and landed on our registration card.

Mac and I got settled into our room and immediately began to dissect the help-wanted ads in the paper. We went around together, applying for jobs at every sort of factory in the area. After three days of applying, we both got hired at Moore Business Forms, a factory that printed computer spreadsheets and various other—well—business forms.

It was shit work. Backbreaking. Printer's apprentices, they called us. *Pack mules* would have been more appropriate. We unloaded stacks of papers as they'd come through the press; hauled huge bundles; cleaned the inside of print rollers—all the sorts of things that most people using the final products would never want to hear about. It was good pay, not great.

We went back to our rat-infested hole each night after work, exhausted and covered in ink that wouldn't come off. My hands looked as if I had been sorting through buckets of black ink for twenty years. The injury to my lower back would begin to heal, then I'd be moving, barely keeping up with the press, stacking product, and—wham—it was right back where it started.

We did this routine for what seemed like years. It would take five, literal, years to move up to the next level. When a pressman who had been at the company fifteen years told Mac one day how much he made, I got even more discouraged. This was not what I wanted to do with my life. I could have stayed in Indiana for this. And for all I got to experience of the paradise of California—the beaches, the mountains, and all that—I might as well have never come West.

The greatest discouragement of all was that I was a million miles away from the entire reason I'd come in the first place—the bodybuilding scene. I'd almost completely stopped working out. After a full day of work, I didn't have the energy. Besides, the only gym in the area I'd found was a racquetball club with a sorry excuse for a weight room. I trained there two or three times, but they only sold year memberships, and it was twenty bucks for a daily pass.

11

I DECIDE TO STAY

August 1995
Seattle

On Monday, I went into the basement closet and pulled out a huge box that for years I'd kept all my old training journals stored away in. I'd started to keep a new journal in May and wanted to be able to read the old ones whenever I wanted, without having to rummage through a closet. So, I pulled them out and organized them by date on some bookshelves in the gym. I also went out into the garage—we hadn't gotten around yet to unpacking the dozen moving boxes that were still lining one wall—and took out all the trophy nameplates. While I was at it, I began going through the magazines and, two hours later, began to realize that I'd been a fool trying to turn my back on the past, stuffing it away in boxes.

In a strange way, this was every bit as bad as if I had plastered pictures and articles—and all the other inflating-ego mementos I had accumulated—on every wall of my home. Anytime I walked into another professional bodybuilder's home and saw that he had turned his place into a temple for himself, I wanted to puke. But I had done nearly the same thing, only in the reverse direction. Instead of constantly reminding myself of my accomplishments by turning my home into a shrine to the self, I had opted for pretending that that life had never taken place by packing it away in dusty boxes.

Tuesday afternoon I took the nameplates to a trophy shop and picked out a wonderful mahogany plaque to have them mounted on. The guy taking my order asked me why I had kept only the nameplates, and I told him that most of the trophies had been so cheap that they fell apart over the years (that was only partly accurate). He said he didn't make cheap trophies.

He finished the plaque in a week and did a beautiful job.

I hung it in the gym, beside the fireplace, where I could see it every day during my workouts. I also pulled my Mr. Universe trophy out of the hall closet, tightened the bolt that held it all together, dusted and polished it, and put it next to the plaque on the fireplace mantel. I took all the pens and pencils out of the silver-plated champagne bucket that was the Mr. Southern California trophy, which had been sitting neglected on my desk for years, polished it, and put it on the mantel too. The punch-bowl trophy for the California Muscle Classic, which I'd filled with agate stones and set in the garden, well, I left that one where it was because it seemed to be doing fine—and it was beginning to look the way I'd hoped it would.

July 1979
Southern California

Doggone, what part of Texas are you from, son?" the guy the other man had called Ron asked, in a fake, stretched-out drawl, not looking me in the eye, but focusing on something behind me.

Where do these people get their manners? I wondered.

I had simply walked in the door to ask how much it cost to work out. While driving through this Anaheim neighborhood a few days before, I had seen a neon sign for the Body Shop at the road edge, in front of a newly constructed strip shopping center. I could see that one of the stores was filled with gym equipment.

On Friday evening, after I'd finished work and was driving by, I saw lights on through the plateglass windows. Walking up toward the door, I could see several people milling around inside. Some of them were pulling on pulleys, picking up dumbbells, or running their hands over the orange-gold paint on the machines—things as silly as kicking the tires on a new car because they didn't know what else to do, but knew that they should do something. Gyms tended to bring out the purest insecurities in those who didn't know their way around inside one—especially in men, who tried not to look desperately lost. I walked through the door, into the breeze of air-conditioning; they were putting the last touches on the interior of the gym.

The first person I encountered was a balding, sandy-haired man, no more than four and a half feet tall and nearly as wide, but mostly solid, like a large human ostrich egg. He introduced himself like someone who expects you to recognize the name. When I didn't, he told me that he was a world-champion Olympic weight lifter, but I didn't follow that sport, so I had no idea who he was. The most I knew about Olympic lifting was what most people knew. Everything was filtered through that

fat Russian, Alexiev or something like that, who, after great shouting
and throwing of chalky dust in all directions, could heave upward of five
hundred pounds over his head. He did this on TV. I'd never met anyone
who would actually do that as a pastime, serious or otherwise. So, I'd
taken this guy at the door, on first sight—since he was hanging out at
a gym—as a wrestler. When it became apparent that I didn't have a clue
who he was or how important his presence at this gym was, he directed
me to a guy, Ron, standing next to the L-shaped front counter. Ron was
a blond bodybuilder who had that young-Republican, blow-dried, tele-
vangelist look I'd already learned was pretty common in Orange County.

"Ron, will you please help answer any questions this young man has."

I could tell by the way he spoke to the guy by the counter that the
short man was the boss, the blond, an employee.

The minute I opened my mouth and asked Ron my question, he'd
shot back a question of his own, and I wasn't in the mood to be made
fun of. I just wanted to know how much the workouts would cost.

"I'm not from Texas, I'm from Indiana. How much is the daily rate?"

"Indiana, huh. Same diff I guess. You sure talk strange," he replied,
switching back into his own dialect—nerdy, mock-surfer. He was also
bouncing his chest muscles. I glanced over my shoulder and saw floor-
to-ceiling mirrors across the room. He was clearly watching himself
perform in them. We caught eyes in the mirror; I gave an embarrassed
eyebrow shrug and quickly turned my head back toward him.

"There's a big difference," I said, feeling emboldened to correct his
geography, having caught him making a fool of himself in the mirror at
the same time he was making fun of the way I talked.

Blank eyes; no comprehension that he should maybe be a little self-
conscious.

"So, what's your name, Tex?"

"First off, it's not Tex. Second off, it's Bobby—Bobby Paris." I was
beginning to kind of like this guy in spite of the fact that I knew he
thought I was a dumb hick. I was getting used to being seen that way
by almost everyone I'd met since arriving in California four weeks before.

"Well, not Tex, Bobby Harris—"

"Paris, actually—like in France."

I had hated my last name since childhood, but I still couldn't stand
for people to get it wrong.

"Oh—well, anyway, Bobby like in France, my name's Ron." He put
his hand out to shake, and after I took it, he clunked us, like a square
wheel, through the whitest soul-brother shake imaginable. "Daily rate's
five dollars. Hours are eight in the morning till ten at night, Monday
through Saturday. Ten to two on the Lord's day."

Suddenly, he turned toward the back of the gym and yelled to another well-built man who didn't look so much like a bodybuilder as he
did a field athlete—like a discus thrower; similar to the stocky build of
the first man I had met, but much taller and smaller-waisted. "Hey, Jack,
come over and meet, uh . . ."

"Bobby," I reminded him.

"Yeah, that's right, Bobby. Jack meet Bobby; Bobby, Jack," Ron said
as if memorizing my name by repeating it a few times. The other guy
squatted down to set on the floor the framed poster he had been hanging. It was the same poster of Frank Zane I'd bought and had auto-
graphed a few months earlier. I had mine rolled up in a mailing tube
back in my motel room.

Jack stood up with a jump and walked over bouncing, as if he were
stepping across a trampoline, his heels never touching the ground; his
right arm and hand were outstretched to greet me.

"How's it goin', bud?" he said, also in surf-cat, as we shook hands.
Despite my trying to do a regular handshake, he only took my fingertips
between his thumb and fingertips and barely squeezed them—a bit like
shaking fingertips with a dead octopus.

When in Rome, I thought.

I answered him, "Pretty good. I'm tryin' to find a place to work out.
Not many gyms in this county—least as far as I've found."

A puzzled look crossed Jack's face. He asked, "Man, where the fuck
are you from?"

"Shh . . . darn-it, Jack," Ron said quietly. "Randall is still here and you
know what he told us about language."

"Ah, fuck him," Jack said much quieter, but looking over toward the
short man I'd encountered when I first came in, who was now talking
animatedly with an older, beer-bellied man who, judging by the enrap-
tured look on his face, must have recognized Randall for the celebrity
he obviously was.

"Damn, dude," Jack asked again, "where the fuck did you say you're
from?"

"See, I told you, uh . . . Bobby," Ron said, laughing a little and speaking louder again. He looked from me to Jack. "Texas, right?"

"Totally bitchin', man," was all Jack could say.

They both stood there as if expecting me to entertain them with
some sort of hillbilly dance.

"So, what's with the handshake?" I asked Jack, breaking the quiet and
interrupting Ron, who had started bongo-bouncing his chest muscles
and was beginning to sneak looks at himself in the mirror again.

"You for real, dude? Lifter's shake, man. Gotta keep the hands from getting crushed. I'm nothin' without my hands. It's what the Russians do—Romanians and Cubans too," Jack explained.

"Jack does whatever the Soviet-bloc guys do," Ron added, twitching his right pec one last time before stopping.

"What are you, a commie?" I asked, teasing.

"No way, dude. Russians and Cubans are just the best lifters, that's all. I'm stoked to go to Moscow for the Games next year," Jack said.

"Jack's an alternate for the U.S. team," Ron cut in.

"Well, I certainly know by that handshake that you're not a wrestler [saying it *rasseler*, just to amuse myself]. So I guess that you're probably, um—an Olympic lifter, right?" I asked, already knowing the answer, since he'd been refering to himself as a lifter, but now enjoying myself.

Jack started beaming. "That's right, dude."

"What's with the *dude* there, Jack—y'all runnin' some kind of a ranch here or somethin'?" I couldn't resist.

"Huh?" Jack asked, looking at me as if I'd inquired about the shape of the galaxy. "What do you mean, dude?"

"That. You know—*dude*—dude ranch. It was a joke. Get it?" I looked at them smiling; got blank looks back. "Never mind. So, how's this equipment?"

"Ah, whoa, this shit is bitchin', dude. You oughta feel how the pulleys work, man," Jack said, looking over at Ron for agreement.

"So, Bobby, you compete back where you came from?" Ron asked.

"Yeah, I did the Teenage Florida a couple of months ago."

"So how'd you do, dude?" Jack asked.

I thought about this one for a bit. It would be so easy to lie and say that I'd won. Who would ever know? My pride got very sticky on these points, but after a couple of beats I drew in a breath and decided to tell the truth. "I took second."

"Cool," Jack said.

"So what's next?" Ron asked. "Teen America?"

"Thinkin' about it. Don't know if I have time to get ready though. Since I moved, training's been a little fucked up. Oop, sorry, Ron, I'll watch my language."

"Where do you live, dude?" Jack asked, looking over at Randall, the man who had greeted me at the door when I first came in to check out the gym. Randall seemed to be signaling to these guys that it was time to get back to work.

"Uh, sorry, guys, " I said. "Seems the boss is gettin' nervous. I should probably book on out of here."

"Naw, man, you're not hanging us up. I get off in a couple of minutes.

Grab a bite? Bitchin' deli three doors down. They'll make you whatever you want. They got all that shit you muscleheads like to eat." Jack looked at Ron, who was shaking his head yes. "So, where you crashin'?"

"The friend I came out here with, we got a week-to-week rental over in Buena Park. Rough place, but, hey, a guy's gotta live somewhere, right?"

"Hell, yeah, dude. Hang out a couple of minutes. Then we can jam."

Jack went back and finished his job; Ron went to help out an overweight man who wanted to know if the place was going to have a whirlpool. I played around with some of the machines until Jack came over and said that he could leave.

As we were leaving, Randall came over, shook my hand, and said, "Come back and see us sometime. Have a workout. My bet is that the Body Shop is the right gym for you."

Sounded like a line he gave everyone on the way out.

When we got outside, the hot, dry summer breeze hit my face and made my eyes feel watery after being inside the air-conditioning for half an hour.

"So, Bobby dude, what brought you to sunny Californ-i-a?" Jack asked as we walked down to Zuckermann's Deli.

"Uh, sorry, Jack. What'd you ask?"

"Whoa, dude—you a stoner? Kinda blanked out there. I asked, what brought you out to sunny Californ-i-a?"

"Sorry. I'm toasted from work—and I was kinda thinkin' about home, you know."

"Well?"

"Bodybuilding."

"Why aren't you in Santa Monica, buffin' at Gold's? Scene's up there, dude."

He held open the door and once again I got blasted by the air-conditioning as I walked through and up to the counter.

"Yeah, I, uh . . . you gonna eat, Jack?"

"Hell, yeah, kimosabe. Hey, Goldie," he said to the middle-aged woman behind the counter, who stood wiping her hands on her white apron.

"The usual, Jackie honey?" she asked.

"Yeah, beautiful," he replied, flirting a bit.

"What will you have, son?" she asked me.

"Let's see . . . I'll have, um, a turkey breast on wheat, hold the mayo, lots of mustard. You have baked potatoes?"

"Yes—like one?"

"Yes, ma'am. Dry please."

"Dear boy, none of my food is dry. My potatoes are as moist as can be."

"Sorry, I meant no butter."

"Oy, another muscleman—right?"

Jack laughed. I blushed.

We sat at a table by the front windows, where I could see the cars passing by in a darkness held off halfhearted by all the streetlights. Cars had a certain look driving down a street in California. A dryness in the air, or a greater obsession with keeping automobiles spotless—maybe because they acted so much as a currency of status here—made them all seem brighter colored, shinier, making me think that all the cars in Indiana must have been dull brown and dirty.

"So?" Jack said as I stared out the window.

"I came out here to bodybuild, and things got a little complicated."

"How?"

"Oh—sorta like, I should be in Santa Monica trainin' at Gold's. When I first got out here, I got a motel room up there and kept it for two weeks, but neither one of us knew anybody and we started to run out of money so, well, Mac had an uncle here in Orange County. He kinda helped us get steered in the right direction, gettin' jobs, that kinda thing."

"Where you working, dude?"

I told him about my ball-busting job at the factory, showed him the ink that wouldn't come off my hands, and told him how at the end of the day it was all I could do to drive back to my room and fall in bed.

"Not what I envisioned when I set out for this place," I concluded.

Goldie brought the food out to our table, said, "Enjoy," and walked away.

"So, bud, what is it you want to do then?" he asked, taking a huge bite out of a fragrant Reuben and talking through the bite.

I shrugged. "I just thought about gettin' out here, startin' to compete. There was this guy, T.J., that trained at the same gym I did in Florida. He said that when I got out here, I should say hello from him to the guy that owns Gold's. I guess he knew him. He told me that maybe, if I ever got out to L.A., that this guy might be able to help get me on the right track. But when I got to the gym, well, there were all the stars I'd been readin' about in the magazines, and I never got up the nerve to go up to the guy. What was I supposed to say—'Hi, my name is Bobby Paris, and you may not know it now, but I'm gonna be somebody in this sport—can you help me out?' So here I am."

He swallowed a big bite. "Who's this guy you came out here with? He compete too?"

"Nah, Mac and I went to school together. He came for the adventure. I get the feelin' he might go back."

"So how is everything, my sons?" Goldie came back over to our table and stood again wiping her hands on her apron. "You," she said, looking at me, "you haven't touched your food yet. It's not good enough or something?"

"No, ma'am. I started yakkin' and kinda forgot. Looks great." I took a big bite of the sandwich and grinned up at her with my mouth closed, but then said, "Mmm, delicious."

"Don't talk with your mouth full. Your mother never taught you any manners?" And then she smiled and walked away again.

"So, how 'bout you?" I asked Jack.

"Me? I'm just a dude who wants to go to the Games next year. Not much else to tell."

"How'd you get started with Olympic lifting?"

"I picked it up in the gym at MIT, first year there."

"You went to MIT?"

"Surprised, dude? Most people are. Track scholarship—I pitched a discus way out there. They liked that. Got my engineering degree there. Graduated with honors, that kind of shit. Want me to build you a bridge?"

So much for first impressions. I figured the guy couldn't find his way out of an exit door. But I guess it was natural that I'd jump to the easy conclusion that he was dumb. Everybody did it to me too; people assumed if you were doing anything that involved lifting weights, you had to have a brain the size of a pea.

"Sorry."

"That's cool, dude. Eat up before Goldie comes back and feeds your skinny ass. Gonna train at our gym?"

"Think so. I need to find a different job, though. I ain't exactly on my dream career path."

"Let me think about that one—see if I can help you out."

"Do you mind if I ask you why you're workin' at a gym? No offense, but you got an engineering degree and all."

"I hate engineering. Five years I was at that school, dude, and you know the biggest use I've gotten out of it all was figuring out the mechanics of the clean and jerk."

"Excuse me?" I laughed. "Generally, where I come from, people jerk first and then clean up."

"Oh, dude, you are way off. Clean and jerk is one of the lifts. Snatch is the other one."

"Um, who named these things, the guy who owns *Penthouse?*"

"Shiiiitt, dude, that's old and cold."

We paid for our food, said good-bye to Goldie, and left. Jack had to get home to his girlfriend. I got in my car and drove back to the motel. On the way back, I decided to quit my job within two weeks; it was time to get on track for what I'd come West for in the first place, even if I had to give up a good paycheck to do it.

I began to train again—at the Body Shop—finding the silent purpose as my hands would wrap around the cold iron bars, and the blood rushed in monsoons to wherever I directed it.

I went in after work, and although I was already worn out, I pushed through the workouts. It wasn't Gold's Gym or exactly what I had dreamed about before I left home, but it was well equipped and the best gym around that area.

Fifty miles away was the center of the galaxy for bodybuilding, but no strong gym culture had yet sprung up in the far suburbs of L.A. After I trained, Jack introduced me to a couple of other bodybuilders who were training at the same time. All these guys could talk and think about was the mecca that thrived up the freeway; they seemed to consider it with the same awe I had when I'd dreamed about it from twenty-five hundred miles away. I wondered why they didn't simply get in their cars and drive up there. They probably wondered the same thing about me.

I gave notice at the factory without knowing what I would do to put food in my mouth. A week later Mac did the same. We needed work.

One of the guys we worked with said that if you stood outside the gate of the Kraft Foods plant first thing in the morning (meaning 5:15 A.M.), you could get the truckers coming in—in tractor-semitrailer rigs, to drop off a shipment—to hire you to unload their massive trailers.

We went out one morning. Mac got picked up first. As I was standing at the gate waiting to get hired, I saw three men across the road staring and gesturing angrily in my direction; they seemed to be talking about me. I approached the next trucker who came in and got the job.

The guy who told us about this said that it took about three hours to unload the pallets of product, using a hand trolley. After six hours, moving at a heart-attack pace, I couldn't even see the back of the trailer. Four hours later I finished. The driver paid me fifty bucks. Mac had finished fifteen minutes earlier. We were both dead. On the way back to the motel, I noticed a car following closely. I made a few turns and it stayed right on my tail. When we pulled into the parking lot, the car came with us. Four guys hopped out and blocked our doors.

"That territory is Fernando's, motherfuckers," one of the guys on my side yelled in my face. "Come around again, and you won't like what you find."

He had pulled out a pistol and had it lying, pointed in my direction, across the top of my half-rolled-down window. They all turned around, got back in their car, and peeled away.

"Guess they don't want us workin' there," I finally said to Mac after we'd sat there silently for a couple of minutes.

"Fuuucck."

"You can say that again."

"Fuuucck."

"They can have it."

Cash became a serious issue.

I was going into the gym each day to train; it was my only escape. Mac and I had both started looking for new jobs, but nothing was happening in that department.

The manager of the motel had turned out to be a major pain in the ass. When we'd first moved in, paying two weeks in advance for a week-to-week rental had seemed strange, but we'd done it. When we went in to pay our rent after we'd been there a few weeks, he said that there was now a new policy—handed down from the owners, he claimed—that you not only had to pay two weeks at a time, but also had to pay that two weeks' rent three days before the last rent was up.

This was a real head-scratcher, but Mac and I were trapped. We hadn't been able to put together enough money to get a real apartment; and everyplace else similar to this motel was much more expensive. Suddenly, we didn't have the money to pay another two weeks. Our new three-day payment time had arrived, and the manager began calling our room every hour, for two and a half days, to find out where our money was. Finally we went down to the office and tried to explain the situation, and the manager said that he was real sorry, but that rules were rules, and oh, by the way, did we realize that we had signed an agreement saying that if we rented week to week, for more than one week, we had to give one week's notice before moving out or we were liable for another rent period, plus damages.

He went into a file and pulled out our registration card—there was still a greasy stain where he'd spit biscuit on it while we were checking in—turned it over, and there on the back, in microscopic letters, was a sentence confirming what he'd just told us. I had never even looked at the back of the card when we checked in. It had appeared to be a normal motel registration card.

Mac and I could only look at each other.

"We'll figure it out," I said to the manager, and we left the office.

When we got back to the room, we were both stumped. Mac started talking about going home. I said that I wouldn't go. A couple of weeks earlier he had bought a used car from a dealership across the street from the motel, so he didn't need me to get back.

"I got an idea," he said, then suddenly jumped up from the couch, went to the phone, and dialed a number. At the end of the conversation, he'd come up with our reprieve. One of the guys whom he had gotten close to at work—he partied with this guy, since I had given all that up—had a trailer in some place called Big Bear, up in the mountains. He told Mac that we could use it for a while and gave him directions and said where a key was hidden. The guy said that he was planning on coming up that weekend anyway and would see us there.

"Now we just have to get out of here without getting arrested," Mac said.

"Tell ya what," I said. "I'll go out to your car and act like I'm goin' to the store or somethin'. Then I'll park it out of sight and we can take all our stuff down the back stairs."

"It's a plan. What'll we do with your car? It'll never make it up in the mountains."

"We can park it over at the gym."

In the small hours of the night we shuttled all our things down the back stairs and into Mac's car. Then he got in his and I walked back through the building to mine—perfectly innocent, I wasn't carrying any luggage or anything that looked as if I were running—and we drove to the Body Shop, parked my car, shifted all my belongings into its trunk, and followed Mac's pal's directions out of Orange County and into the mountains, up to Big Bear.

Beautiful place; forested paradise; the sort of spot that I had come to California to see. Tom, the guy who owned the trailer, came up on Friday night. We had a good time hiking around, exploring; it was the most fun I'd had in months. On Saturday a strange-looking kitten crawled out from under the trailer, and after much discussion, we decided that it was a baby bobcat. We named him Bob-the-Cat; Mac said that he would raise it.

By Sunday I decided that I had to go back down into the city. I wouldn't have minded staying for a while, but all day Friday I had searched the area for a gym and only came up with a small weight room in the high school; the school secretary I spoke with didn't know whether or not I could use it. Paradise or not, I needed a gym.

On Sunday evening I rode back down with Tom. He dropped me off at my car and asked me if I was going to be okay. I said I would—no worries. I didn't tell him that I was afraid the motel had filed a complaint with the local police because we'd violated some stupid rule of theirs. I feared that every cop in the area might be keeping an eye out for me.

For three nights I slept in the front seat of my car, behind the gym, without getting caught. I had neatly folded all my clothes in the backseat, and all the rest of my stuff was jammed in the trunk. I grew more despondent and hopeless with each passing day.

I knew Mac. It was only a matter of days before he would head back to Indiana. I would have bet my last dollar on it. Maybe I needed to go back too. But I couldn't; I had nothing to go back to, except a bunch of people I'd grown up with, trying to justify their own choices in life by taunting me with told-ya-so's.

On the fourth night, at around four in the morning, an Anaheim cop shined his flashlight in my car window and rousted me from my sleep, and car, for a grilling. When my license plates and driver's license were from different states, I had to invent a blend of truth and lies—about a great-uncle in Big Bear (since I'd just come from there, it popped into my sleep-filled mind), a college buddy at the Body Shop, and so on. Anything to keep him from calling my name in on a warrant search.

After I managed to talk my way out of that one, I parked my car in a more secluded place. Right before I fell asleep, I thought that my only two choices were either to crawl back to where I'd grown up, as a failure, or find a nice tall building to leap off of.

When I woke up—the sunlight blasting in my eyes—things could not have been darker.

"What the fuck am I gonna do?" I said quietly.

The car's engine turned over, reluctantly. It had been throwing black smoke out of the tailpipe; the battery seemed on the edge of disaster. If I decided to flee California, it most likely wouldn't get me to Kansas.

I drove back to the gym, parked next to the concrete-block wall that surrounded the parking lot, and went into Zuckermann's Deli to get some coffee and maybe a bite of breakfast.

"How are you?" Goldie Zuckermann asked as I came through the door.

"Swell."

"Well, you don't look so good. Ever hear of a comb? And most people put on shoes before they come into a restaurant."

"Sorry, Goldie. I forgot—kind of a rough night. Can I get a large coffee to go?"

"You think I haven't seen you in your car late at night? You should be getting a place to live, young man."

"Yeah, well, I might not be around much longer."

"Oh."

I went back out to the car. The sun was already making everything boil. I drank the coffee, got some training clothes from the backseat, and went into the gym.

Might as well make this a good one, I thought. I was beginning to figure that I would need to give up on this crazy notion of becoming a great bodybuilder; everything seemed to conspire against it.

I threw myself into a workout and kept pushing. Set after set; the only way I could keep from crying.

I took a shower and couldn't make the water hot enough. I stayed under it for forty-five minutes. Ron was working the early shift and poked his head in the shower room to ask if everything was all right. When I said that it was, he told me to save some hot water for other people, laughed, then left.

The rest of the day, I sat in my car with the local paper in my lap turned to the help-wanted classifieds, but couldn't bring myself to read them. Hours passed; I wasn't wearing anything except shorts and a T-shirt, but the sweat poured off me. The wall that I was parked next to, with its cascading bougainvillea—a flowering vine so beautiful that it could sometimes camouflage the toughest surroundings—didn't make much shade.

Finally, after sitting there all day, I said to myself, "Fuck it. I quit. I can't take this anymore." I then started the engine—which didn't want to do anything except grind, but finally came to life—and headed for the freeway. Mac had the map that we'd bought in his car. I began to cry after I got on the wrong freeway, going in the wrong direction, for the third time.

Two hours later, I was parked in front of Palisades Park, in Santa Monica, getting myself ready to leave for Indiana.

I Decide to Stay

*   *   *

The Santa Monica Mountains curved out past Malibu and faded into the charcoal sky, blending until I couldn't see the difference anymore. A sharp line had remained between the air and the jagged edges for almost an hour as I stood there in Palisades Park, high above the ocean.

Watching those flinty edges, where the top of the range touched the sky, had taken me all the way back to a small tobacco field, bordered by Highway 46 on one side and Salt Creek on the other. Pap-pa Clark and I were clomping through the field back to his Chevy pickup, after he'd spent several hours showing me how to cast my fishing line—just right—to get my lure under a fallen tree, sticking up out of a deep pool in the creek. He guaranteed me that if I could get my line into that one special spot, I'd land a big one. At the end of the day, as we were crossing the field we'd parked beside, he found an old arrowhead crusted in dirt and gave it to me to keep. I imagined—from looking at its jagged edges—that arrowhead was a bunch of mountains. That day in the field, Pap-pa had called me a dreamer. I knew, deep in my seven-year-old heart, that even if he didn't mean it that way, it was a compliment.

I stood all those years later, an entire continent away from the farms and hills where I was brought up, and knew, on that night, high above the sounds of Magellan's violently peaceful sea, that I had truly found my destiny. Barefoot and in serious need of a haircut, I was right where I needed to be. I had almost turned my back on it and reluctantly returned to where I'd come from, to live a life that would have been small and desperate compared to where I thought I would go if I kept following this dream.

I was down to my last few dollars and didn't have anywhere to live except the front seat of my car—a vehicle hopelessly clutching to its deathbed—and I had no idea what the next day was going to bring, but the adventure had truly begun and there was no turning back. I headed toward my car, praying to God—who I thought had only taken mediocre care of me up to that point in my life—that the engine would turn over. It did. Reluctantly.

I waited at a traffic light to turn off Ocean Avenue and try to find my way back to the freeway. Through the passenger window I saw the statue of Saint Monica, standing at the edge of the park, the cliff and ocean behind her, and a floodlight shining up on her marble body. Just for the hell of it I waved at her. It was a hello, not a good-bye wave. I slowly made my way through the unfamiliar streets and got on the freeway to head on back down to Orange County, knowing that even though I didn't have a place to live and that I would've rather stayed in Santa Monica, I'd already begun to set up my life down there in a way that would help me find my path into the future.

"One step at a time, Bobby-boy. You'll be livin' here before you know it," I said as I merged from the freeway ramp into the shining cars that seemed to absorb me into their fold. All I could think about was finding a place near the gym where I could park my car, avoid being rousted by the cops, and get a good night's sleep.

Come morning, I had a killer workout to do.

12

GRASSHOPPER · TURNS
SOME CORNERS

Autumn, 1979
Southern California
___

So who's grasshopper, over there?" I heard him ask Mark, who also worked at the Body Shop. "He ever talk, or does he just space-cadet his days away?" His tone was smart-ass, but not in a bad way.

I was starting to come back from the deep meditative state I'd been in, lying on the floor of the gym near the Olympic lifters' platform, when I heard him ask this question. I thought, *Grasshopper?*—then realized that he was referring to the young monk's nickname on the TV show *Kung Fu*.

I opened my eyes, and it was Rory Leidelmeyer who'd asked the question. He'd been coming into the gym to train a couple of days a week ever since right before I started working there. We hadn't yet spoken because I was intimidated by how huge and outspoken he was. So I went about my quiet business whenever he was there.

The first time I saw Rory in the gym, he was getting ready for the Mr. California the next spring. He was wearing a thermal underwear shirt with the neck cut out, so that the top half of his thick chest and all of his neck and trapezius muscles were showing. His arms pushed the fabric of the long-sleeve shirt until it appeared that the material would fly apart at any second. He had on tight sweatpants that were rolled up to his knees, and knee-high, white socks that let his calves bulge through, as his shirtsleeves did to his arms, and wore a leather lifting belt, cinched tight to make his waist look small. The guy who always came in to train with him was dressed exactly like this also; he appeared to be a smaller carbon copy of Rory. He wore his hair the same and did everything exactly as Rory did it. When Rory had finished his workout that first day I saw him, he began a few poses, with his clothes on, in one of the mirrors at the back of the gym. He was telling his training partner how this time next year, he'd be Mr. Universe. His training partner agreed enthusiastically and told him how great he was. I found this all extremely intimidating, and I told Mark, who'd just been hired to work days, that I didn't think I could ever be that big.

I got a job at the Body Shop almost two weeks to the day after the Anaheim cop had caught me sleeping in my car behind the gym. When I got back to Orange County—after watching the sun set in Santa Monica and deciding to stick it out—I parked my car in a dark alley, got a pretty good night's sleep, woke up the next day, had one of the best workouts of my life, and understood that I'd made the right decision the night before.

I'd become pretty good friends with Jack—the surf-talking Olympic-team alternate with the engineering degree from MIT—since I'd started training at the Body Shop, and the day after I decided not go back to Indiana with my tail between my legs, he took me over to a nightclub where he'd worked as a bartender and introduced me to the manager. Jack knew this guy not only from working at the club, but also from track-and-field circles. The manager had been a world-class shot-putter whose athletic career had been cut short by an injury.

I went there with Jack to interview for a job and knew that I was going to have to lie about my age and say I was twenty-one, when in fact I was still nineteen, because the drinking age in California was twenty-one and you needed to be that old if you worked in a bar. I got a job checking IDs at the door and started the next night. It was only a twenty-hour-a-week, minimum-wage job, and most of the other bouncers were student athletes at Cal State Fullerton. The club was right across the street from campus. I knew that I'd need another job during the day to make it, so after about a week the guys at the Body Shop talked me into applying there, and a few days later I was hired.

I was afraid that the gym would never hire me. A week after the cop found me sleeping in my car, Jack had done me a favor. He knew that I was living in my car and let me sleep in the gym after it closed. I promised him that I wouldn't disturb anything and he told me to lock the doors and find somewhere out of the way to put my sleeping bag. I curled up inside one of the rest rooms. Around midnight, a light went on in the gym and I lazily woke up thinking that maybe I was dreaming. Then the lights came on in the small rest room, and Randall, the world-champion Olympic lifter, who was one of the gym owners, was standing in the door staring down at me. He kicked me out, telling me that I had no right to be sleeping in there, and I spent the rest of the night in my car. But then he hired me a week later.

Jack convinced me that my training would be helped through meditation and guided visualization—like the Soviet-bloc athletes did—so I began to experiment with meditating before my workouts. I'd find a quiet spot, breath myself into a relaxed state, then picture doing perfect workouts, and that sort of thing. It did help my training. Rory wasn't the first guy in the gym to make fun of me for doing it, but I was used to being seen as odd and didn't let it bother me too much.

One Saturday afternoon, about two weeks after he'd called me Grasshopper, Rory was in the gym training at the same time I was, and after we'd both finished, he asked to see what my physique looked like. I joked that I only showed my body to people I knew, so we both laughed and introduced ourselves to each other. I told him that I knew who he was from the magazines, and that seemed to please him. I took my shirt off and did a few poses for him, and he told me that I had the potential to become a great champion.

He began casually to offer me advice on training and dieting and all aspects of bodybuilding when he'd come into the Body Shop. He helped train a bunch of younger up-and-coming bodybuilders, and a number of them had won shows on everything from the local to the national level. He had trained the last teenage Mr. America, the year before we met.

I remained living in my car for several weeks. I'd shower and change for work in the gym, then when night came, or when I got off from work at the nightclub at two-thirty in the morning, I'd move my car to a spot where I knew the cops wouldn't find me. I was getting crafty at this homeless business. Eventually Jack's neighbors let me stay in a bedroom of their apartment for a few weeks while I tried to save money to get my own place. I met them while at Jack's one night; he was letting me crash on his couch because a big storm had moved in from off the coast and it was raining so hard that I might have floated away. While living next door to Jack, I started getting high again. The people I was staying with were frequent tokers, and Jack and his girlfriend smoked pot too, so one night, when a joint was passed my way, I took it. Jack said that most of the athletes he'd ever known were heads.

One day as I was sitting in Jack's apartment, he asked me what drugs I did. I told him that other than the occasional toke of weed, I had given all that up in high school.

"Nah, dude. What 'roids—what kinda cycle are you on?" he asked.

"None," was all I could say. "I'm open to suggestions."

"So you've never done anything, dude?" he asked, his voice disbelieving.

I told him about my brief Dianabol experience in college.

"Ah, dude, that's nothing special. Kids' stuff. Although, for some fuckin' strange reason, the Soviets like the stuff—or I guess they like to trade that shit. Every international meet, these dudes try to trade you Levi's for Russian D-bol. It's the wildest shit I ever saw. I know dudes on the team—pack whole suitcases of blue jeans just to trade with—but most guys think the big D is strictly bush league."

He told me all the names of the anabolics that were popular, then got a couple of small vials of Deca-Durabolin out of the hutch in his dining room and gave himself a shot while I watched. He offered to give me a couple of vials and new syringes to try out and showed me how to give myself a shot in the top of my butt muscles. He said that his doctor would probably prescribe me more if I went to see him.

Within two weeks my strength had dramatically increased. I felt as I had on the D-bol, in college, and thought—as I'd blow through ultra-intense workouts—that this wasn't so bad. I went to his doctor, who had a little sports-medicine practice in some remote part of Orange County, and continued to get more. I took my once-a-week injections with the religious zeal of a vampire chasing fresh blood. My body continued to grow and change, and even though I had passed the point where I could get ready for my last chance at the teenage Mr. America (since I'd turn twenty in December), I trained, knowing that I would get ready for a real show—not just some teenagers' contest, but a full-blown show—the next year.

I went with Jack to paint the interiors of the two other gyms the owners of the Body Shop were opening in other parts of Orange County. We would spend the days talking about training theory—he would tell me how he thought that some of his training for Olympic lifting could transfer to what I wanted to do in bodybuilding—while we worked.

Then they let me go. To this day I can't say why. One day I came into the gym and Randall was there. He pulled me aside and said that he was sorry, but I couldn't work there anymore and offered no explanation—told me I didn't have the right to one. I told him that the gym owed me three weeks' pay, plus all the overtime for helping Jack paint the other gyms, which I'd done when I wasn't working my regular shift. He said I'd have to call one of the other owners to sort that out. I told Mark, who was working at the time, and he couldn't believe it. We speculated that it was because I'd gotten my ear pierced, and the owners were all extremely conservative fundamentalists; other than that, Mark had said everyone there thought I did a good job.

I tried calling the other owner's office for a week, and he either didn't take my calls or had his secretary tell me that he wasn't in. Eventually he came on the line and told me that the way he saw things, they didn't owe me a cent. He obviously practiced the form of fundamentalist Christianity that I was starting to learn was prevalent in Orange County. All you had to do was talk the talk and put one of those little fish symbols on the back of your Mercedes, and you could do anything. I had grown up in the Bible Belt and had never experienced anything like the brand of Christianity I saw in that part of California. I'd heard it called business-aside-Christianity, because as long as you said the right words in the rest of your life—lots of talk about witnessing and praise Jesus-ing—you could do anything you wanted in business, including screwing people over, especially if you determined that they were unwashed heathens. That's obviously what I was, and they screwed me—in the name of Jesus, evidently—out of several hundred dollars, which might as well have been a million bucks to me at the time.

I still had my job at the nightclub, but that would never get me through. The week before I was given the heave-ho at the gym, I'd gotten an apartment right next to the nightclub, and I split the rent with one of the other bouncers at the club. That was nice because he spent most of his free time at his girlfriend's place and I had the apartment mostly to myself.

As if losing my main job wasn't enough, my car finally breathed its last and sat—a pile of useless junk—in the parking lot of the nightclub.

All the guys who actually worked at the Body Shop liked me, so they told me to keep coming in to train and they would simply pretend, if asked by an owner, that they'd never seen me again. At least I still had a place to train, even if I had to get there by bus.

I went to the Department of Labor to file a complaint against the owners of the gym, hoping to get the pay they owed me. The woman who helped me with my claim said that I had an ironclad case, but then my car quit working, and although Mark from the gym took me in once, I eventually stopped going in for my follow-up meetings because it was so hard to get there. It took three changes on the bus to get from where I lived to, an hour and a half later, the Labor office.

* * *

Right after I'd lost my job at the gym, I got an impulsive desire to go back to Indiana. I asked the manager of the nightclub if he could front me a couple of weeks' pay, he said that he could, and before I knew it, I was at the Orange County Amtrak station, catching a train to Chicago. I'd have to take the bus from there all the way down Indiana, because the train didn't go that far.

All the people I knew, at the gym and at work, looked at me as if I'd decided to head back home for good; I hadn't. It might have been in the back of my mind somewhere, but if it was, it was so buried that it would have taken twenty strong men ten years to dig it up.

Just like in the movies, while I was on the train I met some total strangers and struck up a conversation. They asked me if I wanted to smoke a joint with them, and I did. They told me that they were headed for a sacred native site, somewhere on one of the reservations on the Arizona–New Mexico border, to do a traditional peyote ceremony. They asked me to come along, so I said yes.

I asked a conductor if I would be able to get off and get back on, and he told me that the way my ticket was structured, I could.

We got off the train at some little stop, in the absolute middle of nowhere, in the middle of the night. Two men in an ancient pickup met us. These guys asked my new friends who I was and they told them I was cool, so we drove miles out into the darkness to a small shack, where a large fire was burning, in what would have been called the yard if there had been any grass.

We did the ceremony according to all the traditional customs—my friends told me this. And when I had finally woken up from a night and day of the most incredible visions imaginable, the same men who had picked us up drove me back to the train stop. The people who'd brought me there said that they were going to stay for a while.

Back on the train, I rode the rest of the way in a fog, staring out the window and knowing that the things I'd seen during the ceremony had told me that I was on the right path.

When I got home, I knew almost immediately that I needed to turn around and leave. Being back sent me spinning into a depression, and two days later, I reversed my route, back on the bus and train, and almost as if I'd never left, I was once more at the Orange County train station.

That was fuckin' weird, I thought as I stepped off the train. I'd already determined that if there was such a thing as fate, it had gotten me on that trip just for the purpose of meeting those people and taking part in the peyote ritual. I'd come back ready to do whatever it took to secure success in my future. The one peyote-induced vision (or dream fragment or whatever it was) that kept flashing through my mind—that I couldn't seem to block out—seemed to mysteriously hold some secret key to my future:

"Turn around."

"What?" I asked the thin air while looking back over my shoulder.

"Turn around." It vibrated from nowhere.

Just an empty barbell resting across chest-high supports, in front of a metal garage door. Silence. I twisted my frame toward it, then reached out and touched the bar. Warm and soft. It betrayed itself, purposely deceiving me. I allowed it to.

Suddenly, as if the touch had triggered it, I lifted up. There was no ceiling, only deep blue sky. The curve of the globe was in front of me and I swam—moving my arms as if breaststroking through a backyard pool—without resistance, across leagues of distance.

I descended naked and sleek onto a yellow-green, grassy hillside that smelled of freshly cut wild onions, and inside the dream I fell asleep.

I woke straddling a gaping, wild river. One bare foot on one side, the other foot on the opposite bank. I couldn't move because the level of the crushing water kept rising. My feet slid farther apart. I couldn't fly anymore. I wanted to fly. No voices whispered secrets; I was alone. I knew that I needed both feet on one side of the river or the other. Remain like this and I was doomed.

I looked for a branch to grab on to, as Tarzan would when he was sinking in quicksand. Just when he was up to his chin in muck—which would stop the air from entering his lungs forever—a tree branch would appear, as if an angel had lowered it to him. I couldn't find my saving branch and the water came higher, splitting me farther in two. All I could see when I looked up was knife-sharp sunlight.

In another of those twists of fate that can change the course of your life, losing my job at the Body Shop ended up being for the best. First, because the company that owned the gyms went out of business a short time later (maybe the owners didn't prey—er, I mean pray—hard enough). Second, during the last Saturday I worked out there, Rory told me that he had something to talk to me about and asked me to come and see him at an address in Garden Grove the next day. I tried to ask him what it was all about but he just laughed and said that I'd find out the next day. He said that he'd have Frank, the teenage Mr. America, pick me up at my place—since it was well-known that I didn't have a car anymore—and bring me over.

The next day Frank picked me up and we drove to Garden Grove. I asked him what this was all about, but all he would tell me was that Rory was having some physique pictures taken at the address he'd given us. It seemed as if he knew more but wouldn't tell.

We pulled into a business park under the freeway and drove around until we found the place we were looking for. There was Rory, standing oiled-up in a tiny pair of mustard-colored posing trunks, in front of a short, heavyset man who was behind a camera mounted on a tripod. Frank said the photographer was Joe Valdez, who had been friends with Rory forever and took all his pictures. I just nodded and, as we got out of the car, thought, *Rory has the most fantastic physique I've ever seen.*

Frank and I watched Joe take roll after roll of film of Rory doing all these beautiful poses. I asked Frank where Rory had learned to pose so well, and he told me that it was one of Rory's strongest talents. Frank said that Rory was great at teaching people and was probably going to be a Mr. Olympia. Had I ever seen bigger arms, he asked me, and I replied that I hadn't.

After they'd finished the photo session, Joe Valdez introduced himself and asked me what I thought.

"He's the best I've ever seen," I said.

"He's the greatest physique in the world," Joe declared. "He should have easily won the Mr. Los Angeles this year, but the judges—well, they just screwed him over. You should have heard the booing from that audience at the Embassy—why, it must have lasted fifteen minutes. Frank was there—he can tell you. I have a tape recording of all that booing. I'll let you hear it sometime."

Frank smiled and nodded in agreement.

Rory pulled on some sweats and asked me to come inside with him. We went into the building we'd been standing in front of. A gym was inside. Who would've known?

It's so hidden from the street back here in this office park, I thought as he showed me inside. It was a terrific gym; it looked as if it had been there several years.

"Were those pictures he was takin' for the magazines?" I asked.

"No, they're just some progress shots. Joe is doing weekly shots all the way to the Cal, next May."

"Oh." I thought that all those pictures would have to be expensive.

"What do you think?" Rory asked.

"I think you have a great physique."

"Well, thanks, but I meant about the gym."

"Oh—well, it looks like a pretty good gym."

"It's mine—well, I mean I'm going to run it. The owner's a friend of mine."

I just shook my head, in a gee-whiz, sort-of-envious, I'd-love-to-have-a-friend-own-a-gym-that-I-could-run way, as I looked around taking inventory of the equipment—doing what any serious bodybuilder does when he goes into a new gym.

"I want to hire you to work here," he said.

I stared.

"Well?"

"Um—when do I start?" I asked, waiting for the catch.

"Monday. We'll work getting the gym ready to reopen—the people who had it before ran it into the ground. There's another thing. I want to help you with your training."

"Fuck, yes! That'd be fantastic!" I said, not bothering to hold in my enthusiasm.

"There's only one thing."

"What's 'at?"

"If I train you, you have to do everything I tell you to, the way I tell you to—no questions. You get advice from, or listen to, anyone else, and it's over. You follow what I say to the letter—or it's no deal. Understood?"

I shook my head yes and broke out into the biggest smile I'd had in years.

In the beginning, I was purely a student. A sponge, pulling in every ounce of knowledge he would spill. I followed his demands and listened to no one else.

I began to work at Rory's new gym, taking the bus from my apartment to work each day. There are many good reasons why most people get around in southern California by car. Public transportation is one of them. It took me an hour and a half to go to or from work; if I'd still had a car, it would've been a fifteen-minute trip, with traffic. My days revolved around waking up, waiting for a bus, riding it, working a full day, doing my own workout, waiting for another bus, riding it, working my second job, and sleeping. After a month of this, Rory asked me if I didn't want to live closer to the gym. I said that I would love to, but that I needed both of my jobs because my share of the rent was expensive, and I'd still have to ride the bus to one job or the other, since they were in different parts of town. He asked me how much my rent was and how much money I made at the nightclub. I told him. Then he said that he'd been thinking about it and offered to let me live in the storeroom of the gym, if I wanted to. I wouldn't have any rent, and he could increase my hours—so in the end, I'd only have to work one job, I'd have less hassle, and I'd make more money.

Live in the gym? I thought. *Coooll.*

"I'll give notice on my apartment and at the club tomorrow," I told Rory. The next day I let my roommate know that I was going to have to move, and I told the club manager that I'd still work enough nights to repay what I'd borrowed for my train trip.

Living in a gym may be any young bodybuilder's dream come true. For a while it was. I had access to all the equipment anytime I wanted it, and I had the whole place to myself when it was closed; but that was the catch—when it was closed. We opened at 7 A.M. and closed at 10 P.M. I didn't have a car, so if you took into account that I also served as a kind of nighttime security guard and that I was there all day, every day, because the place was in the middle of a business park and the nearest anything was a couple of miles away, I became, in essence, a seven-day-a-week, twenty-four-hour-a-day employee, getting paid for only forty of those hours each week.

As the months passed, I saw Rory get ready for the Mr. California, attended the contest, watched him win by one point, caught my first glimpse of Joe Weider—he even talked to me, in passing, backstage, as I watched Rory pose for photographs.

After his show Rory said that it was time to look for a contest for me to do. The Robby Robinson Classic was a brand-new show, named for the famous pro bodybuilder who'd been one of my muscle heroes when I first began following the sport. Rory and I agreed that this would be a perfect show for me to work toward, since it was still several months away.

Rory was rigid in how he saw things. In his way of getting ready for a show, you took your body weight up as high as it would go, then as a show approached, you went on a severely strict diet to take off all the fat. I remember thinking, as he first told me how I would go about this, that it would probably be far easier to simply work my way up in muscle size while staying closer to contest condition—not in peak contest condition, but at least not forty or fifty pounds over it. But I kept my mouth shut because I was there to learn.

I began to bulk up, taking my weight up to over 230 pounds; I felt like a fat pig. I had a hard time breathing, and all I seemed to do all day was eat: six or seven meals a day. Most of my paycheck was going to groceries. Then at the very peak of this weight, twelve weeks out from the Robby Robinson Classic, fast approaching in September, he had me reverse the process and go on a restricted-calorie diet of mostly protein. I went from feeling like a glutton to starving and craving everything in sight, almost overnight.

The workouts he designed were long, nearly twice the length of any workout I'd ever done before; and he had all these variations on the exercises that he taught me, most of which he'd named after himself—the Rory curl, the Rory extension, the Rory this, the Rory that. When I tried, cautiously, to tell him that I wasn't afraid of hard work, and that I'd always trained hard, but that the workouts he'd designed for me felt way too long for my body—that I wasn't recuperating right from them—he gave me another dose of his "my way or the highway" spiel.

He taught me how to pose, and we worked for hours on a new posing routine for the show that would look as if it were as much ballet, or classic moving statuary, as a contest posing routine. He pushed me hard, and I took to this part of what he helped me with as a young bird takes to flight; I was good at it and had a natural talent for the movements and how to place my body so that it looked its best.

Three weeks before the show, someone who worked out at the gym brought in a whole fresh peach pie and gave it to me as a well-intentioned gift.

How can someone be so cruel, I thought as I thanked him.

Another guy who had done some contests but wasn't one of Rory's protégés came into the office and asked me what the deal was with the pie.

"Hell if I know," I said. "Guy's obviously never dieted before. Doesn't seem to understand that right now, I could eat the eyeballs out of a dead squirrel, if they were covered with sugar. What was he thinkin'?" I kept looking at the pie, salivating.

"Yeah, some people are so stupid. You could always do what the wrestlers back at my high school used to do when they were trying to cut weight."

"And what would that be? Push-ups in the sauna, wearing plastic garbage bags for sweats?"

"Well, that's one way—the hard way. The other's just to eat the fuckin' pie and then go in the can and stick your fingers down your throat."

"Get outta here." I waved him off.

"You wouldn't be the first guy dieting for a show that's done it."

"Yeah—right."

*   *   *

I left the peach pie on the desk. That night, after I'd closed the gym and had my last paltry meal of the day—a cold chicken breast and a tiny salad—the pie won. I got a fork and started in the middle, and before I knew it the thing was gone, nothing but crumbs and a little yellow-orange gel left in the pan. My stomach felt as if it would explode at the slightest wrong move. I ran into the bathroom in the men's locker room and closed and—for some reason—locked the door, even though no one but me was in the gym. I stood in front of the mirror looking at myself, ashamed that my discipline had slipped so badly, then I opened the lid on the toilet and jammed three fingers of my left hand down my throat. The pie came up in rivers of glop, splashing toilet water everywhere, and when I thought I'd gotten it all up, I looked in the mirror and saw that my eyes were bulging red, and my face looked as if I'd been stung by a hundred bees. I went straight to bed and swore to myself I'd never let that happen again.

His diets worked. They got me in shape. It seemed, though, that they were so severe, and my body was so overweight when I began, that in the end I'd sacrificed a bunch of hard-earned muscle. It also seemed to me that he didn't need to be so rigid and get so mad every time I asked a question or tried to tell him something about how I thought my body worked. He said again if I didn't want to do everything he said, without hesitation, then I was free to move on. I'd shrink away and swallow my questions down with a can of dry tuna fish and half an orange.

I did the Robby Robinson Classic. My posing routine was well rehearsed and Rory had helped me get into perfect condition, even if the route did seem severe. I came into the show at around 185 pounds, having lost 45 pounds in twelve weeks.

In the prejudging it became obvious that I would either win or place second. It would be close. At the night show, I became nervous while going through my routine, slipped a bit a couple of times—I doubt that anyone noticed but me—but received thunderous applause as I left the stage.

Once again, just like the teenage Mr. Florida, the emcee made a big production out of how close the result was—one point separated first and second, he exclaimed. I was the one in second.

Backstage at the Embassy, where only a few months before I'd been allowed in as a total outsider, one of the judges from the show came up to Rory and me and said that I'd looked fantastic and that he'd been one of the judges who had me in first place.

"He's gonna be a great one," he said to Rory.

"He'll be one of the best in the world," Rory said, looking away, not seeming interested in what this guy had to say.

"But, Bobby, don't go and blow up now," the judge said to me as he looked back and forth between Rory and me. "You know what I'm saying—try to stay close to contest shape. You have too beautiful of a physique to walk around fat half the year."

"He's going to do whatever it takes," Rory shot back. "Come on, Bobby, let's go eat." And we left.

Big plans had been made, for weeks, about the pig-out feast after the show, and a gang of us—all the Rory clones, as detractors liked to call the people he taught, mainly because most of them tried to dress exactly like him and he demanded such rigid loyalty—all went out for dinner, and I ate until I knew that ice cream was going to pop out of the top of my head.

The next morning, Joe Valdez took photos of me on the beach in Venice. Rory, his wife, Cynthia, and Mary Roberts—whom Rory had trained for the women's contest at the show the night before—and her husband, Dick, all went. We picked up Mr. Robby Robinson himself at his apartment and he went too; Joe Valdez was a friend of Robby's. Now this was a pure and simple dream come true. First off, that I got to meet such a great champ—a living legend, the Black Prince, as they'd nicknamed him in the magazines—and secondly, because Joe asked Robby if he'd like to get in a few shots with Mary and me, and he said yes. Man, was I ever a happy boy.

I also noticed that, even though Robby didn't have a show anytime soon, he didn't hesitate to take pictures. He was totally in shape during the middle of his off-season, not porked out to fifty pounds overweight. I couldn't help thinking, as I noticed this about Robby, that if I had only stayed closer to my contest condition—as that judge had suggested I do now—I would have kept more muscle size and easily won the show, instead of coming in second.

Immediately after the contest, I flew back to Indiana for a short vacation. I couldn't stop eating. Now that my show was over, I could have anything I wanted. It was disastrous. I'd come home triumphant and looking terrific—fit, tanned, glowing. I spent every minute of every day I was there with some kind of junk food in my mouth, and I blew up fast. By the time I returned to California, I had gained about twenty-five—very ugly—pounds. My face began to look like a sumo wrestler's and I was getting the body to match. When I compared that to how I'd looked only a week before, I knew I was going to have to find a better way.

I stayed training under Rory's guidance through the next several months after the Robby Robinson Classic. We decided that my next show should be the 1981 Mr. Los Angeles, coming up in February. It was the most prestigious local show in the country—maybe the world—since so many of the up-and-coming guys came to L.A. to train and usually did this show as an initial step on their way to the national level.

I listened to Rory's advice and began to take my weight back up again. I didn't really have a choice. After the Robby, I couldn't stop eating. The diet for the show had been so severe that I simply couldn't get control of my appetite when it was over. My weight shot up to a roly-poly 240. Rory expressed great concern one Sunday, a couple of months after my contest, when I went to one of those all-you-can-eat brunches with him and a gang of people. I ate as much as I could stuff down my throat—of the junkiest offerings they served. He said that, by then, I should have been switching myself over to trying to gain weight by eating massive amounts of good, bodybuilding food, not junk. I told him that I couldn't seem to stop myself, got ashamed that I didn't have more control, and went back for my fifth plateful of blintzes and pastries.

That night in the gym, long after it had closed for the day, I stripped off all my clothes and looked at my body in one of the mirrors.

What a fuckin' hippo, I thought.

I started on a diet of my own creation the next day. Rory would write out these eating plans for me that consisted of about six thousand calories a day. I took them and then did what I knew I had to do; I followed what I thought was best and ate the same kind of food, only half as much as he recommended. I would take the workouts he gave me and cut them in half. My body responded.

He and I began to struggle because I wanted to skip the L.A. and go straight into the Mr. California, in May. In the end, I heeded his advice on this. He said that I should do the L.A., win it, then decide whether to do the Cal.

Three months before the contest, the man who owned the gym decided to sell. I was going to have to find somewhere else to live. I moved into a house one of Rory's other trainees, Dale, had just rented. Before

I moved, I began to worry about what was going to happen, since I still didn't have a car and now I was going to need to find a new gym to train in.

Two days before I moved out of my room in the gym, Dick and Mary Roberts came in. Rory was helping Mary get ready for her next show, and while they were in the office going over her workouts and diets, Dick asked me what I was going to do now that the gym was changing hands. I told him about my new place to live, but that I was stumped regarding transportation. He said that he had a bicycle-repair business, and that he had a moped that had been returned a year earlier for a warranty repair and had never been picked up. I could borrow it for a while, he told me. So I did. I also found a new gym.

Dan Howard's World Gym was in Fountain Valley. I found it listed in the phone book. I took my newly borrowed moped and putt-putted my way down to this place to check it out. I must have been quite a sight—it was a small moped and I was a fairly big guy—going slowly down the ten miles of Orange County streets, big, shiny cars honking at me to get my silly ass out of the way, and me just kind of ducking my head and pressing on. Didn't these people realize? I had a contest to get ready for. I started training at the Fountain Valley World Gym, which was the best gym I'd ever seen.

I talked to the manager at the nightclub in Fullerton where I'd worked before, and he let me pick right back up, working there again, until something else turned up.

The moped routine got to be too much. In two weeks of riding it, I'd had at least a dozen close calls with cars that seemed to regard me as some sort of object that they needed to speed by at as close a distance as possible; I'd been completely run off the side of the road twice. I called Dick and told him that I needed to return it—thanked him vigorously for letting me use it—but it was simply too dangerous; I would have felt safer walking down the center of the street.

When I took it to their house to return it, Mary asked if I wouldn't stay to supper. Since I only had a bus to catch, I said yes.

During supper, Dick asked if I liked bicycles. I told him that I'd been an avid rider as a kid; we talked bikes. After supper he took me out to his shop and started talking about his business. He went around to a bunch of different chain department stores putting together their bikes and doing repairs for customers. He told me that many years before he'd come to California from Georgia and had gone through many of the same struggles I was going through, trying to set up a life. We stood silently in front of his tool bench for a couple of minutes. I was looking at a Campagnola brake system that was lying there in its box.

"These things cost a fortune," I said. "I used to dream of having a Campy-equipped bike. I had to settle for one with all Simplex instead. It was all I could afford."

"Actually Simplex has gotten pretty good nowadays. I know what you mean though—there'll never be anything like a bike nut's first crush on Campy components."

"That's for damn sure."

"Bobby, I've been thinkin' for the past few days, and, well, how'd you like to come work for me?"

"Wadda ya mean?"

"Doin' bikes—goin' on my route with me. I go all over southern California and Nevada."

"Well—that's kinda a surprise."

"And you know, Bobby, you could probably kill two birds with one stone on this one."

"Oh, how's that, Dick?"

"If you came to work for me, I could let you use the work truck after hours—that's how."

And so began one of the most supportive relationships of my life. They all but adopted me. I worked there. I ate there. Many evenings I'd stick around and watch TV or talk to Dick late into the night. And when I was ready to leave for the day, I drove back to my place in the Toyota pickup that Dick and I would go around in during the days, putting together and repairing bicycles. I would spill my guts to him about how I was feeling—that I really cared for Rory as a friend and that I was grateful for his help, but that following his strict guidance was so hard, because I liked to think and ask questions and know why I was doing something; and I liked to give my input, if I thought something might work better, without feeling as if I were going to be told to get lost if I did. He said that Mary felt much the same way and was doing what I was doing with her training and diet too.

The Mr. Los Angeles was the turning point in my short career.

I won the show with straight first-place votes. I stood onstage, barefoot and oiled up, in the light blue posing trunks Rory had loaned me, listening to the audience's wild applause after my name was announced as the winner. I thought I had the world by the tail.

Most of the judges came up to me after—including master photographer Artie Zeller, who would later become a close friend—and told me that I was the new Steve Reeves and had the best physique potential they'd seen for years. Adjusting the guidance I was getting according to the strong instinct I had begun to develop had worked like a lucky penny. My body had gone through years' worth of improvement in only a few months.

Almost immediately after the show, my relationship with Rory completely dissolved. We simply couldn't be around each other anymore. Whether it was a matter of my having learned all I could from him or his getting sick of my constant—even if mild-mannered—questions, I got my freedom, whether I wanted it or not, without ever having to say a word about it.

He probably thought I wasn't grateful for the help he'd given me or that I'd just used him. If he thought those things, he was wrong. The simple fact was, we were both independent, stubborn young men who each knew what was best for himself when it came to the sport. I learned more from him than any other person had ever taught me about body-building. I learned what worked for me and what didn't.

The truest factor in all this was that we were two of the major "leading men" coming up in the sport and we were each going to have to find our own way to the prize. That prize was winning the Mr. America and Mr. Universe, and getting into the pros.

We would meet again—soon.

Dick and Mary were good to me. They treated me as if I were family. I continued to work for Dick as I kept training at the World Gym in Fountain Valley. Eventually Dick began promoting bodybuilding contests, developing a reputation as one of the best in the business. Mary went on to win the women's American Championships and then became a top Ms. Olympia contender, placing as high as second in the show.

During the time when they became like family, I finally came out to myself as a gay man. What a relief. This wasn't as much of a struggle as I had always thought it would be. One day I wasn't dealing with the information, except to squash it down in the back of my brain, and the next I had worked up the nerve to go into a gay bar, and the walls inside my mind fell away. This quick shift did, however, create a new set of complications. What would I do with the information since I was beginning to become successful in a public career? Should I stay quiet? Those were the rules, after all. Everyone knew that if you were gay and wanted to have any career involving the public, you kept your mouth shut and were damned happy if nobody—outside of the other gay people you knew—found out your secret. I didn't tell anyone, not even

Dick and Mary. Of course, a couple of years later as I came out to all my family and friends, I found out that everyone had figured it out long before I had ever decided to do anything about it. Typical.

I moved from the rental house I'd shared with the guy from Rory's gym, down to Laguna Beach, and continued to use Dick's truck after work to go to and from my new apartment, which I'd gotten by answering room-mate ads in the paper. Everything seemed to be going along fine.

About two months after I'd moved, Dick pulled me aside and said that he was sorry, but his business couldn't support my job any longer. I had been training for the Mr. America in Las Vegas, after deciding to pass on the Mr. California, but now I was, in one second, once more without a job or car. I told him that I understood. I had been suppressing a suspicion anyway that he had been carrying me, hiring me more to be supportive than anything else. Although we worked well together for seven months and everything had seemed—on the surface—to be going smoothly, his decision didn't take me much by surprise.

I began to take the bus from Laguna all the way up to Fountain Valley, so I could train: an hour-and-fifteen-minute ride to a stop two miles' walking distance from the gym. There weren't any bodybuilding gyms closer. I went around and began applying for jobs, but couldn't seem to get one no matter how hard I tried. I was asked what my qualifications were, for even the most menial jobs, and they never seemed to be enough. It was the first time since I was eleven years old that I couldn't stir up work when I wanted or needed it.

The day of the Mr. America came and went. I had continued training and dieting for it all the way up to the last moment—hoping that some miracle would happen at the last minute and I'd find a way to get there. No miracle.

I sulked around my apartment in Laguna during the day and rode the bus up to work out every night. I bought large, cheap jars of peanut butter, generic cans of soup, and five-pound bags of rice to live on, trying to make the few dollars I had left stretch as far as they could. I had fallen a month behind on my rent.

Right when all the pieces of my life had seemed to fall together, they fell as quickly apart again, and I felt hopelessly lost.

I had nowhere to turn. I thought that Dick's message to me was that I had become a burden on his family, so I couldn't turn there. The only friends I had in Laguna were acquaintances, at best, so there was nobody I could turn to there. My family was twenty-five hundred miles away and I felt as close to them as to a distant planet. And I was queer—now it was for absolute sure—in a world that said my kind were the lowest of the low and deserved nothing out of life except contempt.

I was nothing but some guy who—in spite of having kept a promise to his Mam-ma to read at least one meaningful book a week—hadn't gotten what anyone else would consider a formal education and had nothing to show for his life but a Mr. Los Angeles first-place trophy. That and a couple of dollars might buy me a sandwich. I truly believed that ending my life was the only way out. I was like that scared kid once more, searching for a tree that would support a rope and a body.

I believe in angels. I do now, anyway. I know that the image of angels, or whatever you want to call them—living or floating, visible or not— has of late become an exploited cliché. Skeptics will cringe or laugh or both, probably say I'm delusional, then present several logical explanations.

Believers will say, "Aha—see."

But every once in a while, right when life seems darkest and you have searched every corner for a piece of hope and found none, when the waters you thought had long ago receded begin to boil and rise again, threatening to pull you under—out of the clear sky the hand of an angel appears, holding a saving branch.

I could simply swim out into the ocean until I couldn't swim anymore and that would be that. Then I realized that I was scared of being any farther than a hundred yards offshore and decided that it would have to be a more suitable method, something more in line with my personality—a dive off a tall building or a cliff, perhaps. I'd always loved heights, and falling a long distance intrigued me; the notion that once you let go, there was no going back; if you were a bird, you could simply flap your wings, but because you were a useless hunk of human flesh, you would simply splat. I was thinking like this as I walked out to buy a pack of cigarettes. I had started smoking again, rationalizing that, oh, well, once a smoker, always a smoker. I couldn't afford a decent meal, but I could scrape up change for coffin nails. I'd take the slow way if I couldn't come up with a quicker one.

On the sidewalk, right outside my front door, I ran into the mailman, literally. I had been looking down at my bare feet as I was walking, trying to decide if I wanted to go back in and get my flip-flops.

"Oh, sorry," I said when I bumped into him.

"It's okay, I wasn't looking either. One-B?"

"What? Oh, yeah, One-B—that'd be moi." I pointed at myself. "You know, I coulda said *me*, but, well, I didn't wanna sound like I was writing poetry, out here on the sidewalk."

He just looked at me (obviously no sense of humor), then handed me a short pile of mail and walked away. Over his shoulder he said, "Have a nice day. Get out and play."

He gave a half-look back over his shoulder and smiled.

"Exactly," I called after him. "Play indeed," I muttered to myself. "Play in traffic, maybe." I stuck the mail in the back pocket of my shorts without looking at it, decided I didn't need the flip-flops, and went on to the convenience store at the end of the block.

When I got back to the apartment, I went out on the patio, un-wrapped the pack of Winstons, lit up, and sat down, only then realizing that I still had the mail in my back pocket. I pulled it out and set it on the patio table, then decided to look through and see if, by any slim chance, there was anything for me. A bill for Sam, bill for Sam, letter for Sam, junk mail, more junk, letter for Bob, bill for Sam. Letter for Bob? I set the rest aside and blew out a cloud of smoke, crushed out my cigarette, and looked at the handwriting—unfamiliar—and the post-mark, Los Angeles; no return address.

When I opened the envelope, there was a two-page letter with a money order—for two thousand dollars!—paper-clipped behind it.

What the . . . ? I thought.

The neatly handwritten letter read:

> Dear Bob,
>
> I hope you don't mind me addressing you as Bob. I do so hate formality. You don't know me, as we have never met, but I know who you are. Please be assured that I am not a madman.
>
> I have watched your career progress over the last several months. I saw you win the L.A. You have a superb phy-sique, but most of all I think that you have a gift—one that you should continue to pursue.
>
> This may be presumptuous of me, and I hope that you won't take offense, but I was told by a mutual acquaintance that you have hit upon some difficult times.
>
> I have been extremely fortunate in my life. At one time when I was in a position perhaps similar to the one you may now find yourself in, a complete stranger assisted me. I feel that it is only correct that I take every opportunity to attempt to do the same.

Please accept the enclosed gift. I have heard that you are a proud young man. Before you make any attempt to return the check, I would like to ask you to do me one favor—accept my gift for now, with the understanding that when you have achieved all the success you deserve, you may pass this gift on to someone else who is trying to make their way in the world, but is finding the going rough. In this way—you might say—it is both a gift and a loan.

There are no strings attached, other than the favor I mentioned, but you may do that, or not, according to your own wishes. I do not expect to meet you, and if we do someday meet, I will never bring this up or ask for anything in return. Please accept also my best wishes for your continued success. Thank you for your time.

That was it. No name or signature, no address or phone number; a money order—not a personal check—and a letter that, well, frankly, I didn't know what to make of the letter.

I decided to sleep on it. It fell out of the sky, and although my first, and most natural, instinct was to cash the two-thousand-dollar money order, I was torn over what to do.

The next morning I woke up and decided that it would be foolish of me not to accept the gift. I had no way of finding out who had sent it, and even if I did, it had been well intentioned and certainly came at a perfect time. What was I going to do, throw money in the trash because I didn't know where it came from, then jump off a cliff to keep myself from starving to death?

I walked across the street to a bank and cashed it. When my roommate, Sam, got home from work that night, I told him that I was going to be moving and paid him the rent I owed him and apologized for giving him such short notice. He said that was okay. I suspect that he was glad to get anything; he probably thought that the way things had been going, I would simply sneak out one day, owing him money.

I packed a small suitcase of the clothes I wore most frequently, put my three trophies into the duffel bag I'd had since I was a kid, and went out behind the building to throw the rest of my stuff in the trash. When I got out there, a homeless guy I'd seen frequently around the neighborhood was leaning against the wall next to the rusty blue Dumpster, eating out of a styrofoam take-out container that he must have Dumpster-dived for. I asked him if he wanted to go through the clothes I was tossing before I threw them in. He did.

I went back inside, smoked one last cigarette on the patio, and started to throw the rest of the pack away because I'd decided to quit, but instead I got my bags, went back out behind the building, and gave the homeless guy the pack of smokes.

I got on a city bus, headed north.

Several hours and many bus changes later, I was in Santa Monica, reading the classifieds in the Santa Monica paper, looking for an apartment. Everything advertised there was beyond expensive. I bought a *Los Angeles Times* and started looking in areas that seemed close to the beach. Still expensive. I rented a hotel room for the night, changed into my gym clothes, and walked to find Gold's Gym. It had moved to a large warehouse space in Venice. It seemed to take forever to walk there. As I was walking down Main Street toward Venice, I noticed the World Gym, in a two-story, gray, concrete-block building.

So that's where it is, I thought.

World had a reputation as a quiet, serious place. Joe Gold owned it, and he had opened this new gym not using his name because when he had sold Gold's Gym, years earlier, he had contractually agreed not to open another gym using his name. The early Gold's Gym that Joe had started became the mecca, the pilgrimage site, for all the muscle guys coming West to the scene. The new owners of Gold's trademarked the term *Mecca of Bodybuilding,* and so when Joe Gold got the itch to start a new place, he called it World Gym.

I had read in the magazines that Arnold, Franco Columbu, Frank Zane, and several of the other top guys trained there. It seems they all loved Joe Gold's no-bullshit personality and preferred the gym atmosphere that he created over the new "Mecca." I had also read that a number of the best bodybuilders in town trained at both Gold's and World because the places were so different.

I went up the steps that led from the street into the second-story gym, which was above a parking garage.

I peeked in the door, then walked inside. A man stretching his calves on a high wooden block said in a New Yorker's accent, "Help you?"

I recognized him from the magazines: Eddie Giuliani, a great national-level competitor from the sixties and seventies.

"Mind if I just look?" I asked, and came farther inside.

"Nah, go on. Hey, aren't you, uh—no, I got it—you won the L.A., right? You beat my training partner, Joey. Bobby, um"—snapping his fingers, trying to get it—"ah, Bobby Paris. You're Paris, aren't you? How could I not remember?"

"Yeah—hi."

"Eddie." He stuck out his hand.

"I know. Eddie Giuliani. It's a pleasure, sir."

"I thought you lived down—wherever—Orange County or some-place. Rory trains you, right?"

"He did. We went our separate ways a few months ago."

"Oh—yeah? Wait a minute—you trained at Dan's gym in Fountain Valley, right?"

"Yeah."

"You know, Dan used to help Joe Gold build all his equipment."

"I know. Great gym, fantastic equipment—loved it there."

"So, you live up here now?" He went back to stretching his calves.

"Not yet. I'm movin' now." Lou Ferrigno was across the gym, with his shirttail pulled up. He was showing someone his abs. They looked like blocks of granite.

"Well, come in and train anytime."

"Yeah, sounds good."

"Take care."

"Bye, it was nice to meet ya."

He waved over his shoulder as I turned around and walked back down the stairs.

When I finally got to Gold's, the place was packed. Ed Conners, one of the owners of the gym, came over to me as I was paying for my workout and told the guy on the desk that I could train for free. He introduced himself, and I reminded him that we had met, briefly, at the L.A.—backstage. He seemed impressed that I remembered him.

He told me that if he could ever do anything for me, not to hesitate to ask.

I did my workout, but had to wait in line for the machines I wanted to use. The place was noisy, loud rock blaring through the speakers mounted high on the walls.

Walking back to my motel, I decided that I'd most likely train at World.

No inexpensive apartments turned up anywhere inside the muscle ghetto. I decided to pursue other areas of the city. When I'd been living in Laguna, I'd come up to West Hollywood once to go out to the clubs with a couple of the guys I'd become friendly with at the beach.

In the classifieds, the apartments there were almost half as much as at the beach. This presented me with a dilemma. I could get a place that I couldn't afford at the beach and be close to World Gym and the whole muscle scene, or I could get a place in West Hollywood that I could afford (assuming I could find a job) and make do with whatever gym might be there, until I could afford a car.

In the phone book, the only gym listed in West Hollywood was the Jim Morris Gym. Jim Morris was a Mr. America in the early seventies. He had also been one of the judges who came up to me with Artie Zeller, after I'd won the Mr. L.A., and complimented me.

I took the bus up to his gym.

When I walked up, Jim was sitting at his desk, which I could see through the front window. He had his head resting on his hands.

"Hi, Jim," I said, walking in the door. "I'm Bob—"

"Well, Bobby Paris. How are you?" He stood up and a broad smile changed his entire face. I shook his hand.

I told him what was going on with me. He told me how fantastic he thought I'd looked at the L.A. And we kept talking, as if we'd known each other for a long while. After we'd talked bodybuilding for quite a bit, he asked me if I had ever thought about training people.

"You mean like guys getting ready for shows? Nah, I—"

"No, I mean regular people. People with money who want someone to take them through their workouts."

"You know, I was hopin' to start doin' something that pays more than minimum wage. I've just about had enough of barely gettin' by."

There was no such thing as a private trainer at that time, at least as far as I knew. The only people training anyone were guys setting up new workouts for gym members, as I had always done.

"How does twenty to twenty-five bucks an hour sound?"

"You're joking."

"Nope. I do it here. I can set you up with two clients that I know of, as soon as you're ready to go. You take them through three workouts a week, an hour each time, and there's—what?—a hundred fifty bucks a week, right off the bat."

And with that I was in business. A private trainer. Years later the job would become a common part of the culture, but Jim had brought me into something that was, at that point, a fairly new concept.

I got a small studio apartment on the edge of West Hollywood, began to make some money—not a lot of money, since this was still such a new thing, but enough to live on—and began to train at Jim's gym for whatever shows I planned to do next. World Gym would have to wait a bit.

Within a few months I had met someone whom I was dating, had a training partner, a new line of work that I was good at, and I'd managed to save money for a car—a several-year-old yellow Honda Civic. I had become good friends with one of the best sports-medicine doctors in the city and had gotten myself fully back into my training.

Jim offered to help me, if I wanted it, for whatever show I chose to do next. He didn't demand that I only do what he said. He simply offered to help: to check out my condition, to make sure I was on track, to help me correct my poses, whatever.

I took him up on it and immediately did a show that Dick Roberts was producing, the California Muscle Classic. I won—easily.

Next came the Mr. Southern California. Two weeks before the show, Jim took me to meet John Balik at his Venice studio.

When we showed up, John took several rolls of film and told Jim that I had a terrific physique and asked him if I'd met Joe Weider yet. John was asking this as I was standing up under the studio lights, on the shiny black platform, he had set up. When we'd finished, I told John that I admired his work and that it was a pleasure to get photographed by him. He was still one of the two main staff photographers for Weider then, and he said that Joe would flip over the pictures if they came out as he saw them through the camera.

The Southern California was another easy win. The next weekend, the Mr. California, in San Jose, was not so easy. I took second, by the slimmest quarter-of-a-point margin, to a guy from San Francisco, whom I thought I should easily have beaten. Half the crowd booed the decision.

When the night show was over, after I'd done the best posing performance of my short career, and I'd been announced in second, I held my cool and congratulated the winner. I also won the Best Poser trophy.

Yeah, fuckin' consolation prize, I thought, seething, in a young, headed-quickly-for-the-top, spoiled-brat way when I was handed the Best Poser trophy.

After the show, I stormed out the back door of the auditorium; my training partner trailed behind me, asking where I was going so fast.

I looked around to make sure that no one could see, raised the second-place trophy up overhead, and smashed it to the parking-lot asphalt. It broke into dozens of pieces. I picked it all up, tossed the scraps into a nearby Dumpster, and stormed back to the hotel.

When I left the next day, I conveniently forgot the Best Poser trophy, next to a wastebasket in my room.

In only three years I'd gone from a complete nobody—some hick kid from the middle of nowhere—to barely, by the slimmest of possible margins, losing the biggest, most prestigious state contest in the country, and being voted the best poser in that elite show, and I'd already grown to expect that everything I touched would automatically go my way.

13

WORLD BY THE TAIL

The Early 1980s
Southern California

The first time I sat down and actually talked with Joe Weider was over lunch at a Rueben's restaurant in Woodland Hills, near his office. After we formally introduced ourselves, I pulled out a yellow legal pad of notes I'd made for the meeting. I had every intention of getting this relationship off on the right foot. My manager had suggested making notes so that I wouldn't forget anything. We had a lot of ground to cover and I was determined to get everything I wanted to talk with Joe about out on the table.

We finally met after I'd already placed third in the American Championships.

After the Mr. California, where I placed second, I was crushed, because I had planned to have a winning streak that stretched right through the Mr. Olympia. Instead of stopping to carefully plan my next move, I did the wrong thing and jumped right into the next available competition. I also had it in my mind, from my days of training with Rory, that I was a light heavyweight and had to keep my competition weight under 198 pounds, in order to make that class. I wanted to break out of that limit and become a heavyweight.

I had begun to shift away from the cycle of bulking up and then severely cutting down that I'd been taught was the way to get ready for shows, but I still couldn't fully see myself as a heavyweight. But I was determined to jump up a class and compete in the heavyweight class in my next show anyway.

I immediately entered the Mr. USA, being held in Las Vegas. I went into the heavyweight class at 205 pounds and placed third. While I placed higher than other great athletes, such as Mike Christian (who went on to become a top pro, years later), to me this was a disaster. *I was meant to win these shows! Didn't these judges understand?* I thought after the show as I gobbled down a gigantic, sloppy cheeseburger in the hotel restaurant. Second place was unacceptable; third was unthinkable. Something would have to change so that I could get back to winning.

After the USA, I decided that it was time to begin training in the muscle ghetto, that I'd been training out on the edges too many years. Putting myself into a more competitively charged atmosphere would change my current fortunes back to the winning track, I thought.

Driving my old Honda Civic down to the beach each day, I began training at World Gym, early in the morning, and quickly became part of Joe Gold's early crew. The second day I was there, Arnold came into the gym to train, as he did nearly every day, even after his competitive days were behind him. I got so shaky when I saw him that I couldn't finish my workout. Slowly, as the weeks passed, I got used to training around him and my nervousness passed.

The first time we spoke was on a Saturday. I was looking around the gym for a favorite handle that I used on triceps pushdowns. I finally found it on a machine outside on the deck. I took it off, brought it inside, put it on the machine my training partner and I were using, and started doing my exercise. While I was catching my breath between sets, Arnold came into the gym from the deck, looking around, and finally made his way over to the machine I was using.

"So—there's the handle I was using," he said, taking it off and starting back for the deck. "You must not want me to work my biceps," he joked. "Don't you know, Bob, that I must work my biceps?" He smiled, then headed on.

I shot back, in a completely smart-ass tone, "I feel the same about my triceps."

He stopped, turned around, shook his head, and laughed. "That's a good one," he said, and headed on outside.

I was never shy around him again, except one Saturday, a year later, when he complimented me on my condition as I was hitting a couple of poses in the mirror on the gym deck and he came walking out and stopped to look. Other than that, I never had another nervous moment at this place, regardless of who was training there. I was on the inside now and had, at last, found my training home.

I decided to go into the American Championships (the name of the competition was in transition at this point, evolving from the Mr. America and ending up as the National Championships in 1983), confident that I would at least win the light-heavyweight class (I'd decided to return to that class after my placing in the less prestigious USA) and make the Mr. Universe team. I arrived in New York a week ahead of the show and stayed with some friends of my training partner's.

At the weigh-in, before the prejudging, I stripped down to my posing trunks, as all the athletes were required to do, and when I stepped up on the scale, the official doing the weighing said, "One hundred ninety-nine and three-quarters"—a pound and three-quarters over the light-heavyweight cutoff. The scale I'd been using all week had me at 197, a pound under the limit. I was thrown into the heavyweight class—whether I liked it or not—as the smallest guy in a lineup filled with 220-pound, and larger, athletes.

A guy named Lee Haney was the favorite in the heavyweights. I had been the precontest favorite in the light heavies. Lee Haney won the class and the overall title and went to the Universe and won that too. (He continued on to become an eight-time Mr. Olympia.)

I placed third. The guy who won the light heavies lost his class at the Universe. Not only did most observers of the show think that I would have won the light-heavyweight class with a fair amount of ease, but that I'd also held my own in the heavyweights, against Haney and another newcomer named Matt Mendenhall. The fans who liked pure mass said that I placed where I should have; the ones who liked a more symmetrical, classical look said that I could just as easily have won the class. Whatever. After doing some studio photos and an interview for *Ironman* on the Sunday after the show, I returned from New York determined never to make another mistake with my career—ever.

The first thing I did on returning was to shave my head. It was a bootcamp type of symbol of how I was going to approach the next year. I turned myself into a warrior, a man determined to prepare flawlessly and to return to claim the titles that were his destiny. I cut the number of private training clients I worked with back to the minimum that would allow me to survive, but not so many that I couldn't devote all my energies to my training. It was time to get serious.

Every day I'd come into the gym and throw myself at the weights with an aggression I'd never before experienced. Everyone in the gym seemed to think that I was on the verge of greatness and I wasn't going to disappoint them or myself.

I had thought that New York was a failure. Evidently others saw it differently. I was a new "overnight" sensation. Ricky Wayne, from *Muscle and Fitness*, wanted to meet me at World Gym to do an interview for that magazine. Ricky and I hit it off immediately. We did the interview on a Saturday afternoon. When it came out a couple of months later, it was called "Paris Is Burning." Around the same time, an article that I'd done an interview for in New York also hit the stands, in *Ironman*, titled "The Last Time I Saw Paris."

I began to appear in the magazines nearly every month and started to get requests to do seminars and guest-posing exhibitions. Some were in foreign countries. I turned down the ones that were too far away because I instinctively knew that the travel would disrupt my training and intense focus. I gave a few seminars in areas close to California. They were easy. In my mind, I'd had a training seminar ready to go for over a year.

A few months after New York, a friend, Harry Kessler, who was also a personal manager for a famous, major cosmetics manufacturer, asked me if I wanted him to help manage my career. He said that he wanted to help me achieve whatever dreams I had, as a way of repaying me for coming to his rescue one night while he was having a nearly fatal kidney-stone attack. Harry had called me in the middle of the night and said that he was being rushed to the hospital, and would I come and make sure that his house got locked up correctly and call some of his other friends and associates, letting them know where he was and what had happened.

Now he wanted to repay me. I told him that there was no need for repayment, that I'd only done what any decent human being would have done. I told Harry, though, that I'd love to have him act as my personal manager. He said that I could be a huge star, far beyond the world of muscle, that we'd turn the fame in the world of bodybuilding into a film career; I reminded him of a Tyrone Power with muscles, he said. He had to show me a picture of whom he was talking about. I said that would be a swell idea, since becoming a serious actor had been something of a dream even before I had discovered the weights, and I had always thought that it was a natural next step after I'd finished with bodybuilding.

Immediately we began to make plans for how to turn the fame that was beginning to build in the magazines into something bigger and more enduring. As a side business, he co-owned a small sweater company. We agreed that I would start a clothing company directed at the bodybuilding world. It seemed a natural. We made plans to put together ads that would appear in all the magazines.

Joe Weider called. He wanted to meet. Everyone told him great things about me, he said, and the photos John Balik had taken of me were bound to become classics. We set up a meeting. He asked me to meet him for lunch and gave me the address. I hung up the phone shivering with a nervous excitement that had been building since high school.

Harry and I sat down the night before my first meeting with Joe and made a plan of how we wanted the lunch to go. He said that I should make notes and take them in with me, then write notes from the meeting as well, to keep a record of what had happened.

We talked about how it would be great to get *Muscle and Fitness* to do a fashion layout, which would accomplish several things. First, it would use me as the male model, further building my career. Second, I could get my new clothing line into the shoot. Third, I could tell Joe that I would find all the other clothing for the shoot, then do it and show him that I was a can-do kind of guy.

Then we talked about what to do about the "gay issue." We decided that the best route was to tell him; get it right out on the table and then assure him that I had every intention to be "discreet." I wrote extensive notes on a yellow legal pad.

The next day, I met Joe at the restaurant. He eyed me warily when I opened my knapsack and produced the legal pad.

"What are you—some kind of lawyer?"

"No, I just wanted to make sure to talk about everything. This is so I don't forget anything," I said, pointing at the pad. "No trick questions."

After we had talked about bodybuilding for a while, I brought up doing fashion shoots. He said that he had been thinking about doing one. Did I want to go as the male model? (Over the years I learned that he habitually took anything you brought up to him—if he thought that it was a good idea—and acted as if he'd already thought of it.) He said that he could get Rachel McLish to be the female model. I told him that was perfect. He said that we could go to some exotic location— maybe Mexico—for the shoot. I told him that I'd take responsibility for all the clothing. He said that was fine.

When we'd finished eating, right before he paid the bill, I said, "There's one other thing I'd like you to know, Joe—just to get it out in the open."

"Whaat, that you're—"

"That I'm, um, yeah—that I'm, um, well—gay. I didn't know if you knew that or not."

"I knew."

"And?"

"Look, nobody out there knows, right?" He made a broad gesture around the restaurant.

"I stay pretty—oh, I don't know—pretty quiet, I guess you could say."

"Good. Keep it that way, Baab. Those people don't need to know anything. I'm gonna make you into a star, Baab, just like I did for Arnold—you just go along, everything'll be fine."

We did the shoot in Acapulco. Rachel McLish, the two-time Ms. Olympia, was the female model. It was the first fashion layout in *Muscle and Fitness*. I had gone around at the L.A. clothing mart borrowing the newest clothes from the designers. I'd walk into a showroom, introduce myself, and by the time I left, I had a yes. My manager was friends with the owner of Guess and made arrangements to get their latest line as well. The shoot was a success.

When the layout appeared, the muscle ghetto's jealous wagging tongues wondered why I had been chosen to do the photos. They didn't understand that the whole thing had been my manager's and my idea to begin with, and that I'd worked my butt off to pull everything together for it.

The ripples of jealousy had begun, though. I was on the cover of *Muscle and Fitness* and in the magazines all the time. I now had ads for my own clothing company. Why was I getting such special treatment? wagging tongues wanted to know.

Joe and I had the first of several fights during the first *Muscle and Fitness* cover shoot I was on, the week after the trip to Acapulco. He wanted the female model who I was shooting with to be completely draped over me, in a sexual way. I asked why it couldn't be more athletic and not so sexual, and he told me to just take the pictures. He was having photographer Dick Zimmermann do some photos for my ads, so I backed off. The model I was shooting with told me that she agreed—the picture should be less sexual—and between shots we pulled the photographer aside and told him. He agreed. So the three of us tried to quietly convince Joe—pulling him aside one at a time, winking at each other as we whispered to him—that it would be a better cover if it was approached differently. By the time we'd each talked to him, he was convinced that he himself had actually thought of changing it to a much more athletic-looking cover shot.

But this notion of how my cover shots should be done and how my image should be portrayed in his magazines didn't go away. Over the years, Joe and I would have dozens of heated arguments revolving almost completely around these same issues.

Finally after my clothing-company—Bob Paris Fashions—ads had run in Joe's magazines three times, I got a formal complaint from the National Physique Committee and, in the end, pulled the plug on the company.

Summer, 1983
World Gym, Santa Monica, California

I was on the verge. Everyone knew it too. Each morning when I came to the gym, a feeling of momentum, a taste of accomplishment just about to happen, was soaking the air.

The old World Gym was amazing. Small, tight; perfect equipment. I knew its grooves and meanings; its shadows were family.

The National Championships were three months away and I was already in shape; I had been for more than a month. After placing third in New York the year before, I swore myself to a year of focus and intensity that would make everything that had come before seem uncommitted. And it had happened.

I was still relatively poor; every spare penny went toward my training. I had already survived an attempt to have me disqualified from amateur competition because I had used photos of myself to advertise my clothing company. I actually had to undermine the company to keep my amateur status. On the advice of an attorney who was familiar with the bodybuilding world, I not only had to pull the ads, which had cost me several thousand dollars to produce, out of the magazines but also had to discontinue business until after I had my pro card. I had to send a letter to the head of the National Physique Committee, Jim Manion, stating that I hadn't made any money from the enterprise (of course, I hadn't made any money, I had only just started the company. I hadn't had a chance even to get my investment back yet) and that I would stop doing business for the time being. All this simply because of an anonymous complaint that I later found out had come from a close associate of one of the other favorites to win the Nationals. It was all irrelevant, though. At that point I would have given up nearly anything to win that show. It was my gateway to the big leagues.

The only thing I regretted was that the Mr. Olympia came before the Nationals and World Championships this year. If the Olympia came after I had my pro card (which I would get by winning the Nationals and then the World Championships), I knew that I had a shot at taking them all. That would be the equivalent of somehow winning the Big

Ten, the Rose Bowl, and the Super Bowl all in the same year. These were the things bouncing through my head as I banked around into the home stretch. I knew that other guys worried endlessly about who their main competition was and what kind of shape those competitors were getting into. I already knew that I was going to win; I didn't care who showed up or what condition they were in. I just kept pounding the weights, knowing that major change was only three months away.

Come on, two more, two more, that's it—squeeze. You got it—squeeze, push, push, push, I went inside my head as I struggled through the last reps on a set of incline dumbbell presses, at the end of my chest workout. The skin on my chest felt as if it could be played like a bongo. I knew, as I put the hundred-pound dumbbells back on their rack, that beneath the tattered red sweatshirt I was wearing inside out were the goods. When I was in contest shape, I never looked my full size in baggy clothes. I always had a deceptive body, one that only came alive when I made it happen. My deception in clothes had always worked to my advantage in the mental warfare that my more thuggish competitors constantly tried to wage. I was always being written off by them because I looked so unbodybuilderish in the street clothes I wore. I usually ended up beating those guys who wrote me off as more of a pretty boy than a serious competitor because I didn't run around with my body popping through tight clothes as they did. They didn't understand how to play the game, I told myself whenever I'd see one of them, their chest and delts pushing through a shirt small enough for an eleven-year-old boy. They gave it all away for nothing, so they'd never have anything except the momentary looks of strangers. For me, it wasn't about building this huge body so I could walk around flexing my muscles everywhere, or so I could get laid more. This was my sport; the body I built was simply my four-minute mile, which I happened to carry around with me just under my clothes. That's why those guys—the lugs, who might do a little something in competition, but would never turn it into what it could be—underestimated me so frequently. They measured everything only according to their limited rules. I knew their rules, took them into account, then played by my own.

That said, on this perfect California summer morning, I thought, *Oh, why not,* and pulled my sweatshirt off, up over my head, so I could see what I looked like with my chest and shoulders packed full of blood.

I was training on the outside deck of the gym, where I could breathe the ocean wind coming from two blocks away. World had a full gym out on the deck. It would go rusty in the winter, and they'd have to clean it up after the March storms had passed, but the rest of the year it was an amazing place to work out. Usually I avoided the deck because the beauty of being able to see the ocean and feel the air distracted me from my absolute focus and, I thought, hurt my training. But on this particular Saturday I felt like being outside. When I peeled off my sweaty, worn shirt, immediately every man on the deck looked to see what was different; they were used to my quietly—with ray-gun intensity—going about my work, mostly covered up, trying to attract as little attention as possible, then leaving. I hit a couple of poses toward the mirror, where the light was right, in between the doors leading back inside the gym. From my neck to my waist, lines and deep grooves ran everywhere; a few small veins pushed through the thin skin on my abdomen; bigger artery-looking veins crossed my chest, shoulders, and arms in a few places; nothing hung over the elastic of my blue gym shorts. When I could wear shorts with a tight elastic waistband without a dent where the skin met the top of the fabric, I knew that I was on target.

"Jesus, Bob. I had no idea you looked like that," Tom Platz said, a look of surprise on his face. Tom had won the Universe three or four years before and had placed third in (and should probably have won) the Mr. Olympia two years earlier. He was doing sit-ups, but came over, acting as if he were headed toward another piece of equipment. I did a couple of shots while he stood there.

Arnold came out from inside the gym right at that moment. His eyes opened wide, and he smiled at me as Tom walked away.

"Here is our future Mr. Olympia. You look fantastic, Bob," he said in that unmistakable Austrian accent, genuine, unguarded, almost like a kid, as I did three or four more poses toward the mirror, thanked him for his kind words, pulled my shirt back on, grabbed my knapsack, and scurried out of the gym.

When I got down to my car, I realized that I'd forgotten to finish my workout. I still had triceps to do.

Oh, well. I can always come back later, I thought, realizing that being forgetful was probably okay under these circumstances. It's not every day that one of your biggest heroes gives you such compliments and forecasts how great you yourself are going to be.

Did I really tell Arnold, 'Thanks for the kind words'? I wondered as I pulled out of the parking lot under the gym.

"God, Bob, you're such a geek," I said, looking in my eyes in the rearview mirror, turning left onto Main Street, headed toward home.

* * *

In the gym, I was lightning and thunder all combined. From three months out of the Nationals I could have walked onstage with two weeks' notice. My warrior's approach had worked. I was in shape at 225 pounds; the days on the border between heavyweight and light heavy were a distant memory. I was doing everything—including pushing my bodybuilding drugs up to higher and more sophisticated levels—that it would take to win.

After returning from placing third in New York at the America, I pulled out all the stops. I started researching all the chemical potions that would give me an edge. I knew that if I relied only on my genetic talent—combined with relatively conservative-strength drug use—I'd continue to remain an also-ran in national competition. That would never do. So, in addition to finding more cutting-edge steroids, I started experimenting with other drugs that I speculated would catapult my body to the next—and highest—level of development.

March 1983
Southern California

I waited nervously, hoping that no one would come in and recognize me. Dr. William White was the man of the moment, but none of the guys really wanted to be discovered sitting on those 1960s, blue vinyl bench seats thumbing through *Highlights* in his waiting room. I knew it was foolish to hope that no one would find out I'd been here. His nurses and receptionists were known as notorious gossips, telling anyone who would listen whom the doctor was seeing and what he was doing for that person. The doctor was even known to brag about his topflight clientele. That's why I was here. I'd heard about all the top guys coming out to this tiny beach town, miles up the coast from the muscle ghetto, to get it: human growth hormone. Even its name gave me an odd mixture of blind hope and the willies. As I played with the ten one-hundred-dollar bills in my zippered sweatshirt pocket, I pictured radical microscopic close-ups of cells exploding and shifting inside my body: something human in me dying and being replaced by an entity larger, stronger, but less alive.

There had always been something vampirelike in all of this drug business. I was sure that this new one would take over my soul. It was relatively fresh on the scene, very cutting edge. The rumors about growth hormone were that it either didn't work and was an expensive waste of money or that it worked so well that it would radicalize the bodybuilding scene. No one I knew could truly afford it. No one I knew could truly afford to be without it.

I certainly couldn't afford it. My rent was $400 a month (a fortune in those days) on my tiny studio apartment fifteen miles from the beach and the gym. My six-year-old yellow Honda Civic, which I'd spent all my savings paying cash for a year before, was a mess. I saw my mechanic more often than many of my friends, since the damned car was broken as often as it was running. My food bills were larger than my sister and brother-in-law's, and they had two kids.

Any spare money I had was going toward my normal anabolics and training expenses since I was only eight months out from the National Championships, and hopefully the Mr. Universe three weeks later—if I won the Nationals.

I had no idea what effects this new drug would have on my body then or in the future, but I'd found a way to pull together a thousand dollars for a two-week supply and knew I could get another thousand for the two weeks after. Two grand for a four-week cycle. It was supposed to be eight to ten weeks at twice the dose I'd rationalized for myself. It already felt as if I were going to inject rocket fuel and hope for some magic to make it all pay off.

Now I sat waiting to see a doctor who pitched the stuff like a car salesman talking you into a bigger engine on a new Chevy. I was a willing mark. I wanted him to convince me that I had to have a 454 under the hood.

I never wanted to face how I sold my ideals so easily. I had a tremendous capacity, even at an early age, to shut my brain off to any dangerous complicating thoughts about my destiny. No one had forced me to be here. If I didn't like having to take higher and higher levels of drugs to rise to the top, I could just walk away and do something else. But I didn't. Instead I took a breath and dove a level deeper. There was something enticing in all of this. I was not only justifying the means, I was worshiping them. My religion had grown so strong: this dogmatic belief that I deserved to be the best. I could only pray that the sword I lived by didn't kill me. But I tried my best not think about that.

There was nothing really different in my decision to use growth hormone. I had made small and large decisions just like this ever since I had first figured out how to push past just busting my ass in the gym every day to achieve my dreams.

So here I was, waiting to see Dr. White, to push further, to insure that—whether growth hormone worked or not—I wasn't left in the dust of everyone I'd be competing against in the fall. I justified that if I did this through a physician, it was probably okay. After all, what kind of doctor would knowingly do harmful things to his patients?

Two years before the rumors about growth hormone began to surface in, and then sweep through, the sports world, I walked through a mall in Whittier, California, with Rory Leidelmeyer, during the time when he was helping me get ready for my first amateur shows. He told me about an article he'd read in the newspaper that morning. The piece was on how far Olympic athletes were willing to go in their quest for gold medals.

The reporter had asked dozens of top Olympic hopefuls: "If you knew that a drug was available that guaranteed you would win the Olympic gold medal or its equivalent in your sport next year, but the only catch was you'd drop dead from the drug's side effects five years later, would you take it?"

Something like 90 percent of the athletes interviewed said yes. I shook my head in an outward show of disbelief as Rory and I talked about how stupid those people were, but deep inside I knew, at that point in my life, that I would have said yes too.

Even with being in the magazines all the time, I was only an underdog favorite to win the Nationals. Matt Mendenhall, the good-looking, blond heavyweight who had taken second in the class the year before, was the one to beat. Mike Christian, who'd placed fourth to my third in the two national-level contests we'd both done, was said to be doing what it took and was coming on strong. Rory was reported to be training hard for the show as well, and everyone in the sport knew that he could be a major force—if he did everything just right. He had skipped the contest in New York and had placed second in the light-heavyweight class—having lost too much weight during the final weeks—the year before that in Las Vegas.

The year that the show was in Las Vegas was the year when I had been living in Laguna Beach and had suddenly found myself without a job or car and had had to let the show go by, even though I had gotten myself into better shape than I would be in for New York; sometimes these things work out for the best. If I had done the show in Las Vegas, or even won the light heavies in New York, I might never have put myself through a year—"A Year of Training Dangerously," as one article about my preparations for the 1983 shows was titled afterward—where

I did nothing except focus on getting what I wanted. But I was still seen as a dark horse.

The show was going to be in San Jose, at the same auditorium where I'd taken second in the California and smashed my trophy against the pavement of the back parking lot. Winning there would be sweet, I told myself.

All throughout the year I had been meditating and visualizing success at this show, every day, and sometimes two or three times a day. When I'd lie on the tanning bed, the whole time the bulbs were turning my skin darker, my mind would be rehearsing the win. I had it so clearly pictured, so vividly etched on the back of my brain, that my body had little choice but to follow. No other outcome was possible except winning. "Grasshopper" would show them a thing or two.

Autumn, 1983
San Jose, California
NPC National Championships

In San Jose the first thing I did was have Samir Bannout come up to my hotel room to give me his opinion on my condition. Samir had, only a few weeks earlier, won the Mr. Olympia in Munich. We had become friends at World Gym while we both got ready for our shows.

"All I can say, Bob, is that I'm glad I wasn't going against you in the Olympia."

I knew that his saying that meant that I was right on the money.

The prejudging was on one day, the finals the next. The morning of the prejudging, a camera crew, which a friend of my training partner's had hired to trail behind me and tape everything, followed me into the weigh-in, being held in a small conference room of the hotel. Rory was sitting in one of the chairs that were lined up in rows, in front of the scale. He wouldn't look at me as I came into the room. I stripped off my clothes only when I got up to the scale; I could feel all the eyes in the room suddenly shift in my direction. I weighed in—216 pounds. The second I stepped off the scale and turned around to get dressed, I saw Rory headed for the door. He had been waiting just to see me weigh in. He was probably telling the guy he was with that I looked like shit.

The judging was supposed to begin in the afternoon. About half an hour before it was scheduled to start (everyone already knew that the judging was running hopelessly late), Samir found me sitting in the auditorium lobby reading a book. He asked me how my body was looking. Since a contest-ready physique can go through dramatic changes from hour to hour, he was curious. Samir, my training partner, and I slipped into a small rest room off the lobby, so I could show them how I looked. As we went in, I noticed Mike Christian watching us from across the lobby. We closed and locked the door and I stripped off my sweats.

"You're right on track, Bob," Samir said. "Maybe you need to carb up a little more so you keep filling out."

"Yeah, but I gotta be cautious. I don't want to go overboard and be holding water by tomorrow," I said after I'd hit a few poses to show them my condition. Samir had pinched the skin in different places all around my abdominals and lower back—to see if the skin was staying tissue-paper thin. It was.

"You know," I added, pulling my sweats back on, "this whole two-day competition thing is so fucked up. Why can't they just do it all in one day?"

"You're gonna win, Bob. Don't worry," Samir said, and pulled the rest-room door open.

Mike Christian fell into the room, catching himself at the last minute before landing on the floor.

"Uh . . . is, uh . . . is this . . . um, the . . . rest room?" he asked nervously, embarrassed. He must have had his ear pressed against the door listening to our conversation.

"Obviously, Mike—this is the rest room. Get an earful?" I asked him as we walked away laughing. "Jeez, some guys'll do anything for a little drama."

We went into the auditorium and found seats in the back as the prejudging for the lighter weight classes kept moving slowly forward.

The heavyweights eventually came onstage at eleven at night. I had sat around all day, slowly munching on carb foods, letting my muscles fill up. At the weigh-in I had felt flat—as if my muscles were deflated, so I was carefully eating small amounts of food throughout the day to get them to fill out and explode against the skin. I sat thinking that I was glad to be flat at the weigh-in; it would make Rory overconfident.

All day, as we waited hour after hour through unexplained delays, I sat just breathing, sinking into the totally calm place that I'd been practicing getting to all year. I'd alternate between meditating and reading a book, so relaxed that the building could have caught on fire and I would have just serenely walked out an exit and found a spot outside to lie down and continue reading.

My brother, Jim, had flown in for the show. He'd graduated from high school that year and had enlisted in the Air Force; this trip was one last fling before heading off to boot camp. He sat beside me in the auditorium, along with a few of my friends who'd come in to see me compete.

Within the first few call-outs, it was obvious that the class was going to come down to Mike Christian, Rory, and me. Matt Mendenhall was not in his best condition. He said that he had the flu. I stood in the lineup as still and flexed as a statue. I had practiced this in my meditation as well. I would breathe myself into a kind of alert trance, which made standing in a constant state of muscular tension seem as if I were lying in a golden green field that smelled like fresh-cut wild onions.

On the last call-out, it was indeed Mike, Rory, and me. The head judge asked for a side chest pose, and I turned to my right, so I could do the pose from the left side. Rory was on my right. When I turned, he had rotated in my direction. We came face-to-face; at that moment I knew I had him. A brief look of shock or fear or something crossed his face, and he spun around to do the pose from his left side as well. I have no idea what went through his mind at that second, but that was the moment I knew that the student had beaten the teacher.

The next night we stood onstage in front of a wild, sold-out crowd, and Mike Christian had already been announced third. There was a lot of booing; at a show this competitive that was natural; everyone had his favorite.

The audience was deafening, with cheers, hollers, chanting, booing, clapping, foot-stomping, and any other means of noisemaking as Rory and I stood while the emcee stretched out the suspense. I had gone over this moment in my mind a thousand times during the year. When the emcee finally said, "The new NPC heavyweight National Champion is— Bob Paariiss," and the crowd erupted in a hurricane of emotion, and Rory held my arm up in the air and congratulated me—I had already seen the movie of it. Time splintered into slow-motion shards; voices sounded like forty-five records played on thirty-three. Then it all came swooshing back to full speed, and I realized that I was being handed a six-foot-tall trophy and being told to get ready for the comparisons between the class winners for the overall title. I had won by one point.

The pose-down between class winners felt a million miles away. I had seen this movie before too. At the end of it I was announced the overall winner of the National Championships. Even though the NPC didn't call it that anymore, I was the new Mr. America.

*   *   *

Mike Christian would go on to win the National Championships the next year. A few weeks later he'd also become a Mr. Universe and move on to a successful pro career.

Rory never did win the Nationals. His second place in 1983 was the closest he ever got. That was a shame. He would most likely have been a great pro.

Matt Mendenhall's career—after such a promising start at the 1982 version of this show, where he placed second to Lee Haney's first and my third in the heavyweight division—floundered. Within another couple of years, Matt, whom many in the sport had seen as *the* golden boy, had quit competition and faded away.

Autumn, 1983
Singapore
Mr. Universe

The headline on the front page of the *Sunday Times*, the main newspaper in Singapore, read, "Paris Rules the World." There was a picture of me holding up my trophy, arms raised overhead in victory, a medal around my neck. The paper was waiting outside my hotel room door by 6 A.M. I hadn't slept a wink all night. How could I have? I wanted to be awake and taste every second of it. Sweet, like a slice of one of Mam-ma's sugar cream pies—that's how it tasted. I'd telephoned back to the States to let some friends know; they phoned my family.

The IFBB was now trying to call what had always been the Mr. Universe the World Bodybuilding Championships; that was its official name. They thought that the title *world champion* was more in line with the ambitious plans to eventually have bodybuilding in the Olympic Games; it gave the champion more of an international sporting flair, something like world gymnastics champion, perhaps. The title Mr. Universe smacked of being attached to a beauty contest, they felt, and it betrayed the athleticism of the competition. We didn't wear evening gowns or have a Mr. Congeniality winner, after all.

I was the new World Heavyweight Champion, although the papers insisted on referring to me as the newly crowned Mr. Universe; must have rankled Ben Weider to have them use that newly obsolete title.

Singapore was hot and muggy. You could have picked up anything in the whole city—an automobile tire, a baseball, a filing cabinet—wrung it out, and provided yourself with a bucket of water. We had arrived in the early morning or the early evening or the late night. I couldn't tell what it was, since the plane from San Francisco had catapulted us over the international date line, and so far from home that yesterday was tomorrow, or something like that. I had taken two sleeping pills on the flight, put on one of those sleeping masks—like an old movie actress might wear—and didn't wake up until we landed in Hong Kong for a layover.

The whole U.S. team met in San Francisco for the Singapore Air flight. We were all on the team by way of winning our individual weight classes in the Nationals three weeks earlier. Our team was escorted by Jim Manion, president of the National Physique Committee and the IFBB vice president for North America, and a small entourage of others from the States, who were associated with the federation in one way or another.

We had all heard that Singapore's customs officers could be a nightmare, and when you're entering a country where possession of chewing gum is against the law, you can get worried that maybe your underarm deodorant might be too, and if caught, you'll be hauled off for a good caning or maybe be put in shackles in the town square. But we were met by one of the officials of the championships, and since the country was enthusiastically awaiting the upcoming competition—or so the official told us—we were swept right through customs like arriving royalty.

The hotel had assembled a gym for all the athletes, in an outdoor pavilion, where passersby and fans alike could watch everyone train. There wasn't really much training to be done; almost all the best athletes took at least the last two days before a show off from training, so that the body could rest and not be depleted on contest day. I was so thrown out of whack by the severe change in time zones, though, that I went down into the pavilion and fiddled around with the weights, doing some light exercise to work the jet lag out. The spectators seemed to be looking at me as if they expected to see world-record feats of lifting. And the press was swarming all around as well.

Ever since I'd arrived, the local reporters had been following my every move. There were articles in the papers every day, and they had built up this tremendous rivalry between a heavyweight from Holland, Berry DeMey, and me. As far as the press was concerned, the whole contest came down to a showdown between the two of us. They wondered which way the judging panel, which was fairly evenly divided between all the different countries but leaned heavily toward European judges, would come down in the final matchup.

One reporter asked Berry what he thought about me as I walked through the hotel lobby, having just arrived, wearing a pair of Levi's jeans and a red polo shirt. The reporter quoted Berry, who had been sitting on a couch in the lobby, in that night's *Times* as saying, "He has nice pants."

There was also the German, Ralf Moeller, to contend with, the press reported. Ralf fired up imaginations because he was a charming, good-humored man, but most of all, they were in awe because he stood six foot eight and had done well in the contest the year before.

The prejudging was on a Friday, and the finals on Saturday. This arrangement was unpopular with all the athletes because you try to hit your absolute peak on one target day. Holding that peak for two days was difficult at best; anything could happen, and minute changes in condition could mean the difference between winning and only placing.

On Friday I rested in my room while the lighter weight classes were being judged. I'd been given an official time for the start of the heavy-weight prejudging and figured that if I got over to the theater forty-five minutes early, that'd be plenty. The theater was a quarter mile or so across a long overhead walkway, on the other side of the road from the hotel. It was an outdoor theater and I knew that the heat could impact my condition—and I couldn't predict whether the impact would be positive or negative—so I decided to wait to go over, not too early, but with just enough time to be safe.

Right below my room was a Hindu temple, and I could see over its walls and into the courtyard, where some sort of celebration or service seemed to be unfolding. They were burning huge fires, and the smoke of incense rose in puffy, damp columns, and large numbers of celebrants were moving through the courtyard, caught up in whatever it was that they were doing.

I thought, *I should find out if this is a holiday or what's up down there*, as I casually got dressed in my navy blue U.S. team sweats to head out for a gentle stroll over to the theater.

I told myself as I left the hotel and felt the full weight of the equatorial heat smack up against me, *Take it easy. Don't get your adrenaline running—you'll start to hold water.*

I proceeded cautiously because my internal workings were already thrown off enough by the drastic change in time zones and climate. Halfway to the theater, I saw Charles Glass, the middleweight from the U.S. team, running toward me. I thought, *What the hell is Charles doing? He should be onstage about now, in the middle of his prejudging.*

"Bob, come on. You gotta hurry." He was completely out of breath.

"What the fuck's goin' on, Charles?" I was totally confused.

"They're getting ready to start your class. If you're not there, like, right now, they're gonna start without you."

"My class doesn't start for another hour." We began to sprint toward the theater.

"They—finished—early—decided to—move it—up."

When we flew through the stage door, everyone asked me where I'd been. I was trying to pull in some air, after sprinting over, and there was no relief from the heat anywhere backstage. Adrenaline burst through every pore, and adrenaline is one of the great enemies of a bodybuilder getting ready to walk onstage; too much of it at the last minute and the body can begin to send fluid rushing up under the skin, water that can obscure the muscularity of even the most ripped physique. This was sort of the equivalent of a sprinter getting a severe hamstring cramp ten minutes before running the final heat of the hundred meters at the World Track and Field Championships. Months, and even years, of careful preparation could be ruined right at the last possible moment.

They'd been calling the hotel and had sent out search parties to find me. Jim Manion came over, wearing his blue official judge's blazer, and told me that he knew that the heavyweights weren't due for another hour; he'd tried to tell the promoter that when it was discovered that I hadn't yet arrived, but the promoter had decided to opt for efficiency, and since the other classes had finished early, they would proceed with the heavyweights. In the promoter's view whether or not I was there wasn't relevant. His feeling was that I should have been in the theater during the entire judging, and if I wasn't there whenever they began, tough luck.

I asked Jim why they'd bothered with official start times then. I said something to the effect that it would be like starting the Super Bowl an hour early because everything was ready to go and some stubborn pro-ducer insisted on beginning; it didn't matter that the players hadn't ar-rived yet or that the TV hookup wasn't for another hour. On and on I went, all the time stripping my track suit off and spreading on oil. I was sweating profusely, and as I looked in a mirror, I couldn't really tell if it was the poor backstage lights or not, but a fine film of water appeared to be resting right under the skin. That water hadn't been there as I got myself ready—shaving stubble off my body, putting on tanning gel, blow-drying my hair—back in the hotel room only an hour before. In the hotel room mirror my muscles had looked dry as a bone, meaning that the skin was wrapped around them tightly, and I wasn't holding a single ounce of unwanted water. I'd appeared to be in perfect condition, and it seemed that walking across the road and becoming a world champion would be simple. I'd been calm and focused; I'd meditated for more than an hour after breakfast and visualized the entire show, taking my mind into the sort of calm place that had always worked so well for me. Because of unnecessary panic and a two-hundred-yard sprint, all that preparation may well have been tossed in a Dumpster.

Hurry up and wait. That seemed to be the common story at these contests, and this one was no exception. I couldn't stop sweating, and I felt my condition fading by the second, although I knew that feeling could sometimes be inaccurate.

Whenever I stripped down to my posing trunks backstage for a show, I always began to feel small and out of shape, no matter what condition I was in. Someone once told me that happened because the backstage area was so huge at a competition that, by comparison, your body felt small and frail, even when you were in spectacular shape. Because of that I usually kept my clothes on until the last possible minute, so that I wouldn't have my mind overwhelmed and my confidence hurt. Here, though, I didn't have a choice. I had stripped off the second I'd come through the door because everyone was so convinced that if I wasn't ready to walk onstage—right that second—they'd start without me. I'd stayed in my posing trunks and didn't get dressed again because a stage manager kept coming back and saying, "Five minutes. Heavyweights out in five minutes."

I couldn't miss the contest. In fact, I couldn't even take less than first place. I'd worked all year to get there, and in a way it was a jinxed show for anyone who didn't win. The chances were overwhelming that—especially if you were on the American team—if you didn't win on your first try, you'd never win and would most likely never even get the chance to return.

You qualified to be at the Universe by winning at least your weight class at the Nationals. But if you were the overall winner of the Nationals (as I had been), then you were prevented from competing in that show again. If you were in my position and didn't win the World Championships, then at the next year's Nationals, if you wanted to make the team, you'd have to compete separately, not in the contest itself, but as a special competitor, being judged against all the guys in the show, to make the World Championships team. No one had ever made the U.S. team by going that route, much less returned to win this contest on a second try.

A few years later, when the IFBB started drug testing at the World Championships, the NPC changed the qualifying rules for making the

American team because they decided against drug testing the Nationals. When that change occurred, they started giving weight-class winners at the National Championships their pro cards and selecting a U.S. team for the Worlds in a separate contest, making sure to select guys who could pass the drug test, and those guys were only rarely the class winners from the Nationals. Up until that point you had to win a World Championship, be a Mr. Universe, to make it into the pros.

An hour after I sprinted into the theater—at exactly the time it was supposed to start in the first place—the heavyweight prejudging began. The stage manager had continued coming back with his five-minute calls for the entire hour as the athletes milled around, ready to go.

From the outset the contest obviously came down to Berry and me, with Ralf pulling up third. They kept comparing us over and over, and I could see, when I was standing under the lights, that I was indeed holding a thin layer of water right under the skin. That was going to make the contest far closer than it might otherwise have been. Leaving the prejudging, I was only three points ahead of Berry.

Jim Manion pulled me aside once it was over and asked me what had happened to my condition. I told him that all that panic, combined with the hard weather, and probably traveling around the world to get there, had made me start to hold water, but that the run to the theater had truly triggered it all, since I'd been in perfect shape when I left my room. He told me to figure it out and do something about it; he said this kindly and with a great deal of understanding for what had happened. I told him that I'd figure it out. He said that I definitely should, because the prejudging had been far closer than he was comfortable with.

That night the articles in the papers said that it was a toss-up between Berry and me, and that the heavyweight championships would all come down to our posing routines, at Saturday's finals.

After the prejudging finished, I immediately went back to my room and took half a diuretic. Three hours, and many trips to the toilet, later my condition had returned to crystal sharp.

That night, after I ate dinner, I went out for a long walk in the vast park that surrounded the theater where the contest was being held. With each step, through the steaming jungle forest of the park, I breathed deeper and told myself that the heat was not the enemy, that allowing myself to get upset had been the stumbling block. After the walk, I felt calm again, went back, and slept as if I had been awake for years.

The alarm clock went off. At first, I thought that I'd set it wrong, but it was daylight outside, even though it seemed as if I'd only been asleep twenty seconds. I jumped out of bed, refreshed, ready to take on the world.

At the finals, I nailed my posing routine. It may have been the most polished performance I had ever given. The scoring gap between Berry and me held, and given that I was now in the shape I should have been in for the prejudging, it had even grown a few points wider.

When the emcee announced my name as the new World Bodybuilding Champion, I let out a breath and tried to hold back my tears. It had been such a long, hard road getting to that moment. I gave Berry DeMey a hug. I knew exactly how he was feeling right then, getting so close, only to have someone else, with ambitions the same as his, get in the way.

The waves from the audience made the theater feel as if a new galaxy were being started in its midst, what with all the flashing lights from cameras and the thunderous noise of human eruption.

There's no way I'll sleep tonight, I thought as the promoter's daughter brought me my trophy. *I probably won't sleep for a bunch of nights.*

I smiled and hit some victory poses, with my new Mr. Universe trophy, as the flashes kept going.

I could stay here forever, I thought.

14

SECOND THOUGHTS

December 1983
Los Angeles

The change came faster than I could ever have anticipated. After I won the Mr. Universe, there was a dramatic fast-forward shift. I was caught off guard.

A professional bodybuilder. I'd done it. But I'd put all my efforts, all my drive, into earning that pro card. Not much practical thought went into what I would do, as a bodybuilder, once I had it. What would happen in the days, weeks, or months after the National and World Championships? I knew that I wanted to win the Mr. Olympia, but had no plan for how I would make the transition from top amateur to successful pro.

If the Mr. Olympia had immediately followed these shows—as it did most years—and I had maintained my winning condition, I might have gone there and cleaned up. But the Olympia came early that year. A few weeks before the Nationals.

Samir Bannout had won the '83 Olympia after years of trying. He'd been a professional, or at least one of those top amateurs who everyone knew would eventually break through to the big leagues—almost since the time I'd discovered bodybuilding. I remembered him from the magazines; not the earliest magazines I'd read in high school, but more around the time I started college. And he'd made it. Becoming Mr. Olympia put him in a small, elite class of guys; only six men in the whole world could, at that time, say that they had won the Mr. Olympia. Everyone except Samir had also won more than once. Arnold had won seven times. Six of those wins were during the days when the prize money was so small that the show was only really professional in name. The question now remained, at least for me and the people who'd been in my corner, Would my name be added to that list?

*   *   *

"Okay, so here are copies of all the appearance contracts and your plane tickets—the boarding passes are all inside," Harry said while hurrying around his office, stuffing papers in my briefcase. "Once you get to Boston, there'll be a car waiting to take you to the seminar. Now remember, the minute it's over, you've got to get back to Logan. Your flight to Atlanta leaves at nine. When you get down there, get in, do your seminar, and get back to the airport. Don't worry, you'll have a driver there too. The schedule is tight, but then you can get to Brussels, do your guest posings, and catch the train to Paris. Ah . . . oh, yeah, don't—are you listening to me?—don't forget to wrap your mitts around the money. I've let all the promoters know to pay you the minute you arrive in each place. Don't forget."

"I know all this. We've been over it a hundred times—okay?" I said. It came out angrier or maybe more impatient than I intended. "Sorry, Harry. I'm just anxious about the trip. Damn, man, these plane connections are close. Am I gonna make this flight to Belgium? I mean, come on."

"Yes, you'll be fine. Right—okay, so anyway—the translators are all set in Belgium and France. Are you nervous about doing seminars through a translator?"

"No. Not really."

"Now look, you're gonna want to hang out in Paris for a while after your work. Trust me. I've been going there for twenty-five years. You will. But you can't. You must be back here to do that rehearsal for the benefit. And you can't miss your cold-reading class either. I've got meetings set for early January with those other agencies I told you about. They're gonna want to see what you can do. Did you give any more thought to working up a showcase scene?"

"Did you give any thought to when I'm supposed to work out? I am still a bodybuilder after all."

"You'll find time. Oh, that reminds me. Before you go, take a look at these contact sheets. I got the stuff back that John Balik did last week. You look terrific in the shots, by the way. They're exactly what we were after."

Two weeks after I returned from Singapore, I had hired both John Balik and Mike Neveaux to take tons of physique photos while I was still in contest shape. They were for the future. To be stored away. Freezing my Mr. Universe body in time.

Harry had figured that I would probably push my physique up to a higher—freakier—level of development in the year leading up to my pro debut and I needed to own pictures of how I had looked. He figured that it was a much more commercial look than what I would have during the next year. Besides, he had said, none of the other guys worried about owning their own photos. He'd said I'd be glad, years down the line, that I had all these pictures stored away that the public had never seen and that I owned outright.

Harry was a good manager and was working his ass off for me; he'd been there since before it all began to pay off. Already he'd turned all the guest-appearance requests that had flooded in right after the Universe into solid paid dates. Many paid dates.

Too many, I thought as I listened to him while examining one of the contact sheets of photos with one eye and glancing at the schedule he'd typed out—which was lying on the desk next to the photos—with the other.

Things had already shifted. Dramatically; nearly overnight. There hadn't been any moments to simply bask in the glory of my recent success. Harry had said that we needed to get me out working while the fire was hot. He was already working me onto the celebrity charity circuit, doing appearances for diabetes organizations, visiting kids with cancer in the hospital. He was working on something with the Special Olympics. And I had a rehearsal for some famous benefit, which the wives of several Hollywood power brokers produced every year, to do when I got back from a jam-packed two weeks of seminars and guest posings in the United States and Europe.

I was studying cold-reading (the technical term for auditioning from a script for TV or film parts) with one of the top casting directors in town and had already met with three talent agencies. I had decided that I needed to lose my accent if I wanted to be seen as anything other than a transplanted, hick-town muscleman, so I began to vigorously sand the rough edges off the southern-Indiana drawl I'd had all my life. Outside the gym, I'd started dressing only in expensive designer clothes.

Harry had said that he wanted to see me really make something out of myself. One night, about a month before the Nationals, we sat having a glass of wine and brainstorming about the future of my career. I should be driving a Rolls and living in a mansion within three years, he'd said. He was dead serious. I was twenty-three at the time with not much else on my mind except winning the shows and getting my pro card.

The change was too fast. None of the other guys I'd be competing against at Madison Square Garden in the '84 Olympia were thinking about how to get a high-powered agent or how to break out of body-building into show business. I knew most of these guys. All they were thinking about was preparing for battle at the Olympia.

Autumn, 1984
Madison Square Garden, New York
The 1984 Mr. Olympia

The '84 Olympia was my first experience at placing any lower than third in a real competition; I had grown mostly accustomed to winning.

Everybody claimed that my rise in the sport was meteoric; an overnight success story. After all, I had gone from second place in a state-level teenage show to winning a World Championship and qualifying for my first Mr. Olympia in a little over four years.

That didn't subtract from how I felt that night onstage in Madison Square Garden.

The fans had come out by the thousands. Even the ones who hadn't gotten, or couldn't afford, one of the five thousand tickets for the sold-out show were mobbed around the Garden, fanning out all the way into the streets, around the backstage entrance, waiting to see the competitors as they got out of taxis and tried to make their way inside. Some guys got through unmolested, but the ones these fans were clamoring to see would be instantly surrounded. They would tear and scream and stick out papers or magazines—anything that could be written on—to try to get an autograph; hundreds of flashes smacked the air.

"That's Bob Paris," a man's voice cried out the second I stepped out of my cab.

"Bob . . . Bob . . . Bob Paris . . . Paris . . . Bob—" Hundreds of voices all mingled, calling out my name, and a huge section of the crowd shifted into my direction. I signed hundreds of autographs, was photographed scores of times, shook every sort of hand that God ever invented. I tried to work my way toward the door as I smiled, shook, and signed. Three New York cops finally broke through the crowd an hour after I got out of the cab and had made it halfway to the side of the building.

"Come on," one of them said, and they pushed me through as I followed them like a fullback follows his blockers.

"Jesus H. Christ, that was wild," I said, laughing and panting, when we'd made it through the door.

"Damn—you're one popular kid," the oldest of the cops said.

"Hey, Bob, do me a favor, would ya—sign this for my son," another one said

"Your son—yeah, Mikey, right—your son," the third one shot in.

"Nah—it is. Come on, Bob—sign it to Mike Jr. Hey, somebody got a camera?" he asked, in general, to all the people standing by the door.

"Yeah—here, I'll do it. Gimme you're address after—I'll send ya copies," a man standing nearby, with a sophisticated camera around his neck, said.

We took a couple of pictures. They all wished me good luck in the show and headed out the door to see if anybody else needed to be rescued. Through the open door I could see the blond top of Tom Platz's head, in a sea of people. He seemed to be going through what I'd just been through, about twenty feet from the door. The cops pushed their way toward him as a security guard pulled the door shut.

By the end of the prejudging I knew that I wasn't in the top three, maybe not even in the top six. When I left to go back to my hotel, until the night show, I went out to catch a cab on the other side of Penn Station and the Garden from where I'd come in. It only took half an hour to work my way through the fans on that side of the building.

My dad and his wife, Ellen, had come to New York to watch me make my pro debut. Dad and I were only just beginning to heal some old wounds. He'd never seen me compete. We hadn't really spoken but a few words—even though Ellen kept trying to get us back in touch—since the night I'd come back to his house and found all my stuff thrown out on the driveway, four years earlier.

We had dinner together. Dad and Ellen told me that they thought I had the best body onstage, but that one of the guys in the bar, where they'd been waiting while I came down from changing clothes, had told them that the judges weren't going to let me do as well as I deserved, because they wanted to see me pay some more dues.

Pay some dues indeed, I thought, although I smiled and said, "Well, that's to be expected, I suppose."

Dad and Ellen said that they thought I was being very levelheaded about it. Ellen asked me if I had heard her during the judging. I told her that of course I had. Throughout the prejudging, whenever I was standing in the lineup or a comparison, I'd kept a serious look on my face; I don't think I even realized I was doing it. Every few minutes I'd hear this woman's voice yell out, "Smile, Bob." And I always broke out in a wide, beaming grin, only to forget it a couple of minutes later and get another, "Smile, Bob." That woman had been Ellen. Eventually audience members would laugh along or join in with her whenever she'd call out and I'd respond.

Later that night, in front of a sold-out house of rabid muscle fans, I placed seventh. My posing routine, earlier in the night show, to the theme music from the movie *The Natural*, had brought the house down. Joe Weider handed me my prize money, put a medal around my neck, shook my hand, and told me better luck next time. I stood there and wanted to cry.

That night I went out with friends who'd come in for the show, and we tied one on—big time.

I had no one to blame but myself, even if the judges did want me to pay my dues. This placement was my fault. A couple of months after I'd won the National and World Championships—almost exactly one year before—I'd spent nearly six months plunging into a self-destructive pit that I'd only pulled myself out of in barely enough time to get in great shape for the Olympia—great shape, but not overwhelming shape.

I had run away from home, in a sense, ruining the relationship with Harry, my personal manager, who I thought was trying to move me out of bodybuilding and into show business too quickly. I left L.A., lived on the road, and did the appearance work that had begun pouring in after my wins, but turned my back on all the other new developments in my career, then snapped out of my funk in just enough time to prepare for my professional debut.

I should have gotten into the kind of condition that made it impossible for them to deny me one of the top spots—as I had the year before. I knew how this game was played and I'd caused myself to place as low as I did.

I certainly didn't think I was an overnight success; I had lived through every single second of the time while I was working my way to the top. I simply wasn't prepared. I had focused in so hard and smashed ten years' worth of work down into four; I had left a former life behind and begun to shift my identity, like a costume change; by the time I'd gotten to where I wanted to be, I had already begun to ask myself too many questions. Instead of charging ahead, up the same soaring arc I'd been on, I wobbled, then spent years trying to get back on track.

December 1984
World Gym, Santa Monica, California

I think I'm gonna hang it up," I told Tommy.

We were sitting next to each other on stationary bikes at World Gym, two months after the Olympia in New York.

"Why?" he asked.

"I don't know exactly. Something has changed. It's like . . . um, I can't even do the thing that got me here in the first place right anymore. Know what I mean?"

"Bob, it's just one show. If you focus in, you'll be fine."

"Yeah, but see, that's just it. How am I supposed to focus when I spend half the year—what the fuck am I talking about?—*way* more than half the year living out of a suitcase. Have you ever seen the gyms in Europe? Most of them are like dungeons. Oh, and how about trying to get food? Ever try to order a grilled, skinless chicken breast and dry baked potato in Paris? They look at you like you're insane. And I have to stay on my drug cycle so that I can be in shape for my exhibitions. I should be clean—you know, natural—right now, so I can get ready to peak for next year's Olympia. I don't think I can keep this up. I'm tired all the time. Half the time I don't even know what country I'm in. It's just weird. All that work I put into building my business, and now it seems to stand in the way of going further in the same career that launched the business in the first place. How's that for a mouthful? Anyway, I think I just need to hang it up."

"So cut back on your road trips."

"Boy's gotta make a livin'. I don't ever want to be poor again."

"You're a strange man, Bob. I mean, look what happened. It's like, you won the Universe and then you wigged out. My advice would be to cut your guest spots in half and get your ass back in the gym training with the same focus you had in '83. It's like you're looking for reasons to self-destruct or quit."

"Fuck you."

"Nice. You kiss your mother with that mouth?"

"Harry was right. I shoulda listened to his advice. I shoulda been satisfied with becoming Mr. Universe and then moved on. Nobody outside bodybuilding even knows what the Mr. Olympia is. Whenever the media talks about Arnold, they don't say he was a multiple Mr. Olympia. They say he was a Mr. Universe. That's what people understand. Hell, most people don't even know that there is such a thing as professional bodybuilding."

"You just don't know how to appreciate what you have when you have it."

"And another thing—I'm getting sick of the drugs. I mean, I'm not a kid anymore. Did I tell you I got strip-searched at U.S. Customs last week, as I was comin' back from Argentina? When the Customs officer asked what I did for a living, I told him I was a pro bodybuilder, and right away he sticks me in some holding room. Next thing I know I'm naked and they've gone through my bags with a microscope. He thought just because I was a bodybuilder, I was a steroid smuggler."

"Were you carrying anything?"

"No. Well, I mean I had *some* stuff, but it was obviously only enough for personal use, and I had the doc's prescription in my carry-on."

"You need to be careful. Don't do anything stupid when you're crossing borders."

"I'm not a smuggler, Tommy."

"Yeah, I know!" he half-yelled, then caught himself and said quietly, "Just be careful, that's all."

We rode along for a while in silence, but then, right as I was getting off the bike to head home, I said, "I always thought it would be so simple. I'd rise to the top of this sport, live at the beach, make great money, and do nothing but train. Now here I am. I've had my pro card just over a year and I don't even know if I want to keep going."

"The grass is always greener, my friend."

He smiled, hoping—I think—that it would be contagious, but I walked away, went downstairs to my car, and drove home.

At World Gym, I trained for the 1985 Mr. Olympia as if my life depended on success in the show. After Tommy and I talked, I had gone home, pulled out my date book and training journal, called half the promoters I'd been negotiating appearance dates with, and canceled them. After those calls, I started working on my '85 Olympia training strategy.

Immediately, I started pushing myself extrahard in the gym because I'd made a leap and decided to reduce the amount of drugs I was willing to take, to the barest minimum. The decision to do this had been coming for nearly a year. First of all, I had become fairly close friends with a pharmacist, and he was always telling me how potentially harmful the current crop of fashionable bodybuilding drugs could be. Other friends who knew this guy would listen to what he was telling me and they'd try to convince me that I needed to get away from that world. Secondly, the strip search at Customs had me paranoid and feeling as if I were doing something wrong, something that I could get into big trouble over.

I decided that since I was always reading in the magazines about how much natural potential I had as a bodybuilder, I'd put that supposed genetic talent to the test by training on the lowest drug doses I could get away with.

But I still had my dream, and a big part of that had always been to win the Mr. Olympia. In spite of that dream, though, I wasn't able anymore to justify doing whatever it took, as far as drugs were concerned, and I hoped that I was making the right decision. I knew, on a practical level, that decision would put me at a disadvantage in the show, but it was a risk I'd grown willing to take.

There were just too many horror stories circulating about the hideous side effects of growth hormone, although I got the feeling that most of the stories were started by competitors who didn't want anyone else doing the drug. You would think, to hear all the guys deny ever having used it, that GH would have disappeared from the scene. Not only had it not disappeared, but anyone observing the sport could see that the style of bodies was changing, growing more radically freaky, and most insiders speculated that this was directly tied to the drug everyone denied using.

In any event, I wasn't willing to take a chance, since the major side effects that most people described were changes in the facial structure and bones of the body. GH seemed to have the potential to make the bones of the face and body grow, making the sufferer begin to look like Frankenstein. It was medical phenomenon called acromegaly, or giantism, and all I knew was that I wanted no part of that business. I still had major ambitions that went far beyond my bodybuilding goals, and I liked the way my face looked and wasn't anxious to sport a protruding brow and massive jawbones—which the rumors said you might get by using GH. The unaccounted-for growth of the elbow bones and jaw of one top competitor was said to have come from too much GH, and I knew that this athlete was a star client of the famous Dr. White, the doctor I'd gone to for my short course of the stuff in the spring before I won the Nationals and Mr. Universe. I could certainly see in the magazine photos of this guy that when he'd won one of the top shows, his elbows and jawbone did indeed look larger, as if they had grown more than his muscles had.

I thought that I must have been lucky during my one encounter with GH, back in 1983, but then I'd taken it in such low dosages (only because I couldn't afford any more) that I had serious doubts whether I'd experienced any effects, positive or negative. At least my face hadn't changed, and I didn't have to buy bigger shoes or have my shirtsleeves lengthened, from my bones' growing in an erratic fashion.

So I decided to cut steroid use down to a minimum, and to avoid GH at all cost. I thought that if I just worked harder, I could get every bit as developed without heavy doses as with them. I kept telling myself that I was genetically advantaged, and that I didn't need all those drugs to achieve my potential. I'd also already decided that if I couldn't be successful on these terms, then I'd have to leave the sport.

All year when I wasn't out on the road, doing the appearances that I still had scheduled, I trained my ass off at World Gym. Eddie Giuliani and I had started working out together. We pushed each other hard, plowing through some of the most intense workouts I'd ever had. When one of the other guys in the gym would ask me what drugs I was taking, I'd patiently explain what I was trying to do. Depending on the guy, he'd either look at me as if I were a liar (I had managed to get huge during the months leading up to the show), or he'd tell me I was crazy and ask me why, since I'd come this far, didn't I just do whatever it took to win. This last guy had a point.

My athlete's logic should have told me to keep doing whatever I'd been doing if it had worked and worry about moral quandaries over how I'd done it after retiring as a legend. But I couldn't shut my mind up, and it had gotten hooked on this one topic and wouldn't let it go. And this whole dilemma, which had begun almost exactly at the point when I got my pro card, was starting to seep into other areas of my life as well.

April 1985
Beverly Hills, California

While I was waiting for an appointment to get my hair cut at the swanky salon I'd been going to for a couple of years, an acquaintance—who was also waiting for her appointment with the another hairdresser at the same salon—and I decided to go down the block to an ice cream shop we both liked. Both of our hairdressers were running an hour behind.

I was huge at the time; I must have weighed at least 245—and (by normal standards, not bodybuilding competition standards) I wasn't in the least bit fat. It was the heart of the off-season, six months before the Olympia.

I was standing in line, wearing a normal pair of khaki pants and one of the V-neck sweaters from the clothing line I'd started—dressed like any other man walking along, going about his business in Beverly Hills—and these two teenage girls, three places back in the line from my friend and me, started laughing. I didn't think anything about it, but after I'd finished my nonfat chocolate frozen yogurt, I went to the rest room, and when I came back, those same two teenage girls were standing at my table talking to the woman I was with. The girls got nervous when they saw me coming back and left, giggling, as I got close to the table.

"Nervy little bitches," Sheila, my friend, said.

"Wadda ya mean," I asked, thinking that they'd somehow insulted her.

"You know what they just said to me?"

"No. You gonna tell me?" I sat back down, putting my napkin back across my right knee, even though I was finished eating.

"They said that my friend, meaning you, could be cute, if he didn't have all those awful muscles. They said that they thought you were *ga-rossss*—their emphasis, honey, not mine—and that you looked like a monster, but that if you didn't have all those drugged-up muscles, you'd be a real looker." She said this shaking her head in disbelief. "Oh, yeah, and then they asked if you were rich. Well, I told them that—and, oh, baby, did I tell them to keep it just to themselves, 'cause of, you know, security problems and all that—that you were the only heir to your dying Greek billionaire daddy's entire fortune. Well, that put a whole new light on the subject." She stopped to laugh, then looked at me. I was staring vacantly at the front door of the place.

"You okay?"

"Yeah."

"You sure?"

"Yeah, I'm just tired of getting laughed at, that's all."

"Hey, look at me," she said, reaching over and turning my sullen face back toward her by putting her index finger under my chin and pulling me around. "They're just a couple of kids. Don't pay any attention. I think you look great."

"Oh, I know . . . no, I mean, um, thanks—it's just that I get tired of being seen like I'm some freak or something. Look at me. I'm dressed like a normal successful guy, but even when I wear real clothes, I still bulge out of 'em like I'm Frankenstein's monster trying to disguise himself in a tuxedo. No matter what the monster thinks he looks like, no matter how normal he tries to feel, people still look at the bolts in his neck. I'm just sick of only feeling like a person, and not some sideshow exhibit, when I'm around friends or at the gym. And you know what the ironic thing is? Half the hard-core people at the gym think I look like a model who—maybe—works out some. They think I'm way too small and need to get bigger. I can't imagine. I'm already uncomfortable enough at this size."

The seeds had been planted. I would never look at bodybuilding or myself—as a bodybuilder—the same way again. Even though I continued blasting away at the weights each day, eating all the right foods, and keeping up my public enthusiasm for what I was doing, my outlook toward the sport would never return to the innocent view I'd held during my late teenage years.

Everything had gone into overdrive and there was no way to slow it all down. Momentum had already taken over.

I had worked years to get where I was, and when I got there, my life still went plodding along one day at a time, even though the pace of my life had been dramatically altered. The *anticipation* of success had turned out to be far more delicious than the *achievement* of success.

Autumn, 1985
Brussels, Belgium
The 1985 Mr. Olympia

The Olympia was in Brussels that year. Friends in London asked if I didn't want to come over and stay with them for several days before the contest, so that I wouldn't be negatively impacted by jet lag. It was a good idea, so I flew to London ten days before the show, knowing that I'd have plenty of time to stabilize from whatever impact the long flight from L.A. might have.

In London, my friends Wag and Diane Bennett took me straight from Heathrow Airport to their house in the East End. They had grown to be good friends ever since my first seminar tour through England the year before. Their lives revolved around bodybuilding long before the days when they got to be good friends with Arnold Schwarzenegger, before he left Europe for America and stardom. They lived in an old manor house. On the ground floor they had a commercial gym, an old hard-iron gym filled with eccentric equipment accumulated over forty years in the business. Next to their house, in a small abandoned church, they had built a new gym. It was filled with all the sparkling new equipment that people had grown to expect in modern gyms. Above where the altar had been, they'd had an artist paint huge, fantastical physique pictures of some of the legendary bodybuilding stars; anyone training there did so under the images of the greats. Wag told me, as he was showing me the new gym, that he was planning on having my picture painted up there in the near future. I told him that I thought that was a tremendous honor.

That night, after I'd finished my workout, I showed Wag how my physique was looking. He said that I looked terrific, and that when I'd stepped out of the shower, I had reminded him of Arnold. I did some poses for him, and he commented that I had the best shapes he'd seen in a long time. But I could tell by the way he was avoiding talking about my condition that he probably felt that I wasn't freaky enough.

When I'd been in England the year before, after I'd finished all my seminars, I spent a week at Wag and Diane's house. Wag and I had many talks about the changes in the sport, and neither of us thought that the changes were necessarily for the better, since increased drug use was helping create the shift.

As we sat in the locker room after I'd shown him my physique, I started telling him about my decisions during the last year regarding drugs. He listened patiently and told me that he agreed with how I felt, but that I might suffer in competition, given the current environment.

He was right. I had made a decision, and it was perhaps a fine moral decision, but when I went to Brussels that weekend, I placed ninth. Now ninth place in the Mr. Olympia—in a lineup of the best physiques on the planet—was no disgrace, but I was supposed to be headed toward winning; becoming Mr. Olympia was my preordained destiny, and I had placed ninth.

A couple of months later, Robert Kennedy, the publisher of *Muscle Mag*, wrote in his analysis of the contest that many in the audience felt that I was the only true physique onstage that day. Ricky Wayne, the editor in chief of *Flex* and senior writer for *Muscle and Fitness*, who had come to stay at Wag and Diane's house the last three days before the show, said in his articles about the show that I was built like a Greek god, but I just wasn't in the kind of ultrafreaky condition that would win a Mr. Olympia in that era. Other muscle writers lined up behind these two, saying that I had the kind of body that people—whether they were hard-core muscle fans or not—could look at and say, "That's what I want to look like." Nearly every writer did say that I could easily have, and should probably have, placed much higher in the show. All of them agreed that my muscle shapes, size, symmetry, and posing ability—and the fact that I was in great shape, just not freaky shape—should have weighed heavily in the judging. By this point, though, most of the pro level judges had begun to reward everything according to how monstrous and ripped—how far beyond human reality—the athletes were, and none of the other factors that went into having a great physique seemed to be given more than passing consideration.

Outside the auditorium in Brussels, before and after the show, I was swamped by hundreds of fans wanting me to sign their programs or a magazine. They tore at me as if I were a rock star; they told me in so many ways to keep doing what I was doing, because they really appreciated what I brought to the sport.

On the Sunday evening after the Saturday show, I was traveling through the night, on a crowded train to Italy, to begin a two-month whirlwind appearance tour through six countries. I was chugging along through the obscured countryside with the Fassi family, who were sort of the Weiders of Italian bodybuilding. Franco Fassi was president of the Italian federation and owned the largest gym equipment and supplement company in the country; he had arranged the Italian portion of my tour. We were going by train because all the flights had been canceled out of the Brussels airport. The city was paralyzed by a heavy fog that seemed to suck the life out of everything it touched. The weather exactly mirrored how I was feeling as we rushed from the airport to the train station, driven by cabdrivers who couldn't see to the front of their cars.

As we scrambled to find seats on the packed train, Franco's son Claudio, whom I had become friendly with when he trained for the summer at World Gym the year before, asked me why I hadn't come in superripped as I had at the Olympia the year before in New York. I started to explain to him about my drug decision, but it was beginning to sound, even to me, like a sour-grapes explanation. I told him that I'd just mistimed my peak. He told me that, no matter what, I should definitely have been placed higher, and that he loved my posing routine. He said that it was like watching a ballet, changing the subject because, as a friend, he didn't want to make me feel any more uncomfortable than it was obvious I was already feeling.

We went to the bar car to get a couple of beers, and Claudio's sister Nadia came to find us about an hour later, to tell us that one of the men traveling with our party had pulled off a miracle and found some open sleeping compartments. I got the distinct feeling that some conductor had suddenly acquired an extra million or two lire for magically producing these golden accommodations on the overflowing train.

Claudio and I had another couple of beers and talked about the contest, and how he thought that I'd show them a thing or two next year, and then we went off to get a couple of hours' sleep.

I lay awake, listening to the frequent *cha-chu, cha-chu* sounds when we'd cross over track switches, and the occasional noise of another train whizzing by in the other direction, feeling the car shake left and right as it moved toward Italy. I thought that the beers would help me sleep, but they only made my mind go into overdrive. I finally got up and went out into the area between the cars and tried to look out the window of the passenger door but only saw darkness, and I couldn't tell if it was still miserable out, but it wasn't foggy because I could see scattered lights in the distance. I looked at my reflection in the window, made all the more intense by the overhead light, and thought that I looked like the very picture of a fool, standing there in my fancy-schmancy designer clothes, having once again let escape what could probably have been mine.

Summer, 1986
Around the World at 39,000 Feet

May I get you anything else, Mr. Paris?" the Qantas flight attendant asked as she passed through the business-class cabin on her way to the galley.

"Yes, please. Could you bring me another beer?" I shook the empty can in front of me. I handed it to her, then brought my seat forward some, trying to look around a man standing in the aisle talking in German about business with the man sitting across the aisle, two rows in front of mine, in the window seat. The man standing was talking loudly over the head of a woman who was shooting him annoyed looks, as if she'd been trying to sleep, but he was ignoring the hint. I was watching this scene play out with one eye, and the movie on the screen—which I'd already seen and was vaguely following without headphones on—with the other eye. I could only see half the screen anyway, with this bozo parked there blocking everyone's view. About an hour before, I'd finished reading, for the second time, the second book I'd brought with me and was getting ready for my fifth or sixth beer since waking up three hours into this twelve-hour leg of the flight. I looked at my watch. We still had a little over six hours to go until landing in Frankfurt.

"Foster's or Four X?"

"Excuse me?" I asked, caught a bit off guard by the flight attendant because she had seemed to leave and then reappeared.

"Sorry, sir, would you like to keep drinking Foster's, or would you like a Four X?" she asked, holding up the empty can I'd just handed her. She looked up the aisle at what I was so fascinated with, then looked back at me with an understanding look. I couldn't tell whether she was just humoring me. Didn't matter.

"I'll stay with Foster's, please." Then when she began to walk away, I changed my mind. "Excuse me please, actually could you just skip the beer and bring me a double Jack Daniel's on the rocks."

"Sorry, Mr. Paris, we've run out of Mr. Daniel's finest. Shall I have a look-see at what we do have in the American whiskey department?"

"Uh—no, that's actually fine. I'll just have the Foster's then, thanks."

"Very well, sir."

Getting shit-face drunk on an airplane. How dignified. I was bored, so I drank. I didn't care what strangers on an airplane thought about it either. I knew I'd regret it, though. I hadn't had more than two or three beers at a time in at least three years.

The year had turned out to be incredibly exhausting, but then so had the year before that and the one before that. I hadn't been home more than three days in a row since spring. It seemed as if I lived on these flying cattle trains. So what if my purposely changing my ticket home from Japan to one that went all the way around the planet contradicted my travel weariness? I needed some time away from what had become my ordinary life. In my younger days I would have packed my backpack and headed off into the woods somewhere by myself to find some peace, but I hadn't been out in the woods in a few years, since I'd been putting every ounce of my focus and energy into my career. Instead I climbed on an airplane and circled the globe, watching movies I'd already seen, reading books I'd already read, and getting drunk.

"Be careful what you wish for. You might just get it." Isn't that how the old saying goes? I got exactly what I'd been working and hoping for and I was burnt-out—with a capital B.

Here I was making a living off of my sport—a sport that led people unfamiliar with it to ask frequently, "Can you make a living doing that?" Who was I to complain about anything? Mom had asked from time to time, when I was beginning to gain success at this thing—about the time I won the Mr. Los Angeles—if I ever planned to get a real job. How do you explain the entrepreneurial spirit to someone who can't conceive of ever doing anything more bold than screwing a nut on a bolt or tallying spreadsheets?

This thing was in my blood. I loved the edge, the fix of having to wake up each day and go find my own living; hunting down each meal or new pair of pants like a primitive tribesman heading out on the savanna, taking the prey and then putting every last fiber of the bounty to use. But now here I was, getting what I'd wished for and being bone weary, wondering if I would ever get back to the soul of the thing that had led me here.

Making a living at this sport was a tightrope walk without a net. Even at the professional level it wasn't really the contests that paid the bills. Sure there was prize money for those who won or placed well, but the real money was to be made out on the road doing guest appearances, giving seminars, guest-posing at amateur contests.

The ability to parlay contest success into a moneymaking enterprise was what separated the superstars from the guys who had the stuff onstage, but wound up hanging out at the beach all day wondering how to pay the rent. I learned early how to make a living at this. I had my first seminar ready to go long before I was ever hired to give one. All those years on the speech team and in drama club and school plays paid off. But I was tired.

Funny how life seems to be filled with times of longing. If you don't want to leave one place or circumstance, you'll want to get to another. Even on this plane; I seemed to sit still, yet I was shooting like a bullet toward somewhere else. Very little of life seems lived in between, enjoying whatever it is you craved to get to, once you've gotten there. I suspect that if most folks were truth-serum honest with you, they might admit to the same feelings—the green, green grass of yonder, let me find it now and leave this misery behind. Then I'll be content. I promise.

Thirty-nine thousand feet. Three more cans of Foster's come and gone. Five more hours to Frankfurt, where I connect with a flight to Vancouver, leading me to a plane back to Tokyo, just to reconnect on the same flight (different day) I was supposed to take home from Tokyo in the first place when my ten-day appearance tour in Japan ended. Why didn't I go on home to L.A. once I got to Vancouver and stood again on North American soil? Because I was compelled to go all the way around in one continuous circle, start to finish, just for the hell of it, even if it took a little extra doing to do so. Circling the globe was like being in a decompression chamber for me; like an astronaut coming back from Mars and needing time to readjust to Earth's atmosphere.

That tour in Japan was the tail end of a milk-run trip around the galaxy. Ten days in Japan followed three weeks in Germany, four and a half weeks in England and Scotland, and eleven days in Australia. Seventy-some-odd days I hadn't slept in my own bed, trained in a familiar gym, or seen my friends. Nearly one-fifth of a year where every day I was in a different town, different hotel, giving a seminar or greeting hundreds of strangers, signing pictures and magazines and posters, answering the exact same questions over and over, under constant scrutiny, rarely finding an hour each day to spend totally by myself, except when I was sleeping. Oh, I had made money all right. I got paid well for my work, but I was worn-out.

When I got home, I needed to decide if I was going to stay with bodybuilding or enroll full-time in the acting conservatory I'd been studying at—off and on, whenever I wasn't on the road—for the past year. I was hankering to become a movie star, as everyone in my life expected me to.

The trip wasn't as restful as I'd hoped, but at least it took me away from the world for a while. During the last week of my long tour, I'd sunk into a depression that I would hide behind proper public manners whenever I was doing an appearance, but in private I couldn't seem to shake it. When my flight from Frankfurt landed in Vancouver, I considered changing my ticket again to head back to L.A., but as I sat in the flight lounge, I decided that I'd started this thing and would finish it. By the time this flight had landed in Vancouver, I'd had so much beer that I wobbled with double vision into the lounge, crashed myself across two seats, and faded off to sleep.

The flight to Tokyo was uneventful, except that at first I turned down the offer of alcohol from the flight attendant, but when she kept asking every ten minutes, I finally gave in and ordered a Labatt's, then drank one after another when I wasn't sleeping.

In Tokyo, I at last boarded my plane for L.A., after a painfully long and twisted discussion with the check-in counter attendant in the United lounge. She insisted that I had reservations on this particular flight, but three days earlier. I patiently explained the changes I'd made and how I had decided to go all the way around the world and so forth, which she couldn't seem to grasp. Finally, a supervisor came over to ask if she could help with anything and got it all straightened out. After the supervisor handed me my boarding pass, I saw that she had me sitting in a first-class seat.

"Excuse me, I probably shouldn't bring this up since it's a pleasant surprise—if it's a mistake, then it's a good one—but you have me in first class and my ticket is business class," I said to the supervisor, while the other woman helped another customer with his ticket.

"It is no mistake, Mr. Paris. Please take this upgrade with my compliments. I'm a big fan. I read about you in the Japanese and the

American *Muscle and Fitness*. I came to your appearance at my gym last week. You were kind enough to sign one of your posters for me, sir," she said, looking down, a bit embarrassed.

"Of course. I'm sorry, it's just that—"

"Sir, please do not apologize. There would be no way for you to remember me. There were so many people at the appearance that day. I happily put you in a first-class seat. Please enjoy your flight. But if it is not an insult to you, sir, you look very tired. I hope that you are not overworking yourself. You must save your strength for your training."

I smiled and let out a little laugh that might have made me seem slightly insane.

"I am sorry, sir, I have offended you."

"No, not even in the least. You're right, I do need some rest. Thank you so much for the upgrade and for your kind words of support."

"Your plane will be boarding soon, Mr. Paris. Please have a nice flight and do your best to win the Mr. Olympia this year, sir."

"I'll try," I said, even though I already knew that I wasn't going to do the show this year. I had made up my mind during the Frankfurt-to-Vancouver flight to stop competing and start studying acting full-time. "Thanks again, and take care."

After the plane took off, the man in the seat next to me, who'd had a few too many himself, tried continuously to strike up a conversation. I had been lucky the whole trip around the world and had only sat next to people who either didn't speak English or were just as uninterested in midair chitchat as I was. I tried my best to nod and look away when he asked me questions, hoping that he could take a hint. It worked for a while.

Of course it had to change; "when it rains, it pours," and I don't mean that old saying in a bad way. There's nothing wrong with getting recognized, that's not what I mean. After all, I was sitting and being even more pampered than I had already been on the other flights because I was fortunate enough to have a fan check me in. I just mean that it all seems to happen at once. I'd gone around the planet, all the way around, and not one time did anyone ask, "Are you some kind of a weight lifter?"

I watched as a male flight attendant came up the aisle holding a *Muscle and Fitness* and smiling right at me. I was on the cover, smiling out at the world.

"Excuse me, Mr. Paris . . ."

I interrupted, "Bob, please. You know the line that goes something like, 'Every time you say Mr. Whatever, I look around for my father'?"

"Sorry, Bob. I wanted to ask you, if it's no problem, if you could sign my magazine. I'd really appreciate it."

"Sure. What's your name?" I asked as he handed me the magazine and a pen.

"Ken, um, please sign it to Ken, keep on training, or something like that."

"That's not you, is it?" the friendly guy seated next to me interjected. "Can I see that?"

"Sure," the flight attendant told him, since the man had already pulled the magazine out of my hand.

"Wow, that's you?" He held the magazine up to my face. "Hey, it is you. You famous or something?"

"In a very minor way," I said.

"No way, Bob, you're one of the biggest," Ken said, not being very helpful in my quest to stave off conversation. "He's Bob Paris, Mr. America and Mr. Universe. He's in all the magazines, sir. A superstar." With that Ken snatched his magazine back and looked at my inscription to him. "Thank you, Bob. I really appreciate this. Listen, I'm working coach, but can I get you a drink or something?"

"Well, I wasn't going to drink on this flight, but can you bring me a beer, please," I said, a bit exasperated. If what I thought was going to happen was going to happen, I needed to drink to bear it.

I predicted it would take to the count of ten. I got to eight.

"So, you're a famous muscleman then?" the guy next to me asked. "Name's Hank, how do you do. I figured you were hard of hearing or mute or something, earlier."

"Yes, well . . . my name's Bob." I shook his outstretched hand.

"I caught that already."

Ken brought back my beer and another Scotch for Hank. "I thought that you might want one as well, sir," Ken said to him, setting down his drink and taking away the empty bottle in front of him.

What glorious efficiency, I thought.

"Thanks again for the autograph, Bob," Ken said.

"You're welcome," I said as he turned around and left.

"That woman on the magazine cover with you, she your wife or girlfriend or something?" Hank asked, smiling.

Fan-fucking-tastic, I thought excitedly, *here's my chance to get rid of him.*

"No, actually she's just a model. It's the way they do those covers. I don't have a girlfriend or wife—actually I'm gay." Count to ten again; he'll be gone.

"Well, whatever floats your boat—'s what I say."

Drats, of all the times for someone not to be a bigot.

"How come you got your body all covered up?" I always wore baggy clothes whenever I traveled or was in any situation where I didn't want to get into the exact conversation we were now having. "Man alive, if I was built like you, I'd walk around with my shirt off all the time."

"Now that might be a bit inconvenient, don't you think?"

"Well, at least I'd wear something so that all the women—or, I guess in your case, all the men, huh? Say, was that stewar . . . uh, flight what-chamacallit, was he, you know . . . ?"

"Well, he is a flight attendant."

"Right, gotcha. Anyhow, I'd run around in clothes that let all the ladies see what a great bod I had."

"Would you?"

"Sure."

Should I keep going? I wondered. What the hell, he seemed harmless.

"Hank, let me tell you something. You see this body?"

"Well, yeah, now that I know it's there I do."

"Okay, this body I walk around in is like—how can I say this?—well, it's like a product."

"You mean like a can of Coke or a bag of chips or something?" he asked, puzzled.

"Yeah, I guess—something like that," I said, wondering where this would end up.

"I don't get it."

"Okay, let me ask you this. What do you do for a living?"

"I guess you could say that I'm a barber. I own some salons, which is a fancy way of saying upscale barber-shops—you know, around L.A. But I started out with a two-chair shop years ago. Now I've made so much goddamn money, I can't even count it. I was over in Japan for a product convention."

Hair salons. No wonder he didn't flinch when I said that I was gay, I thought.

"Okay, so you're a barber, and let's just say for the sake of conversation that you're the best barber in the world, or at least in the city—right? You follow?"

"Yeah, sure, just for the sake of conversation, 'cause I can think of a couple who are better, but—"

"But that's not my point. The point is, see, if you are the best barber in the world, are you going to go around giving free haircuts to every person you meet?"

"Huh?"

If my muscles were this dense, I'd have been Mr. Olympia five years ago, I thought. "All right, let's see if I can make this more clear. Say you're walking down some street—"

"Which one?"

"It doesn't matter."

"Well, I like Melrose. My first shop was right off Melrose, back before it was all trendy, you know. I have fond memories."

"Okay, Melrose, whatever—now stop and listen to me so I can clear this up." We were both slurring our words a bit already, but Hank signaled the flight attendant to bring us both another drink. "Let's say you're strolling down . . . oh, say, Melrose."

"Yeah, I like that. I got fond memories there."

"Right, so you said. Now you're strolling down this street—Melrose—wearing a shirt that has 'World's Greatest Barber' written on the front, and you're carrying all your clipping gear—right out—wanting people to notice. And then to top it all off, you start giving out these free haircuts to every person who passes by—whether they ask for one or not. You're always offering free haircuts to everyone, and say you do this nearly every day. Do you think anyone would ever pay you for a haircut?"

"Probably not."

"No, you're right, they wouldn't. Well, it's the same with my body. I make my living from this body. If I walk around showing it off all the time, why would anyone pay to see me compete or guest-pose or buy a magazine I was on the cover of? Follow me?"

"Oh, so that's what you mean when you say your bod's like a product. I gotcha. Your body's like this, this—briefcase, or something like that? Nobody's gonna be paying to see it if you're giving it away free, by walking around in skimpy clothes or with your shirt off."

"Exactly." *Sheesh.*

We talked a bit more. He still insisted that if it were his body, well, he'd probably show it off more, and eventually, three drinks later, he passed out until we landed at LAX. We said good-bye the way people always do on planes, diverting eyes and touching carry-on bags far more than is needed, waiting for that door to open. He gave me a card for one of his salons and we never saw each other again.

15

FIRST COMEBACK

The Late 1980s
Los Angeles

I left competition and announced in several magazine articles that I thought I'd gone as far as I could on the pro circuit. I was retiring to study acting. It was what almost everyone expected of me anyway. All the articles that had been written about me had always compared me to Steve Reeves, the fifties physique star turned movie Hercules, who'd starred in a bunch of low-budget Italian sword-and-sandal epics that remained famous for their deliciously campy awfulness. Steve Reeves and I were supposed to look a lot alike, which was a compliment since in his youth he was a handsome man. Given that his movies were so stilted and ridiculous and his voice was dubbed over, he was certainly not what anyone in Hollywood would consider an actor, although in the muscle world he might as well have been a multiple Academy Award winner. Until Arnold Schwarzenegger came along, Reeves was the only guy from the bodybuilding world to make even the slightest dent in the motion picture business. I wanted to be the next, but I also wanted to be a real actor, so I auditioned for the best theater conservatory in L.A. and started going to classes. I went part-time, sporadically while I was touring, but when I finally decided to stop competing, I began to go full-time.

For years I'd been avoiding the inevitable auditions for commercials and bit parts in the movies because I knew that all those productions ever wanted a muscleman for was as a butt of a joke—a lug who was nothing more than a prop; doing stupid poses or lifting barbells in absurd situations; bouncing, oiled-up chest muscles as a device to grab the viewer's attention. I didn't want any part of that nonsense, and plenty of guys were around who wouldn't mind doing those jobs. I wanted a career, not simply a string of gigs that, even if they paid well, led nowhere except to letting the world know that you thought you were as big of a joke as they thought you were. So I threw myself into my studying with extraordinary energy, using the discipline and focus I'd learned as an athlete to push myself into rapid progress. It mostly came easily, and whatever didn't I worked hard to conquer, since I'd already had experience working consistently in front of live audiences doing scores of bodybuilding seminars, which I viewed as being as much about giving a lively performancè as passing along information.

While I was away from competition, I kept traveling some to give seminars so I wouldn't have to get a normal job to pay for school and to live, but my travel schedule was light compared to what I'd been doing for the three prior years. I found, though, that as bodybuilding dropped out of my life, I heard hardly anything about it, unless I was in front of a bodybuilding audience, and sometimes, even then, someone from one of those audiences would ask me a current-events-type trivia question about the sport and I had to either make up an answer or admit that I was clueless.

I was a news junkie, hopelessly addicted to politics and social issues, so I read four different newspapers each day. It didn't matter if it was the *New York Times, Los Angeles Times, USA Today*, or the *Washington Post*, I never saw a word written about the sport of bodybuilding. And since I'd also stopped reading all the physique magazines, it was as if the sport that had occupied my whole adult life had disappeared from the planet. During those two years I probably couldn't have told anyone who asked who'd won the Mr. Olympia, or even if I did realize—because I was still going into World Gym three or four days a week to train the few private training clients that I'd also taken on to help pay for school, and the guys there tried, against my indifference, to keep me up on the latest news—that Lee Haney was still mopping the floor with all the other competitors, I wouldn't have been able to accurately say who had taken second, third, fourth, and so on. The hunger to know had vanished; my mind and heart had moved on.

The sport had moved on as well during my time away. It gradually changed as the top physiques grew freakier with each passing season. The crop of judges who dominated the pro contest scene had a decided taste for the exaggerated. It wasn't enough anymore for the elite guys to have tremendous development, they had to be twenty miles past the realm of human possibility. It was no wonder I didn't see the sport written about in the sports pages of the nation's leading newspapers; no layperson could identify with these physiques. But for nearly two years, I barely thought about this.

My own workouts were cut back to the barest minimum because I was consciously trying to reduce my body down to a more normal size. Everyone I knew in Hollywood made it clear to me that I would never even get considered for any serious jobs if I stayed so physically huge. Even actors with only minimal development could get branded as being overly pumped up if they weren't careful. It took massive reductions in physical size on Arnold Schwarzenegger's part for him to be taken seriously, and even then people who didn't know better would still talk about him as if he were in Mr. Olympia condition; they should have seen him when he really was a muscleman. So I piddled in the gym with the lightest weights possible and eventually stopped lifting altogether, since every time I did a remotely intense workout, my muscle memory would kick in—all the muscles were lying in wait to be stimulated once again—and I'd counteract weeks of purposeful shrinking.

Then, right at the point when I'd gotten my body reduced down to a completely normal size—altered so dramatically that it appeared as if I'd never lifted a serious weight in my life—and after I'd moved through all the levels of the conservatory I was attending up to the most advanced classes, filled mostly with solid, working actors, I began to have vivid dreams about competing again. The dreams occurred over a couple of weeks, and I don't know if they were packed with heavy meaning or were simply the residue of a previous chapter of my life, but after having woken up to them several mornings in a row, I began to take them seriously. In giving them the power of having deep meaning I suddenly changed the course of my life; but I had been doing that with great frequency around that time.

The biggest change in my life during this time—until those bizarre dreams began—was that I allowed myself to fall madly in love. I'd always run from love in the past, believing that for me my career had to come first. I'd had a couple of serious boyfriends, but I always knew those relationships would eventually fade and never allowed myself to be swept away by total commitment. But, boy, when I fell, I landed hard.

I met Rod Jackson while I was giving what was supposed to be my last bodybuilding seminar ever, at a gym in Denver. I'd been supporting myself as I went to classes by still giving these lectures because they paid so well, and I could give one or two a month and, along with my savings from all the touring I'd done, I could live a fairly comfortable L.A. lifestyle. And I figured that after another six months at the conservatory, I'd be ready to begin to pursue work as an actor, so I could stop working until then and in the meantime live off what I had in the bank.

Rod and I met when I came into the gym to give my lecture, and the chemistry was immediate and overwhelming. He was working as one of the managers at this gym to help supplement his salary as a social worker and to pay back his school loans. He didn't know who I was and had recommended to the gym owner that he not hold the seminar because my fees were too expensive. But when I walked through the door of that gym and we were introduced, I knew that my life had just rounded a major corner.

The seminar went extremely well—there was an enthusiastic crowd of a couple of hundred people—and afterward, as was traditional whenever I did an appearance, I went out to dinner with the owner of the gym; Rod and one of the other managers went too. Rod and I sat down at our table and started talking about social issues and politics, and the books we both loved, and we were hitting it off so well that I'm afraid we neglected the other two. Rod said that he was moving to L.A. the next week—his social work job with hard-core street kids had him burnt-out and he was looking for a fresh start. He'd signed with one of the top modeling agencies in the city.

So he moved to town and never got in touch with me, but a series of coincidences kept throwing us into each other's life. He enrolled for classes at the same school I was going to; he started getting his hair cut at the same place I did; he moved within three blocks of where I lived, without realizing that I lived in that neighborhood; friends kept asking if we had seen each other. I guess everyone else around us saw that we were meant to be together, but even though I made it fairly clear that I had a major crush on him—crush, hell, I was head over heels—he seemed to be avoiding me or running from me or something.

After six months passed, all the time seeing each other as we'd each go to our classes, or around the neighborhood, I decided that if I didn't ask him out, I'd bust. I thought that I'd wind up ninety years old, sitting in my rocking chair thinking about this great unrequited love—Rod—that got away. So one night as I was leaving a classroom and he was coming in, I got up the nerve to ask him to dinner. Surprise—he said yes; he came over that Friday to dinner, and from that night on, we threw our lives together. Now, we were both career-oriented, driven guys who'd never given ourselves away to anyone heart and soul, so the transition from single to couple was difficult, to say the least.

After we'd been together only about a month, I started having a vivid dream about competing again. It always came right before I woke up in the morning. Inside this dream, I'd be standing, in fantastic shape, onstage at the Mr. Olympia, and I would be the only guy onstage. The rest of the pros I had competed against would be sitting in the front row of the audience in their posing trunks, and they were all painted or dyed every color of the rainbow. It didn't matter if, in reality, they were black, white, brown, or yellow; in this dream they were green and bright red and purple and so forth. I would do an intricate posing routine, then Joe Weider would come on the stage and hand me a trophy. Joe would look as he had in old magazines—maybe forty years old, with black, slicked-back hair, and wearing a blue pinstripe suit with wide lapels, like men wore in the fifties. And then I'd wake up.

That was the whole dream. And it would happen night after night, exactly the same. Amateur psychiatrists could have a field day. I didn't know what the hell this dream meant. I did, however, enthusiastically invest it with meaning. I told myself that it meant that I was supposed to go back to competition. Now that I'd reached this point in my acting studies, and since I hadn't yet started auditioning for parts and developing my new career, I could afford to give competition one more shot—before it was too late.

I gave those dreams more meaning than they probably deserved because I was searching for just such an excuse to return to some familiar ground. This new relationship that I'd entered into was intense and tumultuous enough. I don't think I could have handled embarking on a brand-new career in such an uncertain profession, where progress was going to be as big of a crapshoot as my success in bodybuilding had been. So I looked for a way to reach out to something secure. I understood that I could start bodybuilding again, and since I already knew that world inside out, I could concentrate completely on these tremendous changes happening to me as I merged my life together with this other human being's.

There was also a deep-seated feeling that this was not a relationship that I was going to be able to be "discreet" about (discreet being the operative code word meaning that gay people in any realm of public life were to stay in the closet, particularly about their personal relationships). In those days, and those days were not so long ago, most gay people in Hollywood, or in other careers that dealt with building a public image, knew how to play the game. You were, at the very least, to pretend you hadn't found the right woman yet (or man if you were a lesbian playing this game), and you were encouraged to find an escort of the opposite sex to take to public events—and you were never, ever, to talk honestly about your "personal life."

Rod and I both had tremendous ambitions to become successful in Hollywood, but we both knew that, especially since we were both just going to be starting careers, it would be impossible to have the relationship we wanted and play the Hollywood closet game. We would never have allowed each other to get away with it, and the relationship would most likely not have survived. So I invested my dream about coming back to competition with much greater meaning than it probably merited and decided on the spur of the moment—after spending two weeks considering exactly what the dream meant—that for the sake of sanity, I'd put acting on hold and return to bodybuilding.

With the sport's insiders, my being gay was no secret. Of course, it was never mentioned in any interviews I did. In fact, from the time when I began appearing in all the magazines until my first retirement, in all the interviews and articles in the bodybuilding press, I had no personal life at all. Instead an image was built of me being this extremely private, sensitive, artistic type. And even though those things were true, what the words implied was in the same code as Hollywood's unwritten, but widely understood, laws of discretion. The language allowed any reader to put into the words whatever he wanted to project. No one wanted to shake up the fans with anything they might not want to know or hear, but it still allowed gay fans to read between the lines and draw their own conclusions. I went along with it all—all in the name of my success and ultimate destiny. But then I fell in love, with a man, and I had the distinct feeling that as I came back onto the sure ground of a sport where I was still considered something of a hero, this time I might just take a chance and break the unwritten code.

At that time, there was no way to accurately know just how much violating those rules would change my life.

The comeback was swift. I threw myself into full-bore training with an enthusiasm I hadn't felt since the year I won the National and World Championships. Muscle memory kicked in and my physique returned to its fullest dimensions after only four months of killing myself in the gym.

Rod had been disappointed at my decision to go back into the world of bodybuilding. He fully admitted that he knew little about it, but what he did know, from having been around competitive bodybuilders at the gym in Denver, led him to conclude that it was bizarre beyond description and definitely beneath my talents. He also questioned how serious I was about making a comeback, since I had already left the sport once and was so motivated toward a new career. Once I convinced him that I was serious, and that all the bodybuilders he'd known were amateurs and that the professional world was different, he said that he would support me in my decision. We started training together at World Gym, every day, after I picked him up from work. He'd been an athlete all his life and we pushed each other hard in the gym. My body blossomed from the two-hour workouts we'd do, and I began to call on my old contacts in the sport to let them know that my comeback was well under way.

Within two weeks of my putting the word out, I was booked for three solid months of exhibitions and seminars in Europe. It would be the perfect place to get myself back into the groove—far enough out of the spotlight that I could keep progressing without the unrelenting scrutiny of the muscle ghetto of Venice and Santa Monica, and enough in the spotlight that I could rebuild my reputation with the fans as a serious contender.

I wanted Rod to go with me to Europe, to share in the adventure. He didn't want to go. It was probably selfish of me to ask him to drop everything and come with me, but I didn't want to be apart. On a deeper, unspoken level, I thought that I'd come back to the sport to simplify my career life, so that I could work harder on building my personal life, and I thought we'd have a great time exploring all the European countries together. We fought about this up until two weeks before I was supposed to leave, and finally he called his agent and had him set up modeling work over there, so that Rod felt as if he had something equally productive and moneymaking to do, instead of just following me around while I was working.

Within two weeks of my letting people in the sport know that I was returning, I got a call from a medium-size fitness and vitamin company trying to expand into the territory that Weider dominated. They wanted to sign me to an endorsement contract, to use my pictures in their ads and have me do appearances for them to hawk their goods, so I began negotiating with one of their officers.

I also called Joe Weider to let him know that I was planning to compete again. I told him that it would be nice if we could do business together. In the past we had never been able to come to terms on any contract. Joe had a reputation for wanting everything for nothing; we could never get past his calling me ungrateful and neurotic whenever I tried simply to negotiate a dollar figure, or what was expected of me for any money I was to be paid if we did sign a contract—and he flat out refused to negotiate with managers or agents—so we'd never done an endorsement contract during all the years that I'd known him. Maybe things could be different this time.

He told me he'd have to think about it. I said that maybe he'd better move fast because this other company was trying to get me under contract and they were talking some pretty good money. He said that I was difficult and neurotic, and that I'd been stupid not to go further with my clothing company—how I could have been rich if I'd just kept going with it. I reminded him that when I had the company, I was still an amateur, and since there had been threats to suspend my amateur status right when I was on the verge of winning the America and Universe, because I was using my own image to advertise with, I thought I'd made the right decision. I had been more concerned with winning my shows and getting my pro card than selling a few sweaters—and wasn't that all sort of irrelevant now; what had happened, happened. He called me neurotic and difficult again and hung up on me.

So for the next week I went into the office of the man who was negotiating my contract with this other company. The company had been in the fitness and vitamin business for quite a while, but mostly they'd concentrated on owning gyms and making workout clothes, shoes, and gloves, those sorts of things. Now they really wanted to branch out into supplements in a big way, and they were planning an entire ad campaign and new label launch around my endorsement. Going into the negotiations, I knew that the company had a reputation for sometimes not paying its bills, and I asked the guy I was working with— in the politest manner possible, of course—if these rumors were true. He said they were false and were spread by competitors to try to drive them out of business. We continued to hammer out the details of the contract until late on a Thursday evening. The next morning I was to come in and meet the full board of directors, sign the contracts, and pick up my first check, which was going to come in handy since I'd spent all my savings living a pretty good lifestyle while I was still in school full-time, and my appearance work in Europe didn't begin for another week.

That night when I got home, four messages from Joe Weider's office were on the answering machine. Three were from his assistant, someone I didn't know; he changed assistants quite a bit. On the first message, she asked me to please call Mr. Weider; the second one was just checking in to see if I'd gotten the first one; and the third one said that it was urgent that I call Mr. Weider and hoped I wasn't out of town.

Then on the fourth message was his voice: "Hallo, Baaab, this is Joe Weeeder. Listen, Baaab, ya wanna gimme a caaall. If I'm not here, try me at home—you got the number." Some muffled yelling in the background followed, as if he were covering the receiver and chewing someone out for not producing me on his demand. Then the line went dead. I loved his voice. I played the message three times before I went to pick up Rod from work and head down to the gym.

The next day I went for my 9 A.M. contract-signing appointment. Around a large boardroom table were a dozen men in various types of clothes—from sweats to blue suits. The vice president, Jim, whom I'd worked with all week, wouldn't look me in the eye as he introduced me to everyone. I knew a couple of them from around town. Then I sat down and Jim hurried to the other side of the table and took a seat; still no eye contact.

Oh, shit. What's coming? I thought. I'd been around the block enough times to know that his not looking me in the eye, after we'd struck up a good rapport during the week, was not a good sign.

"So, Jim, why don't you tell us all about the details of Bob's contract?" the president of the company said. I knew him as a frustrated former competitor, who'd gone into business and made a small fortune, but had never seemed to let go of his bitterness at having never won a major amateur show nor moved up to the pro ranks.

Jim began to read each clause of the seven-page document, but Harvey, the president, cut him off after about a minute and told him just to give them an overview of the details. So he did. I had to wonder why Harvey was having Jim do this. Jim had already told me that the board had approved the most important elements of the agreement, which were my pay and the number of public appearances I'd be required to do.

When Jim had finished, Harvey said, "Sounds good overall—a few minor changes and we're in business."

"Excuse me, Harvey," I said before he could go any further, "but I was told this meeting was a contract signing—that all the details had been worked out."

"A couple of changes, that's all," Harvey said, giving me a used-car-salesman smile.

"Uh-huh," was all I could say. Maybe they were minor. I decided to listen to what he had to say.

"First, we're going to have to cut your monetary compensation in half. Then we'll need to double the number of appearances you do for us, and—"

"Now hold on just a goddamn minute," I interrupted, barely able to keep from exploding. I knew exactly what he was doing. "Jim, did you know about this?" He wouldn't look at me, he just shrugged. "Do you realize that I have worked—with Jim, an officer of this company, who assured me on the day we started that he had full authority to come to terms with me—I have worked on this agreement all week. I negotiated in good faith, and now you bring me in to a signing meeting and you want to screw me over. This was your intention the whole time, wasn't it? It's a bait and switch. Bring me in on one set of terms, get me all the way up to signing, and then change everything. You think I'm desperate, don't you, Harvey? You think I'm gonna take whatever money you offer now, 'cause I'm desperate."

"Bob, if I could just interrupt, please," a guy I didn't know on the other side of the table said in a quiet, well-oiled voice. He'd been introduced as the company PR and advertising man. "I guess I don't see the problem, Bob. It seems to me that a contract is open to negotiation until it is signed. We have done nothing wrong."

"No, now, you see, that's where you're wrong . . . sorry, what was your name again?"

"Glen."

"You see, Glen, you can believe whatever you want, but what we actually have here is one of the oldest con games in the book. Goddamn—the old bait and switch, and you all thought I'd just fall for it. Well, it didn't work. You underestimated me, gentlemen—and I use that term . . . oh, never mind, you wouldn't even get it." I got up and headed toward the door. "This meeting is obviously over. It didn't work, you dishonest motherfuckers." And I slammed the door behind me.

I was supposed to meet Rod at a nearby restaurant for a celebration lunch. After lunch we were going shopping for some new clothes for our trip to Europe, which was only a little more than a week away. He was waiting at a table when I got there. I sat down and the whole story came pouring out.

"You did the right thing, Bob. I'm proud of you. It would have been easy to just let them have their way, but you did the right thing."

"Now do you see why some people in the sport think I'm difficult? You look out for yourself in this game and you get branded as hard to work with. I mean, that's why Joe Weider calls me neurotic and difficult all the time. He's used to the guys doing anything he asks without question. I can't be like that."

"Did you ever call him back?"

"No, but you know something—I'm gonna go call right now. This game might not end badly after all."

I called Joe from the pay phone in the restaurant, and his assistant put me through immediately. Well, surprise, surprise; he wanted to know if I could come out to his office that afternoon. Seems that he had some business he wanted to talk with me about. I told him that I'd be there at two. Well, okay, I acted as if I were going to have to change some commitments around to get there, but that wasn't really deceptive—Rod and I did have some shopping plans for the afternoon.

When I got out to Joe's office in Woodland Hills, I was thinking that this had better be worth the trip, because the traffic was a nightmare on the Ventura Freeway. It was a hot, smoggy August afternoon, and the Jeep didn't have air-conditioning.

It was worth it. The minute I came through the front doors of the building, I was swept into Joe's office. He usually kept everyone waiting outside his door for at least half an hour while he rushed around inside doing fifty things at once. He seemed to be in a good mood and asked why I hadn't come to him right away instead of going to this other company, and didn't I know that he could do so much more for me than they could, and why hadn't I kept my clothing company—I could have been rich by now—and didn't I realize that he'd always been supportive, and so forth and so on. I just sat there nodding my head, not bothering to remind him that I had contacted him as soon as this other company had called me. I didn't even start on the clothing company—that was a continuously repeating conversation loop from hell, which I knew I'd hear from him, every time we talked, as long as he was in my life. At the end of this one-sided conversation, he wrote something on a slip of paper and handed it to me—as if we were secret agents passing information in a smoke-filled East Berlin café. On the slip of paper he'd written a number. I knew that it was what he was offering to pay me for a year's contract. It was the exact same figure that I was supposed to sign for at the other company, before they decided to play me for a sucker. I left the building that day with a contract and my first check. He never even called me difficult or neurotic.

16

MOUNTAINS AND
GREEN PASTURES

The Late Eighties and Early Nineties

Many of us top pro athletes had always been tremendously frustrated over our lack of say in how our sport was run. In all decisions the athletes always came last. It was as if Ben Weider, as IFBB president, thought that the athletes were mere pawns in a game that was all about him. He flew first class everywhere he went on IFBB business; the athletes, most of whom were twice his size, flew coach. He stayed in luxurious suites; the athletes got normal rooms. He got profits from the Mr. Olympia or other contests by way of huge sanction fees; the athletes got no share of any profits. In fact, any of the guys who placed out of the top spots, where the prize money was, usually got nothing, not even as much as they might get paid for a guest-posing appearance, all while the promoter and the IFBB walked off with suitcases of cash from ticket sales and concessions.

It also seemed as if Ben's position as president of the organization, which proclaimed itself democratic (I never got to vote on anything), was permanent. The IFBB rule book clearly stated that the headquarters for the federation should be in the city where the duly elected president resides. For decades, the IFBB has had its permanent headquarters in Montreal—the city Ben Weider happens to live in. That's quite a stable democracy.

There was always talk about starting an athletes' union, but solidarity was consistently undermined by guys who would sneak back to the IFBB administrators and say that they were against a union, even after having been all gung ho for one around the other competitors. These guys figured that if they could suck up to the top administrators and judges, they'd place higher in shows than the troublemakers. It worked too, because every attempt to organize the athletes—not to take over the sport, but simply to get the share that they deserved—failed as, one by one, guys would defect from the cause.

October 1988
Nottingham, Great Britain
The English Grand Prix

This issue was supposed to have been taken care of during the athletes' meeting the night before the Mr. Olympia the year before. Typical though. Promises made, promises broken.

The IFBB officials had promised to resolve who would pay taxes on prize money earned at contests (in particular, since most of the guys lived in the United States, contests outside the States). Several of the more outspoken guys at the Olympia had been pissed and threatened to take some kind of action, so the officials made their promises, and then of course, once enough time had passed, the IFBB left another bunch of guys to deal with the exact same issue all over again. And they had the nerve to act clueless, as if we were doing something wrong.

We were backstage at the English Grand Prix, the second show on the European tour that followed the Mr. Olympia. A sold-out house of more than twenty-five hundred fans was waiting in the theater. The show was supposed to start any minute, and we had to sit around fighting over something that was supposed to have been resolved. If we didn't fight, then the IFBB guys would just think we'd roll over for anything.

"It's not right that I have to pay taxes on the prize money I earn in Britain or Belgium—or wherever—twice," I said. "Look, my CPA told me distinctly that taxes I pay in a foreign country don't count when it comes time to pay Uncle Sam. This was supposed to have been resolved last year."

"Exactly," Lee Labrada added. "I was at that meeting, Wayne. You guys made an agreement that the promoter would be responsible for all domestic income tax for guys who weren't from the country where the contest was being held."

"Whadda you want me to do?" Wayne DeMilia, the IFBB vice president in charge of the tour, asked. "The promoter isn't going to pay them. He says they're your responsibility."

"Then maybe we won't be goin' out onstage," someone yelled from one of the dressing rooms.

I couldn't tell who'd said it.

"Yeah. Or maybe we'll go onstage and tell the audience what's goin' on and how we're gettin' screwed," a different voice yelled from the same dressing room.

We were going to need more than anonymous voices.

"Listen, Wayne, I don't know why the fuck we're having to do this twenty minutes before a show, but here's the only thing that's at issue," I said while looking around the room calculating which guys would hang tough if this came to a showdown. "We're not supposed to pay any foreign taxes on prize money. That was the agreement you guys made at the Olympia. It doesn't matter if the country we're in has to collect taxes on the money. The promoter was supposed to factor any domestic taxes into *his* gross expenses. The advertised prize money would then be the net of the gross minus the taxes. It all comes down to one simple thing: if European promoters want guys who live in the U.S. in their shows, they must deal with this issue—we won't pay taxes on our prize money twice. I, for one, will just stop competing outside the U.S. But— Jesus H. Christ, why are we going over this again?"

I was getting pissed. So were Lee Labrada, Berry DeMey, and Mike Ashley—all top pros and stand-up guys. Most of the other guys had been vocally angry to begin with, screaming for justice as we all discussed the situation before Wayne came backstage, but I could see that several had already decided to break away and not get caught up in the fight.

A few were sitting quietly, staring at the carpet. Some were hiding in dressing rooms where they could act as if they were involved but still remain anonymous—and therefore be blameless with Wayne and say that they weren't one of the troublemakers—if the situation went south. A couple of others had already changed into their posing trunks and were oiling and pumping up—getting ready to go on stage. Typical.

The main problem here was only tangentially about taxes or broken promises by the IFBB. Too many of the guys were insecure beyond measure. Their big, strong bodies were a facade; deep down they didn't think they deserved *anything* and they were willing to take crumbs. And a lot of these guys would grovel for those crumbs because they believed that if they didn't, some other guy would snatch away their microscopic share.

It would only have taken a couple of years of complete solidarity between all the athletes and everything would have changed. Never happen. Three or four guys always seemed willing to see a tough situation through to the end, but the rest would always fold under the slightest pressure.

"To hell with it," Wayne said, acting angry. "I can't take you guys anymore. When this tour's over, I'm out. I don't want anything to do with this anymore. Look, I'll talk with the promoter, see what can be worked out. But that's it."

What the fuck does he have to be mad about? I wondered. *He was one of the officials who promised that the issue had been settled.*

He walked out of the room, slamming a door.

"Yeah, he's really gonna leave bodybuilding. Right," I said. "The guy makes a fortune off this sport. What's he gonna do, go back and work at the phone company? We have to hang tough. He's gonna try and bluff us."

Four more guys stripped off their clothes and began pumping up. A minute later three more followed. Lee, Berry, Mike, and I were all who were left. Wayne came back in with the promoter and said, "The taxes must be paid by you guys. They'll be deducted from your checks, but I think you should be able to get a refund if you send in for it."

"That isn't the issue," Berry said between bites of the chicken and rice he was eating out of a Tupperware container.

But it was over. Only the four of us were left, and without a majority we had nothing. The other sixteen guys had vanished before any real pressure had even been exerted. Wayne and the show's promoter said that they would make sure all of us got the proper forms in the mail to request our British tax refunds.

The four of us looked at each other, shrugged, and shook our heads.

"Fuckin' cowards," I mumbled, looking around the room.

And the show went on.

A year later, I asked several of the guys who had been there if they'd ever gotten those tax refund forms or a check from the British government. Not a single one of them had. Neither had I.

Not only did the athletes have no true say in how the sport was run, but one of the only places where any grievance could be aired was at the athletes' meeting, held the night before a contest (or in the case of the English Grand Prix, twenty minutes before the prejudging). If you raised a complaint, legitimate or otherwise, you knew that the very people you were complaining about or to would either be in charge of a completely subjective system of judging or were actually judges themselves. That, combined with the IFBB rule-book clause stating that simply criticizing any IFBB official was justification for an athlete's suspension, and the fact that all judges' scores were kept secret (never to be released to the public because, the administrators claimed, some athletes might threaten judges whose scores they didn't like with physical violence), made the guys around whom the whole sport revolved feel impotent and abused. It also didn't help that the president of the federation and his brother owned the largest publicity company by way of their magazines, and that the athletes counted on those magazines to build up their public recognition and therefore their income; or that all of the other non-Weider magazines were, in effect, forced to toe the IFBB party line, because the IFBB controlled media passes to all the big contests and could deny blasphemous reporters access.

Then along came drug testing, and the way it was instituted in the men's professional ranks pleased no one. The guys who were for true drug testing grew frustrated because the system was so easy to cheat. The guys who were against it thought that nobody should be able to tell them what they could put in their own bodies. Most of the top administrators and judges privately expressed displeasure with having to support this testing, even though in public they had to say that they were all for it; the vast majority of them liked the freaky bodies that had grown so common in the sport.

This complicated construction of precariously balanced pieces was ready for the first major wind to come along and blow it over. Amazingly, though, it survived a massive hurricane—a storm that should have changed the face of the sport forever—and from the athletes' perspective, the only alteration was that drug testing went away. Depending on which guy you talked to, that was either a great thing or a tragedy that would prevent the sport from achieving any further growth. Other than that, not one single thing changed.

August 1995
Seattle
———————

In the end, it felt like I was chasing ghosts," I said to Tommy.

He'd called to invite me to attend the premiere of a movie he'd worked on, knowing that Rod and I had finally gone from a year of living separated in the same house to really breaking up and selling the house a few months earlier. Tommy wanted to make sure that I was still holding up. He'd asked how my decision about making a comeback was going, probably thinking that with all the other turmoil in my life, I'd already worked my way through it all and wasn't going to start in on a fresh set of complications.

"What does your gut tell you to do?" Tommy asked.

"Not to forget about how I ended up feeling during the last three years on the circuit. All the frustration with the drug stuff, the judging, the politics—all that bullshit."

"Last time got pretty complicated, didn't it—what with all the political stuff you got into?"

"Yeah. I mean, I used to think it was just me. But then I started putting all the pieces together—disappearing from the magazines, never, ever catching a single break with the judges. I mean, there are at least a half a dozen contests I can name—right now—where my placings were at least two or three spots lower, or more, than they should have been. Gee, what a coincidence that it all happened after I came out and we started getting more public with our activism.

"But you know," I continued, "to hear the IFBB guys tell it, I'm just paranoid. And all they have to do is say that I wasn't in shape and that's that—end of story. It'd be like if I were black and every white person I worked with who was less—or at least no more—qualified than me kept getting promoted and I just languished. Is that racism or paranoia? That's what so fucked about this kind of thing. I know that I was discriminated against. Hell, right after I came out, my appearance bookings dropped by seventy-five percent. Weider only signed me to my last contract to keep me away from the competition during that federation war. Anyway," I sighed, paused for a couple of seconds, and added, "maybe I shouldn't worry about competing and just concentrate on my fitness stuff."

"What's Joe Weider have to say?"

"Oh, him—who knows what the truth is with him. He repeats the same thing every time we talk: he never discriminated against me; he has gay people working at his company. An endless loop of total denial. Let's just say, he proclaims his absolute innocence a little too loudly—a bit too quickly. Maybe he really does think that telling me he had no use for me anymore, after I'd stayed loyal—and was . . . ah, fuck—I don't know. Blah, blah, blah . . . it's boring." I fell silent and Tommy didn't say anything. After a couple of minutes, I finally said, "I keep thinking that I can come back again and make the past disappear—make that whole three years go away—and maybe they'll treat me fair this time. Maybe I'll get it right this time, and we'll all live happily ever after—the end."

"Maybe you will get treated right this time. A lot's changed the past few years. Maybe things changed there too. But you know, Bob, you were treated badly. You didn't deserve that. They all know it too—they just can't admit it because it might say something awful about them. But look at how much things have changed. Ten years ago people would have given Weider a standing ovation if they even suspected that some openly faggot athlete was pushed out. Now they get nasty letters for doing it because more people noticed—and cared—than they ever counted on."

I should have had a charmed career in bodybuilding. If I had been straight and stupid—or maybe not even stupid, but less obsessed with chasing ideals—I would most likely have had that magic career and would have allowed myself to move on by now. But at the end of my bodybuilding rainbow, instead of a pot of gold there was complication; beyond that, frustration.

Things got complicated almost immediately after I decided to go back to the sport, following my first "retirement." I had already built a reputation, long before having left competition, as someone who had a well-defined set of notions about my approach to both the sport and life. The muscle-magazine writers always wrote about my ideals as an athlete and as a man; many of them speculated that having those ideals stood in the way of my winning—or even placing high in—the Olympia. Those ideals included my antidrug (or at least pro–drug-testing) stands, which I'd begun to make several years earlier, and the way I always said in TV or magazine interviews that bodybuilding, as a sport, would grow faster if those running it would place more judging emphasis on its artistic qualities and less on the size-for-the-sake-of-size trend that was developing into the set standard.

I was also outspoken on matters dealing with the rights of the athletes. The IFBB administrators were constantly making the guys sign away their rights on such things as TV contracts for contest coverage. The IFBB's competition contracts were also one-sided documents— which the athletes were required to sign committing to a particular show—that guaranteed, under penalty of sanctions and fines, a guy's participation in the show but didn't hold the IFBB to any commitment. If the IFBB canceled a show at the last minute, there was no penalty at all for the organization. If a contracted bodybuilder canceled at the last minute, he could—and most likely would—be suspended and fined. I always seemed to be the one who would speak up at an athletes' meeting the night before a show and say something like "You know, guys, you shouldn't sign this TV contract. It gives the producers and the IFBB the unquestionable right to use your image for anything—forever. If they wanted to use footage of you from this show in an ad for some product—that you don't know anything about—signing this paper gives them that right. And they get it all for free. Look at clause number seven. And while you're at it, read number three and four too."

Half the guys would have signed the agreement without even reading it. They'd start asking me questions about it while the IFBB official running the meeting would glare at me and claim that the contract didn't mean that. Then I'd go on to face some of these same officials during the next day's judging. If anything—especially after having spent a couple of years away from competition where I was able to develop a better perspective on the athlete's place in the sport—this outspokenness had grown even more intense. But my feeling had always been, from my first year in the pros, that the athletes needed a union or at least a collective-bargaining representative who would look out for the guys instead of the IFBB interests.

As Rod and I toured Europe while I was getting myself back into the scene, it became obvious that if our relationship was to survive, I was going to have to say in the media that I was gay and that this was the person I was in love with. We made no secret of being a couple. Everybody knew.

In 1989, I officially came out in the media as a gay man; and I also talked about being in a committed relationship with Rod—in an article in *Ironman* magazine.

My life changed forever; most of the change was for the better. I truly believed that doing the article would make the whole issue go away and that I would be able to get on with my life, and especially with my career. At the time, my comeback to competition was right on track. I had placed high in some Grand Prix contests in the spring of 1988. In the fall, I did the Mr. Olympia, and even though I'd placed tenth in that show, on the European Grand Prix tour that followed, I dug in, worked and dieted my ass off, improved with each passing competition, and by the end of the seven-contest tour had pushed my way up to fighting for one of the top places against the same guys who'd taken second, third, and fourth in the Olympia. The same thing happened in the spring of 1989, right before THE ARTICLE hit the stands. In the Arnold Schwarzenegger Classic—the second-biggest show, after the Olympia—I placed a controversial fifth. Most of the people I talked to after the show told me that I should have been, at the lowest, third.

I was happy, though, because obviously I was on an upward arc once again, if I hung in there and kept fighting. On the Grand Prix tour that followed that show, we went to Australia, where I took third in the Professional World Championships, and then we immediately headed off for another series of shows through Europe, where I was fighting for the top spots again. Twenty competitions in one year, and although I was physically exhausted, I thought that I was once again headed toward what I had felt during my earliest years of bodybuilding to be my ultimate destiny.

Then things got complicated. The IFBB decided to begin drug-testing the men's pro shows—a policy that I wholeheartedly supported; Rod and I had a wedding ceremony, which, although we did it totally for ourselves, ended up pulling us both into intense activism; a short time after the coming out, we decided to move away from L.A. and up to the Northwest, because we had decided that having chosen our relationship over trying to become big stars also meant that we didn't need to live in L.A. anymore. So we headed for Seattle, which took me away from the muscle ghetto.

Rumors of a new federation—one that would rival the IFBB and bring some real money to the athletes in the sport—began to surface. The emergence of the World Bodybuilding Federation (WBF) should have been the hurricane that broke the IFBB's domination of the sport wide open. Another federation would not have been needed at all if the IFBB had only given the pro athletes more say in how the sport was run and didn't give the guys the feeling that they could either go along or move along.

When World Wrestling Federation (WWF) mogul Vince McMahon started his own bodybuilding organization, plenty of guys were ready to move along. McMahon posed a tremendous threat to the Weiders' domination of the sport since he had as much—and maybe more—money as they had and had already turned the circus sideshow of professional wrestling into an ultrasuccessful business. McMahon hired former IFBB pro star Tom Platz to act as a liaison to any and all IFBB guys who wanted to cross over. The WBF promised that it would be all about the athletes, and that it would use the resources that had been built for wrestling, including all its television outlets, to get greater exposure for professional bodybuilding. They promised to take bodybuilding boldly, with fulfilled potential, into the next century.

Thirteen guys crossed over. I stayed loyal to the IFBB, even though the WBF had contacted me and wanted to negotiate a contract. They were talking serious money. The WBF was signing guys to contracts five to ten times larger than any Weider had ever offered.

Winter, 1990
Seattle

Look what came in the mail today," Rod said when he came back from the postal center where we received all our business mail.

He held up a yellow-beige envelope. "Open it," he said after I'd stood looking at the letter for several seconds. "Well?"

"It's from Tom Platz. An invitation from the WBF to start negotiating on a contract."

"So, call him."

"I don't know. This whole wrestling connection kinda gives me the willies. I don't wanna be a circus clown. I've worked too goddamn hard to flush it all down the toilet."

"Oh, Bob, for God's sake, it doesn't hurt to hear what he has to say. If you don't like it, then it doesn't need to go any further. What's Joe done for you lately?"

"Nothin'."

"Exactly."

My endorsement contract with Weider—which had been signed only when I was being courted by another company when I was first coming back, and was then renewed for another year—had lapsed nearly a year earlier. Joe had told me at the time it expired that he didn't want to renew again, saying that I was just too hard to work with. This wonderfully enlightening news had come just a few months after the *Ironman* interview.

I went into the office and called Tom's number at the World Wrestling Federation headquarters in Connecticut.

"Hi, Tom. Bob Paris."

"Hey, Bob. How've you been? Did you get my letter?"

"Just today. That's why I'm calling."

"You know, Bob, we're really trying to do something great back here. We'd like to have you be part of it. We want this to be fresh, dynamic. Let me ask you something. Wouldn't you like to be sitting in a first-class seat on a plane and when the guy next to you asks what you do and you say you're a pro bodybuilder, you get the same respect from that guy as if you were in the NBA or something? Wouldn't that be nice?"

"Yeah, it would. But I gotta be honest, Tom, the ties to pro wrestling—they don't sit too well with me."

"The only way one will have anything to do with the other is in the TV connection Vince has built for the WWF. Otherwise this is a whole separate deal."

"What about athletes' rights? I think you know that this is one of my main gripes with the Weiders."

"This is going to be all about the guys. Promise."

My other line was beeping.

"Hang on a second, Tom."

I clicked over to the other line. "Hello."

"Hello, Baab. It's Joe Weeeder."

"Oh . . . oh, hi . . . Joe." What was *this* all about? And if it was what I suspected it was, how in the hell did it always happen so fast?

"Listen, Baab—"

"Sorry, Joe. I'm on the other line. Just a second."

He grumbled, but I still clicked back to Tom and said, "Gee, guess who I've got on the other line."

"Amazing, isn't it?" Tom said without a trace of surprise in his voice. "Tell you what, Bob. Talk to him, but then give me a call back. I think you might like what I have to say."

"Okay, Tom. Talk to you later." Click. "Joe—still there?"

"Listen, Baab, when are you gonna be down here again?"

"Why?"

"There's something I need to talk to you about. It's important. It's better in person."

"I'm supposed to come down next week actually."

"Come in early. I'll buy the ticket. We need to talk."

"I'll see what I can do, Joe."

When I got off the phone, I told Rod what had happened. He couldn't believe it.

"Believe it," I said. "Weird old world, ain't it?"

During the frenzy of both sides competing against each other to try to sign as many of the top guys as possible, Joe flew me in from Seattle, brought me into his office, told me that he wanted me to stay loyal. I told him that my loyalty to him and his brother was strong, and that I also wanted to stay. We hammered out a new two-year agreement and signed it a week later.

Far beyond any desire to remain loyal were the disturbing facts coming in about the WBF. I'd heard from a couple of the guys who were in active negotiations with the WBF that the contracts they were proposing had you sign away all your rights to anything to do with your image: videos, books, movies, photographs, and so forth. They would own it all, in perpetuity. Forever. Once you signed with them, they owned you, even long after your contract had expired and the big monthly checks stopped coming. They were worse than Weider.

I decided to give the WBF a wait and see; if they were still around in a couple of years and the guys who'd crossed over were happy, then I'd rethink the situation. And, as the old saying goes, better the devil you know than the one you don't. Besides, it'd be fun having to watch Joe sign me to a new—and much larger—contract when it had already been obvious that he didn't know what the hell to do with a guy who was so outspoken and openly gay.

I received another letter from Tom Platz—several weeks after Joe and I worked out a new deal—saying that he and everyone at the WBF wished me success in my work with the Weider organization.

The WBF lasted less than two years. Vince McMahon knew nothing about bodybuilding, and the two contests they held were ridiculous. He tried to stick the round peg of bodybuilding into the square hole of the phony sideshow of professional wrestling, and it didn't work. The athletes, who'd been wined and dined and flown everywhere first class while they were negotiating contracts, had all that quickly disappear. The promise that athletes would have some level of control vanished; they were back to being powerless pawns. Guys began to complain that the new federation was worse than the one they'd left behind, and that the contests were embarrassing, more sleazy burlesque than athletic competitions.

It *was* embarrassing. All these top guys who had worked so hard for so many years were turned into glorified circus clowns.

During his posing routine at the first WBF contest, Berry DeMey, who had placed as high as third in the Mr. Olympia but had decided to cross over, was accompanied onto the stage by two female string-bikinied bathing beauties who—well, I'll simply say that these young ladies possessed the potential ability to nurse several very large infants for a very long time, and leave it at that. He was wearing a towel around his waist, as if he'd just stepped out of the shower, and his companions liberated him of this towel as he began to bump and grind his way through a—sort of—posing routine. Even though he had on posing trunks under the towel, it was nothing more than a male strip routine. Here was one of the most respected pro bodybuilders in the world reduced to virtually stripteasing for his paychecks. All the rest of the guys did similarly silly things like this onstage. And—oh-so-coincidentally—the placings in their competitions almost exactly duplicated the sequential order of highest- to lowest-paid athletes: the guy with the biggest contract, Gary Strydom, won; the one with the second-biggest monthly paycheck, Mike Christian, placed second; and so on down the line. This was the new horizon bodybuilding was supposedly headed toward. This was the WBF.

Many of the guys had crossed over because they were promised that WBF contests would never be drug tested. Four weeks before their second (and final) show, all the WBF guys were told that the competition would have testing. The wrestling federation was coming under intense media scrutiny about heavy drug use by their guys, so the WBF decided to demonstrate that its athletes could pass a drug test. This last-minute decision left many of the WBF bodybuilders scrambling to clean out their systems—quickly—to pass the test. They had all been promised no testing—most likely as an inducement to cross over, since the IFBB was supposedly performing drug tests in the men's pros now—but most of them still had clauses in their contracts giving the WBF the right to test, and the right to cancel the contract of any athlete who tested positive if the clause was ever exercised.

The WBF had to give away tickets for their shows and still played to less than full houses. It was a complete flop.

As quickly as it came, it was gone, and not one thing about how the IFBB treated its athletes changed. Drug testing in the IFBB men's pro division disappeared from sight.

The guys who stayed with the IFBB and Weider during this federation war were told that their loyalty would always be remembered and would definitely be rewarded. Ben Weider had sent out regular updates on the WBF, telling us how they would make a circus out of our sport. He ended up being right, but you could tell by the vehemence of his letters and the way he tried to make fun of this new organization that he was worried. He also banned for life all the athletes who crossed over, vowing that they would never be allowed back into the IFBB after such a great betrayal.

At the end of my two-year contract, after my total loyalty to Joe and Ben, and with the end of the WBF in sight—and therefore no more need to keep athletes away from a competitive organization—I flew down to L.A. to begin negotiations on a contract extension. Joe had promised me two months earlier that my contract would continue.

So, what can I do for you, Baab?" Joe finally asked after I'd waited patiently for him to finish two long phone calls.

I'd been sitting across the conference table from him. He had handed me the latest *Muscle and Fitness* to read when I first walked into his office. I'd flipped through it without interest for a couple of minutes, then pulled my work journal out of my briefcase so I could get something useful done while I waited. He'd already kept me waiting in the hall for forty minutes before he finally let me in for our appointment, then he continued taking phone calls once I was in his office.

"I'm here to start negotiating our contract," I said, flipping to a clean sheet of paper in my journal so I could take notes of our meeting.

"Wadda ya mean?"

"Well, Joe, the last time I spoke with you—let me see . . . on"—I looked at the date section of the journal where I kept a list of all my business calls—"November third, you said that we would definitely extend my contract. I mean, I asked you about it point-blank. That's why I'm here. It expires this month."

"Ahhhh," he grumbled, then got up, went to the window for a few seconds, and came back over to the conference table.

"What's goin' on, Joe?"

"Ahhh . . . um . . . look . . . I don't have any use for you anymore," he said, each word frozen in ice.

He wouldn't look me in the eye and was trying to find something on the table to busy himself with.

"You made a promise, Joe. What about that?" Nothing but more grumbles. "What about my loyalty during the WBF thing? You and Ben always said that the guys who stayed with you would be rewarded. Is this what you call loyalty?"

"You're just too difficult—too neurotic. I don't have any use for you."

He waved his right hand in my direction; a dismissive gesture.

"Real nice, Joe. It's been such a pleasure." I got up and started to leave, putting away my journal, closing the briefcase. As I started out his office door, I noticed that I'd inadvertently picked up the *Muscle and Fitness* he'd given me. I turned around and said, "Here, I won't be needing this," slammed the magazine down on the desk, and left.

So much for the promise of reciprocated loyalty. One thing my history with Joe proved was that he was only loyal when one of his competitors was seriously interested in doing business with me. He only wanted me around so that the competition couldn't have me. That wasn't loyalty; it was megalomania. And now with the WBF suddenly out of the picture, he, his brother, and the IFBB had no more competition, and I was once again of no interest.

Discrimination is a hard thing to pin down. To make a solid case, you need a smoking gun of some sort. There wasn't one here. It was like trying to wrap my arms around a ghost; you could hear the chains rattling and see it there, walking up the staircase, but try to actually touch it and all you got was cold air.

I had heard the stories, long before the *Ironman* article about judges sitting in their meetings or at one of their parties after a show and saying that they'd never let a queer win a contest—and that the one gay man who'd been a Mr. Olympia, several years before, had slipped through, and they'd certainly never let that happen again—especially a gay man who talked so openly about it. I had five different people swear to me that they'd heard IFBB officials saying these things, some of it supposedly being said by a couple of the IFBB officials who'd come to Rod's and my wedding. These people were my friends. Hearing the stories broke my heart.

I disappeared from the Weider magazines, even though I was still getting between twenty and thirty thousand pieces of fan mail a year. I wrote a long letter to Ben Weider, telling him about how all these things seemed to add up to discrimination—my low placement in shows, even when I was competing in shape; Joe's telling me that he had no use for me anymore, in spite of promises of reciprocating my loyalty; judges and officials reportedly saying some damaging things about me. He wrote back telling me, in so many words, to prove it or shut up. When I would call the people who'd told me about officials saying things that could be construed as contributing to an atmosphere of discrimination, all of them said that they'd never come forward publicly—they liked being a part of the IFBB (especially since it was the only game in town once again) and wouldn't jeopardize that—sorry. That's what is so difficult in these kinds of situations; there was no interoffice memo saying, "Get rid of the faggot." This was all wrapped in fog, and the world had already moved on.

In the real world, it was too petty. So what, some muscleman claims discrimination? Who cares? Tell him to get a real life. In the muscle world the idea that it had happened, whether on a blatant or subtle level (or a complex combination of both), was too scandalous even to consider; the Weider mouthpieces wrote items in the magazines that intimated I was a crazy, disgruntled man who'd squandered his potential by never competing in shape. That's all anyone in the bodybuilding media needed to say about any athlete who complained about the judging system, the IFBB administrators, or the Weiders—*he just didn't compete in shape, so he deserved what he got.* It's what they did to me. The world turned another notch, and it was gone.

In frustration, I stopped training and promised myself that I would never step on a bodybuilding stage again, never allow those people to have the slightest control in my life again. I didn't publicly announce another retirement; I simply let it all fade away.

A few months later, every single athlete who had crossed over to the upstart WBF and supposedly been banned for life was back in the IFBB, with no penalties, no fines, nothing. Most of them got fat Weider contracts, to boot. I guess that's what you get when you're loyal.

For two years I blocked bodybuilding out of my mind. I tried to tell myself that I'd wasted all those years, years that I could have been putting to far better use, but then, right when I thought I'd finally gotten rid of it, like a boomerang, it returned.

September 1995
Seattle

The '95 Mr. Olympia is next week. The show is in Atlanta; a weekend-long extravaganza, with the newly created Master's Olympia (for pros over forty), the Fitness Olympia (for women who don't want to take their bodies to the extremes of competitive bodybuilders), and the Ms. Olympia (for the women who do), all being held—along with the planet's most prestigious men's professional bodybuilding competition—over two days.

The total prize money, in what was once an obscure sport, has reached nearly three hundred thousand dollars. In an era when major athletes in more mainstream sports can make that kind of money in a month, that figure may not seem like much, but the checks that the best of the Olympia athletes take home represent quantum leaps over a relatively short time. When the Mr. Olympia started in the sixties, there was no prize money at all; then it went up to a thousand bucks (winner take all), stayed at that level for several years, then began to inch up as the sport grew.

Hard-core fans will come from all over the world to watch and cheer for their favorites. Newspapers will probably write about the weekend—if they write about it at all, in mocking tones, emphasizing the overbuilt weirdness of the men and women putting their hearts and souls into a dream that many outsiders still see as being roughly equivalent to a circus sideshow. The media will most likely mirror those views. It generally does. Yet most of the people going to Atlanta to see their muscle heroes, and those athletes themselves, won't give a flying damn about what a bunch of reporters have to say about them. The athletes know the value of what they do, and the fans know what they like to see.

I thought about going down to Atlanta to see the show, but in the end decided not to. I still don't really know why. I've never sat in an audience and watched a pro show; I just never did. It might have been fun to go see one.

*   *   *

A vision—a fantastical, imaginary movie clip—has continually run through my mind during this last year. I am climbing, climbing, climbing all alone, to the top of this enormous mountain. I fall sometimes—a lot, actually; hurt myself; get up; climb some more; fall down again. It seems as if I've been climbing this mountain forever. After a while, when I'm close enough to the top to see it through breaks in the cloud cover, I pull out my map, to see where I am, and discover that I've gone up the wrong mountain. Now, this mountain that I'm on is a high one—I can tell this from the map—every bit as high as the one I thought I was climbing. It's just not the right one. The other mountain is the one that many dream of climbing because the hand of fate has lent it greater prestige. It is easy to get them confused; the way my map is drawn the two look a great deal alike. But it's still the wrong one. And I get mad at myself, and I cuss out the mountain, and I cuss out the mapmaker, and I cuss out all the rocks I've tripped over and the crevices I've fallen into on the way up. But in spite of all that cussing, I'm still on this mountain.

I obviously have several choices. I can take the time to go back to the bottom and search for the right one; but that might take a long time and it may be dark by the time I find it—if I'm even able to. Or I can stay right where I am and cuss at the sky and everything else, in the name of horrible mistakes and wrong decisions. Or I can decide that, even though it's not exactly the one I counted on, this mountain is here and it's real, and it may not be as famous as the other one, but it's still exhilarating and challenging—and I can keep going forward toward the peak.

Joe Weider called last week and said that he and his board of directors were going to decide about my endorsement contract sometime after the Olympia weekend (who knows, maybe it'll be on a Tuesday). I didn't ask him why because, you know, I thought, *Oh, well. We'll either do business or we won't.* Either way, it won't change the past; that's already crumbled into dust and blown away.

I keep having to remind myself that Joe's not the mountain; he might be the mapmaker or maybe an expedition financier or maybe he's a frustrated, armchair climber; but not the mountain.

The mountain is my dream.

I still have to decide which way I'm going: on up toward the peak, back down to start climbing a different one, or sit on my ass and cry.

I am no longer innocent or naive. I've been through too much to ever lay honest claim to those traits again in this lifetime. If I decide to continue up this mountain, I will hate some things about it; there'll be ethical dilemmas and the going won't always be smooth. I accept that. The thing that I wrapped my hopes and dreams around for so long has its dark side, but I've never known any field of endeavor that didn't.

I can move on to other things, other goals. I can even call them greener pastures. I can try to forget the past and say that part of my life is now a closed chapter, but in spite of all the aspects about this thing that bother me, I can't escape what it did for my life.

During the past few years I have successfully branched my life and career out into all sorts of new areas, and I could blow my own horn with a long list of accomplishments, but doing that would serve no purpose, other than naked self-promotion. That's not why I raise the point. I mention it for two reasons. First, my time in the sport of body-building taught me that I was capable of doing almost anything I set my mind and my disciplined efforts to. Second, and I think more importantly, in spite of achieving success in other aspects of my work life, not one of these accomplishments can even come close to the feeling I had when I heard the emcees announce my name as a national and a world champion in my sport. To some people that will sound like an incredibly stupid statement, but to anyone who has ever been—or has ever imagined being—in a similar situation, it will make perfect sense.